THE 21ST CENTURY VOTER GUIDE TO CANDIDATE ASSESSMENT

Howard J. Gunn

Published 2019
Printed in the United States of America
Print ISBN: 978-1-951490-09-6

Canoe Tree Press
4697 Main Street
Manchester, VT 05255

www.CanoeTreePress.com

THE 21ST CENTURY VOTER GUIDE TO CANDIDATE ASSESSMENT

DEVELOPING YOUR PERSONAL KNOWLEDGE AND THE VOTING SKILLS NEEDED TO HELP VOTERS FIX THE 50-YEAR VOTING DISASTER LEGACY LEFT BY THE BABY BOOMERS AND GENERATION XERS AND SAVE THEM, YOURSELF, AND POSTERITY FROM FASCISM.

By
Howard J. Gunn

CONTENTS

DEDICATION

This guide is dedicated to our federal republic form of government and the elected representatives of the people who served and will serve in the Congress and the Executive branches. The guide is also dedicated to the Voter Eligible Population (VEP) that is responsible for electing Representatives and their resultant contributions to society.

The protection of our national culture, the development of our economy, and the results from the government's promotion of the general welfare that is produced by extending pathways from the economy to the people are unique achievements of our form of government.

The notion of American exceptionalism, though, has been under attack for nearly 50 years by representatives from both political parties and the republic has been losing most of the battles to American fascism, according to the Gallup Poll ratings of the Congress of the United States and the Growth of Real Income and its Distribution over the same period.

Hopefully, the Millennials, who now represent the largest single voting bloc in the VEP can learn and develop their candidate selection skills and even teach the Baby Boomers (grandparents) and Generation X (parents) better voting skills, so they too can help repair the damages they produced, by their disastrous voting record over the last 50 years.

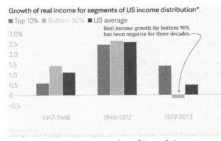

Figure 60 *Growth of Real income and its Distribution*

I also want to offer my sincere thanks to those citizens who register and vote in elections and, my parents, my teachers, my friends, my relatives, my work associates, and the American cultural environment that taught me civics and instilled my patriotism.

The guide is also dedicated to helping the VEP identify and elect better representatives who actually "promote the general Welfare" ideals of our founding fathers and support the Constitution's mandate to produce liberty, justice, and a higher quality of life for the people and posterity, in the face of the ever-present Fascism threat to our Democratic Republic.

INTRODUCTION

Thanks for buying *The 21st Century Guide*. With your help, 2020 can be the start of a great new decade "for the people" and bring an end to the nearly 50 yearlong "for the accumulation of wealth for the wealthy" era in America.

From the author of *Principles of Traffic and Network Design* and *The Basics of IPTV*, in which he explained the building blocks of producing today's mobile information network and the Internet of Things, comes the new riveting work of political non-fiction, *The 21st Century Voter Guide To Candidate Assessment*.

The guide is designed to inform Millennials and provide them with better candidate selection and voting skills, while also providing the general voting skill improvement tools, to also help improve the voting quality of the Baby Boomer and Generation X voters who produced the poor Gallup Poll job performance ratings and real income disaster over the last fifty years.

The guide provides the Voter Eligible Population (VEP) with insights to gain a better economic and political understanding of personal ideologies and political parties. It also provides the knowledge-based skills to assess and better evaluate the attributes and voting proclivities of candidates for the Congress and presidency.

The improved candidate assessment skills will enable the VEP to better predict the behavior of individual candidates and ultimately help voters select better representatives, or at least representatives who will earn better job performance evaluations and job approval ratings in the Gallup Polls, in comparison to the results produced over the last 50 Years.

The Voter Guide to Candidate Selection offers voters an "up to the moment" historical review and understanding of the constitutionally mandated role of government to "promote the general Welfare" for the people, in contrast to the conservative's view that the role of government is too facilitate "the accumulation of wealth by the wealthy."

The voter guide explores the historically "failed" national governments from the royalty, aristocracy and Church-based plutocracies of the past and present, to better understand the current elected Republic models that are focused on the accumulation of wealth by the wealthy strategies for exploiting their general population.

The book's core contention is that the Baby Boomer candidate selection and election processes took a fundamentally wrong turn in the 1970s, when voters began adopting the Cult of Ignorance and Barry Goldwater's conservative worldview, as a way for the elite richest class to put a stop to Medicare, veteran rights, civil rights, voting rights, human rights, women's rights, Social Security, pension benefits, unemployment protection and the building of the "Great Society" through education, the elimination of poverty, and the development of pathways to the economy for the people.

Conceptually, the conservative "for the rich" and the "for the accumulation of wealth by the wealthy" political paradigm got elected into Congress in ways that enabled Congress to create the current federal debt ($22 Trillion) over the last 50 years. (Federal debt is uncollected taxes, created by borrowing money to pay the bills and pledging future taxes, as the collateral.)

The systemic debt burden process of Congress also produced new income inequalities, favoring the rich, via the tax-collection loopholes and the Congressional failure to protect or promote pathways for the people to the general economy, over the last 50 years. The dual failure is evidenced by the shrinkage of the middle class and the expansion of the working poor class, via income inequality generating tax legislation, over the last 50 years.

The numerous "for the rich" tax cuts and the deregulatory economic policies replacing the "for the people" policies, since the 1980s, generated the growth of the right-wing evangelical conservatism and the rise of fascism, to maintain and protect their ill-gotten tax gains

Socially, the misinformed and misguided Baby Boomers and Generation Xers derailed the growth of ethnic equality, income equality and the protections of justice and liberty offered to the people by the US Constitution and the nation's previous 179 years of legislative actions. Moreover, the right-wing radicalizing of a major national political party has also prodded misguided state voters that elected state legislatures for exploiting citizens and their families.

The purity of the American fascist transformation did more than just drive moderates out of the Republican Party. The first "tax cut for the rich" in 1981, the attack on unions, the pension abuses, and the deregulation of Wall Street, plundered 11 trillion dollars of net worth from the people via the S&L collapse and doubling of the Federal Debt. The new-era evangelical conservative Cult of Ignorance political rapscallion leadership and the poor VEP voting choices, also set in motion a new conservative Congress that cut taxes for the rich, again, in 2001.

This second tax cut produced the Great Recession of 2007 that plundered 16 trillion dollars of net worth from the people and replaced the Federal Surplus run rate in 2000, with a new 1 trillion per year borrowed funding run rate, trying to replace the lost taxes from the tax cut for the rich. The 2017 tax cut for the rich and the return to the trillion plus deficit run rate in 2019 reflects the continuation of the fascist fiscal exploitation of the people, right up to today.

The good news from the review is that we are not the first republic to vote in fascism, but we can be the first to vote it out of office, when we do. And, although it is too early to tell for sure, we may have gotten a good start on it, in the 2018 elections.

While we may have had a good start, the current evangelical conservative political ideology to maintain the class structure and the income inequality motivations of many of the Plutocrats in the Cult of Ignorance political movement, strongly support the fascism model that is still driving today's income inequality, racial inequality, and gender inequality.

As mentioned at the start of the introduction to the book, the millennials have the opportunity to help the Voter Eligible Population (VEP) unwind the fascist radical conservative economic attack on the people and save the previous generations and posterity, by making 2020 the start of a great new decade "for the people."

On the other side of the coin, if the VEP with the Millennials' leadership do not end the current model, we the people will surely enjoy our own Roaring 20s decade, just like our ancestors 100 years ago. The original Roaring 1920's set a record-breaking stock market collapse that produced a massive net worth wipeout and 12-year depression. The 2020 version if left to the conservatives could dwarf the Great Republican Depression and the Great Republican Recession and wipe out both of their record setting negative performances.

BACKGROUND AND ABOUT THE VOTER GUIDE

As members of the Voter Eligible Population (VEP) in the federal republic of the United States, you are a key contributor to a unique voting system created by liberal Federalists in 1879, over the objections of conservative Anti-Federalists. With over 200 years of growth, development, and expansion of the economy and the population, very little has changed in the worldview and government perspective in the conflict between liberals, for the people and the conservatives, for the accumulation of wealth by the wealthy.

In any case, the adaptable federal system created in 1789 uses the nation's land mass, broken up into voting districts, states, and territories. Today, most American citizens who reach voting age (currently 18) are now eligible to join the VEP. About 70% of the people who have reached voting age eligibility are also registered to vote (170 million out of 240 million people).

The voting system uses a "popular" voting process to elect the Congress and the Electoral College representatives who elect the president. The College use the same land mass guidelines and popular vote processes to select non-federal government people to be the representatives who are empowered to vote for the selection of the president and vice president. The Electoral College process was set up separately, so that the sitting Congress, a newly elected Congress, nor the people could staff the incoming presidency.

These two voting processes provide the VEP with the opportunity to evaluate candidates and vote for a candidate who the voter thinks will best represent them, their family, their community, and their nation in the Congress of the United States and the Electoral College. The anomalies and frailties of our federal voting processes are discussed throughout this guide.

Voters from the various generations of people have been jointly responsible for every elected candidate and selected federal representative, since 1917, when the Senate selection was converted into a popular state vote process, replacing the original state appointed plutocrat model in the Constitution. In addition to being responsible for selecting the representatives, the VEP is also indirectly responsible for the legislative actions produced during a congressional session and the executive branch actions taken to carry out the Will of Congress.

Various generations of voters in the VEP have been given descriptive names, to reflect their unique eco-system and cultural ties to an era and point in time. Not everyone uses the same definition and delineations for generations of people. This book uses the following names, timeframes, and key events impacting their attitudes and their voting behaviors, in their lifetime:

The GI Generation (born 1880 - 1920)	- Progressivism & Great Depression
The Greatest Generation (born 1921 - 1945)	- The New Deal & WWII
Baby Boomer Generation (born 1946 - 1964)	- The Square Deal & Great Society
Generation X (born between 1965 - 1981)	- Conservatism & Great Recession
Millennial Generation (born between 1982 - 1997)	- Mini Boom & Conservatism
Generation Z (born in or after 1998)	- Selfies & Partisan Politics

The generational makeup and group dynamics of the VEP changes, as the members die off and new ones are added. Just as importantly, economic dynamics are producing changes in attitudes and creating new learning experiences that impact the voting skills of the VEP.

Since 1974, the Gallup Poll has taken opinion surveys that let the VEP rate the perceived job performance of their representatives and the president, while they are serving in the federal government.

Objective data from the job performance ratings of the representatives that were created by the people being governed, and the declining opinion trends over my lifetime, motivated me to research history, to find out what went wrong with our representative system. The discovery led me to publish this guide to help the VEP understand the problem and how voting can fix the poor job performance problem that the voters created over the last 50 years.

The purpose of the guide is to also help the VEP develop a better understand of their civic role, their responsibilities to the people and posterity, and how their voting actions impact their contribution to the quality of life in their country and the quality of life in the future.

The guide also provides information that can help voters hone their candidate selection voting skills and improve the collective voting skills of the VEP, in ways that improve the job performance rating of our federal institutions and the quality of life of the people and posterity.

PART I

INTRODUCTION TO THE VOTING OPPORTUNITY AND ISSUES

Claim

*"Let us never forget that government is ourselves and not an
alien power over us. The ultimate rulers of our democracy
are not a President and senators and congressmen and
government officials, but the voters of this country."*
—FRANKLIN DELANO ROOSEVELT

Rating

Mr. Roosevelt's observation that government is ourselves and
voters are the rulers has been somewhat true in the United
States since 1920, when women were finally granted the right to
vote in federal elections. The plutocrat-patron operation of the
political party system, the gerrymandering, the slandering, the
partisanship politics, the special interest group leverage, and the
various voter interference and suppression efforts aside, actual
voters from the VEP do formally elect the 435 House members
and one-third of the Senate every 2 years. Every 4 years the federal votes are also used to staff the Electoral College to select the
president/vice president.

Governance and government are very complex political forces created by people. These forces directly impact and generally determine the quality of life of the governed.

Governance itself is the operational processes originally established by the elders, tribal leaders, witch doctors, and the richest people in the tribe to control the economic use of resources, the societal culture, and the behavior of the people in a community.

Government, on the other hand, became the institutionalized political structure and the processes used to extend the economic, political, and social controls over large land masses with many diverse tribes and groups living in the governed territory.

The primary role of every national government since the dawn of time was to facilitate the accumulation of wealth by the wealthy. The nobility, aristocracy, and special interest groups (military/big business/Church) based plutocracies (from the Greek -Ploutos, meaning wealth, and -Kraytos meaning rule, strength, authority and power) ran the state government for the benefit of the rich.

The political objective of every national government was to maintain control over the economic, social, and political environment that produced their wealth. Today, this rich royalty, military and special interest model of government is generically referred to as a dictatorship, plutocracy, or a fascist state form of government run by the plutocrats.

The control of the national economy and the social order for the government's benefit generally produced an ultra-rich plutocrat class (small number of people called 1%ers, in the aristocracy, nobility, church) whose power and authority were derived from their wealth, a rich operational plutocrat management class (10%ers), a marginal merchant trading class, a working poor class, an ultra-poor vagabond class, and slaves.

The "accumulation of wealth by the wealthy role" of national government and its effort to maintain the status quo social and class environment can be traced throughout pre-recorded and recorded history, all the way to even modern-day plutocratic governments whose main claim to fame is that they ended the practice of slavery in their society.

The federal republic government model for the benefit of the people replacing the "accumulation of wealth by the wealthy" government model was first written as a proposed new law in 1787. The new "law of the land" would create "representatives of the people" who would replace the aristocracy/nobility elitist class and fill the national government positions with representatives who manage the government operations for the people.

The **liberal** plutocrats who wrote the federal law and the "social contract" of people-empowering government also created the notion of political parties and patrons for funding candidates who would attract voters to their national political agenda.

The first new political party was formed by the liberal Federalists, trying to get the Constitution written and adopted. The second political party was created soon thereafter, by the conservative Anti-Federalists and the Cult of Ignorance Patrons, trying to stop the adoption process.

For clarity, it should be noted that the conservative plutocrats had already adopted a Constitution, in 1781. The original Articles of Confederation Constitution facilitated the stand-alone nation-state plutocracy-oligopoly (special interest groups) government model for the accumulation of wealth by the wealthy. The representatives serving in the Confederation's Congress had no authority to pass laws or impose taxes. Congressional actions required the unanimous approval from the states.

The proposed second Constitution granted the necessary powers and the authority to legislate, operate, tax, and adjudicate nationally over the states that would join the union of the people. States that "voted" to join would forgo some of their sovereignty over commerce, the printing of money, people and the operation of military.

The second United States Constitution was initially adopted into a national law by 1,071 liberal plutocrat voters over the objections of the 577 conservative Anti-Federalist plutocrat voters (per Wikipedia) in the original 13 nation-states. Thirty-seven additional states and 16 territories have subsequently adopted the US Constitution.

Upon the adoption, the new plutocrat-operated political party system evolved to capture control of the government through voting constituencies. The liberal Federalists evolved into the Administration and Whig parties, while the Anti-Federalists, the Cult of Ignorance Patrons and the secessionists evolved the Anti-Administration Party (1792) that produced the Democrat-Republican Party (1794).

The popular vote election to the House of Representatives enabled the elected representatives to work together with others from the various states to develop laws and legislation favorable to the best interest of the nation and its people.

The winning liberal plutocrats and the new federal representatives initially focused on the development and leveraging of the new political party processes, as Federalists and liberal Whigs in the administration. The conservative plutocrats and the Cult of Ignorance Patrons against the union of the people, formed the Anti-Administration Party, the Democrat-Republican Party, and the Secessionists. These Political Party processes have produced a number of political parties, with various liberal and conservative inclinations. Moreover, they continue to operate alongside of the Constitution. and remove processes have survived, along with the Constitution of the United States, since 1789.

A portion of the conservative political forces against the union still subscribe to secessionist and the plutocracy class model "for the accumulation of wealth by the wealthy" versus the "for the people" model in the Constitution. Many also favor the class hierarchy and the maintenance of the status quo feudal like economic and social order.

Historically, the second Constitution began operations in 1789 with elected and appointed representatives who were chosen from a list of plutocrats and patron-based candidates. The then-new republic governance and government model for the benefit of the people would ultimately prove to be a unique political ideology inflection point, pitting liberal plutocrats representing the best interests of the people, against the conservative plutocrats, representing the accumulation of wealth by the wealthy.

The writing and adopting of the new law also produced a turning point in history away from the traditional inherited and appointed plutocracy/oligopoly model to an elected national government with a meritocracy process designed and staffed with representatives of the people, for the benefit of the people, in the union of the people, living in multiple nation-states.

The role of the new plutocracy-based federal government was empowered by the Voter Eligible Population (VEP) of the day, with clear governance and government objectives and the role of the new Federal government clearly expressed.

"We the people, of the United States in Order to form a more perfect Union, establish Justice, insure domestic Tranquility, provide for the common defence (sic), promote the general Welfare, and secure the Blessings of Liberty to ourselves and our Posterity, do ordain and establish this Constitution for the United States of America."

The new law to "form a more perfect Union," "establish justice" and "insure domestic Tranquility" created the new Congress of the United States (consisting of the House of Representatives and the Senate). The Congress was empowered in Article I to legislate and fund the operations of the government.

A separate operational branch of government called the executive branch was empowered to run the operations needed to carry out the Will of Congress and "insure domestic Tranquility," provide a "common defence," and "promote the general Welfare." The law also enabled a new legal adjudication process for resolving economic and behavioral issues between the state and the federal government (the Supreme Court).

The new federal institutions were empowered to produce the legislation, funding, and operations needed to 1) "form a more perfect Union" of the people, 2) generate justice for the people, 3) produce the necessary law and order processes that would 4) "insure domestic Tranquility" and protect the people, and 5) "promote the general Welfare" of the people via the elected and selected representatives operating the new Federal Republic.

The congressional model of legislative government for the benefit of the people and posterity, separate from the executive branch responsible for operations, became a unique government institutional arrangement with the ability to impact the quality of life (the general Welfare) and the personal liberty of every person in the United States.

As a point of constitutional clarity in history, the president and vice president were evaluated by a referendum vote per state and an award of Electoral College seats, based on the results of the House of Representative and president voting processes.

The number of seats per state in the Electoral College was based on the House seats awarded to the state via its population and its slave count. An additional 2 seats per state were also awarded to represent the Senate appointments. The political value of seats in the House and Electoral College are discussed in detail in Chapter 6.

The separate plutocrat body (Electoral College) was created to convert the state congressional seats into executive staff "votes" into the four-year executive term in office. The term limit created a VEP review cycle and a way to confirm their employment.

The House of Representatives was staffed by a popular vote of the qualified adult white males (VEP) living in the territory. The representatives were elected for a two-year congressional session, term in office. The Senate portion of Congress (the upper chamber) was empowered with overseer responsibilities and approval processes that converted the House legislation into the all-powerful Acts of Congress. It also has control over Supreme Court and other key federal job appointments.

The Senate initially consisted of two appointed plutocrats representing each state. Senators served a six-year term in office. The Constitution was amended in 1917 to change the appointment process into a per-state, direct popular-vote election of Senators.

Based on the 4-plus decades of Gallup Job Approval Rating Polls (Gallup Poll process was created in 1974) about the Congress (covering 26 full congressional sessions and a little over half of the 27th), it seems clear that the voters in the United States are somewhat disenchanted with the job performance of Congress.

Moreover, since the voters elected them, it also seems rational to point out that the voters seem to need better candidate assessment skills and voting skills to elect better representatives who can improve the job approval ratings of Congress.

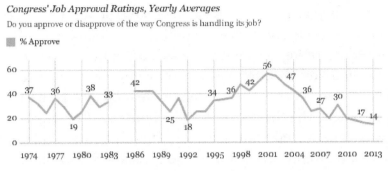

Figure 1 *Congress Job Approval Ratings*

Congress's approval ratings by the people, while not generally high, has declined to mediocre levels based on the perceived poor job performance of the representatives and the failure of voters to elect <u>better representatives for the people</u>.

Given the job approval ratings, it is not surprising that there is little confidence that the Congress of the United States can adequately perform its legislative responsibilities.

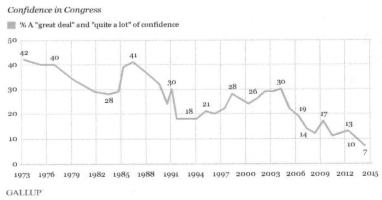

Figure 2 *Confidence in Congress*

In any case, the low approval ratings and the low confidence ratings have had very little impact on the re-election rates of the poorly performing representatives or the overall rating of the institution called the Congress of the United States.

In fact, the re-election rates shown below seem to be highly correlated with the low rating the Institution receives, in comparison with other institutions in American life.

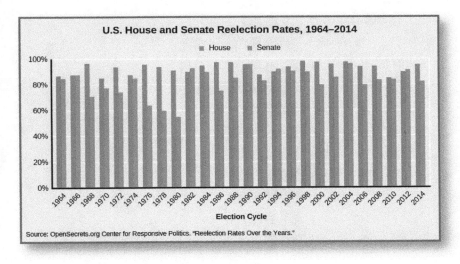

Figure 3 *US House and Senate Re-election Rates*

I am going to read you a list of institutions in American society. Please tell me how much confidence you, yourself, have in each one -- a great deal, quite a lot, some or very little?

June 1-5, 2016

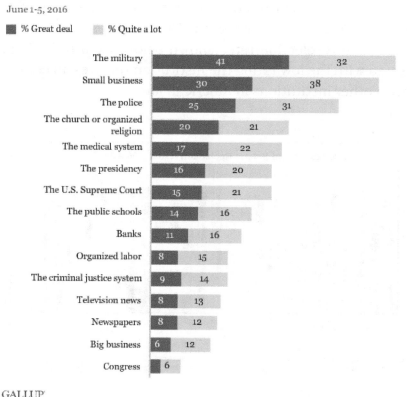

Figure 4 Gallup Institutional Ratings versus Congress

The Electoral College process that selects the executive branch of government has not had the same poor Gallup Job Approval ratings problem as Congress. Although there have been one-term presidents and the recent highly contentious election and poor rating performance of Mr. Trump, the approval ratings of the executive branch have been quite different in comparison to the lawgivers in Congress, over the last fifty years.

As shown below, most presidents have opinion poll swings from positive to negative approval ratings, during their terms in office. On the average, presidents start and end up near a 50% approval and 50% disapproval. In fact, a 50% average approval rating is what would mathematically be expected from a normal two-party statistical curve.

The figure also shows that on the average, the presidential approval and disapproval ratings, at least before Trump's partial 3-year term, were about the same as the approval ratings received by a TV star playing the president (West Wing TV show).

The ups and downs around the average overall rating, over their term in office is shown here. It clearly reflects their actions and their approval ratings, while serving in office. The unique three-year chart of Mr. Trump has consistently shown uniquely different approval disapproval ratings, in comparison to a TV Star playing president.

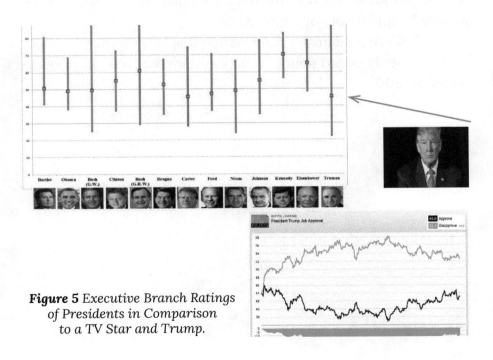

Figure 5 Executive Branch Ratings of Presidents in Comparison to a TV Star and Trump.

The good news for America is that the second Constitution of the United States currently demands the voters formally get the opportunity to evaluate the congressional, executive branch, and political party job performance every two years.

The information in this guide is intended to inform and educate voters and provide them with insights that can help them improve their candidate assessment skills and voting skills. The new less ignorant voters (ignorance is the lack of information and understanding) will hopefully use the skills to elect better performing representatives.

Most of the material that follows in the chapters will refer to the political performance of the elected representatives and the plutocrat/patron-driven political party system that serves as the proxy battleground for selecting candidates for elections in the never-ending political ideology conflict between the "for the people" mandate and the "for the accumulation of wealth by the wealthy" mandate of government.

The following summary information displays the development of the Duopoly-based political party system that was fully operational by 1800.

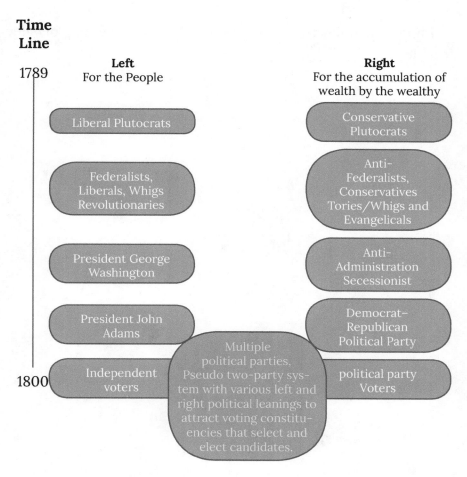

Time Line

1789

Left
For the People

Right
For the accumulation of wealth by the wealthy

Liberal Plutocrats

Conservative Plutocrats

Federalists, Liberals, Whigs Revolutionaries

Anti-Federalists, Conservatives Tories/Whigs and Evangelicals

President George Washington

Anti-Administration Secessionist

President John Adams

Democrat–Republican Political Party

1800

Independent voters

Multiple political parties, Pseudo two-party system with various left and right political leanings to attract voting constituencies that select and elect candidates.

political party Voters

The various chapters in the voter guide will examine how the constitutional charter for the benefit of the people has performed, over the 2-plus centuries of its existence. They will also compare the "for the people" successes versus "the accumulation of wealth by the wealthy" successes.

The first chapter will explore voters, civics, government, and the voting impact on government and how the two outcomes "for the people" and "for the accumulation of wealth by the wealthy" interreact and play out over time.

I hope you enjoy the information and learn something of value from it.

CHAPTER 1

Voter and Voting contributions to Effective Governance, for the Benefit of the People and Not Just the Accumulation of Wealth by the Wealthy.

Claim

"If voting made any difference, they wouldn't let us do it."
—MARK TWAIN

Rating

Probably false today in most of the United States. Voting results do make a difference.

The "voting" observation attributed to Mark Twain was clearly true for most of recorded history. The countless emperors, kings, monarchs, patriarchs, potentates, and the religious cleric staff of the various **plutocracies** simply did not let anyone vote.

While there are subtle operational differences in the birthright, military might, and emperor-based plutocracy models, they are all memorialized for their development of a hierarchical class-based society, a nation-state economy, and an oligopoly-market shared by a few aristocratic (nobility) and plutocratic (other rich) buyers and sellers.

Other memorable "national" traits of the non-voting plutocracy models were a hierarchically distributed governance and a local-to-national economic control system that enforced the **conservative political ideology "for the accumulation of wealth by the wealthy" and the maintenance of the status quo social class structure** over a large land mass with a preponderance of the general population (90%) being poor or slaves.

Older plutocracies would usually get the church and deity to grant the richest or strongest "plutocrat" sovereignty over the land and dominion over the people living on it. The other plutocrats in the hierarchy simply got grants of nobility and land grants and fiefs along with the authority to help the royal family operate the local, regional, and national government and the national economy, for the accumulation of wealth by the wealthy.

The modern "elected" plutocracies use the **republic government** model where the **power and authority to govern is vested in representatives who are selected through an election process**. Most of the elected plutocracies were created in the last two centuries by plutocratic families whose political powers were derived from their wealth without the divine grants from a church or a deity.

Most of the "elected" plutocracies were initially created by liberal plutocrats after a revolution for the benefit of the people. The liberal plutocrats (open to new behavior or opinions and willing to discard traditional values) were generally opposed to the embedded conservative plutocracy for the accumulation of wealth by the wealthy.

The "elected" plutocrat-based government model has produced both **liberal democratic republics (from the Greek word *demos*, meaning "people")**, operating for the benefit of the people, and **conservative autocratic republics (from the Middle French word *conserver*, meaning "adverse to change and holding to traditional values and methods")**, operating the same way as traditional nonelected plutocracies for the accumulation of wealth by the wealthy, except they hold elections.

Some nations, including the USA have had both democratic and conservative plutocratic voting outcomes in their history. Other nations, like Russia and China have stuck with the conservative plutocracy model throughout their "voting" history.

To avoid the danger of misinformed or uninformed voters and/or the secret plutocrat/evangelical cults electing candidates who facilitate the conservative plutocracy model for the accumulation of wealth by the wealthy is the reason behind *The Voter's Guide to Candidate Assessment* and effective governance for the benefit of the people.

This book provides a Baby Boomer's hindsight into the legislative, economic, and social outcomes that the various generations produced as the new generations aged in. The Boomer's and Generation X were the largest voting bloc and the primary source of the poor federal candidate judgments and Gallup Poll ratings, over the last fifty years.

The guide will analyze a variety of historical events and information to help people "learn from history" how to recognize and understand the economic and societal differences between the "for the people" liberal governance behavior and the "for the accumulation of wealth by the wealthy" conservative governance behavior.

This new knowledge and insight into the role of government and the observed political behavior of representatives will hopefully motivate Millennials and help reprogram the thinking of the evangelicals and conservatives in the older generations of voters. The older generations have already produced the 50-year national decline and they need to join with the millennial voters to rescue the United States republic for the people, from the conservative ideological government mandate, supporting the accumulation of wealth by the wealthy.

Assessing the ability, skills, and quality of a candidate's future legislative behavior requires voters to have a rational intellect plus a general awareness of economics, math, science, and some level of understanding of the difference between effective governance for the people and effective governance for the accumulation of wealth by the wealthy.

The book uses examples from history and science to improve your awareness and understanding of the two governance ideologies and how the "for the people" role of government produces different results and ratings of government performance, versus the "for the accumulation of wealth by the wealthy" role of government.

The opinion polls on the effectiveness of the 115th Congress that just ended (2018), reflected a massive disapproval rating of people elected in 2016, even though there was a massive re-election count (93%) from the poorly rated 114th Congress.

What caused voters to clean the House in 2018 versus 2014 or 2016 is complex and will be analyzed throughout the book. How voters might have fixed the problem sooner and better are also questions that are considered and examined in the book.

While many voters are calling for term limits to stop the poor staffing decisions of voters, the term limits idea does not address the other "voting anomalies" that contribute to re-elections and our poor federal voting results (see Chapters 5-6 for voting insights).

Limiting terms would not have fixed the poor performance of our plutocracy, nor the poor performance of the **political party Duopoly (a political situation in which two major suppliers dominate the market for governance)** over the last 50 years.

The voting anomalies within the Duopoly range from re-electing poorly performing incumbents to conferring the title of president-elect on candidates who do not receive a popular majority of the votes in an election. In any case, this guide suggests that better-informed and skilled voters can learn how to avoid the incumbent and voting anomaly problems built into our federal election system. The Millennial-led voter rescue of the House in 2018 is an example of how to overcome a political party problem with votes.

In terms of historical timing, the governance role for the benefit of the people and voting are both relatively new ideas, created in the last couple hundred years as an alternative to the traditional "accumulation of wealth by the wealthy model." Voting made its entrance into history when liberal plutocrats in North America got a bunch of immigrants to vote with muskets in the 1775 Redcoat shootouts at Concord, Lexington, and Bunker Hill.

The musket-ball voters began the American Revolutionary War (1775-1783), pitting the liberal plutocrats against the conservative plutocrats in the colonies. Ralph Waldo Emerson called the original musket ball voting, "the shot heard around the world" in recognition of the musket ball vote's potentially earth-shaking consequences.

The liberal Founding Father plutocrats, referred to as Patriots, Revolutionaries, Continentals, Rebels, American Whigs, Scoundrels, and Traitors demonstrated that representative voting could also make a difference in the lives of the people.

The Continental Congress representatives, for example, voted 56-0 to release the Declaration of Independence on July 4th of 1776.

The liberal representatives declared their personal response to human events, based on the self-evident liberal heretical belief that all men are created equal and an equally heretical liberal governance idea that people empower government "for the benefit of the people."

Only a king with divine rights from God and the "accumulation of wealth for the wealthy" governance plutocracy in the colonies stood in their way.

The same liberal heretic "representatives" resolved the divine rights issues by declaring the king's personal colonies to be free and independent states that were now bound together by the people in a new nation called the United States.

The liberal plutocrat "vote" for independence from the conservative plutocrats in the colonies, in 1776, set in motion key events that became the first steps toward the introduction of the <u>new liberal governance ideology based on equality, justice, and the rule of law for improving the quality of life of the governed people and not just the rich.</u>

The equality of men and the social contract from the people empowering government for the benefit of the people was clearly the liberal political governance model at the opposite end of the conservative political governance ideology model, for sustaining the status quo class model operating for "for the accumulation of wealth by the wealthy."

Given this obvious political dichotomy between "for the people" and "for the wealthy," the war with Great Britain also generated a local plutocrat "political" war between the liberal Patriot Whigs and the conservative Loyalist Tories and Whigs in the colonies.

John Dickenson, a well-known plutocrat of the time, suggested that the economic and social issues of equality and income inequality could be resolved "among prudent men of Property" as a part of Great Britain and the divine right governance model.

For him, there was no need to change a successful working model of governance that had been producing wealth for the wealthy since at least the start of recorded history.

The Continental Congress that had approved the Declaration in 1776 produced the Articles of Confederation Constitution in 1777. Only 16 of the 56 original signers of the Declaration voted for the Articles, as written in 1777. The Articles, prepared by John Dickenson, a non-signer of the Declaration, were adopted in 1781. It formed 13 independent nation-states and formally disemboweled the Operating Continental Congress, to create a new limited, Articles based Congress.

The defeat of Cornwallis by George Washington's Army and the

French Navy, at Yorktown in October of 1781 signaled the end of the shooting hostilities with Great Britain. Peace terms and the king's giving up his divine rights in the colonies was signed in Paris by the Free States (1783) and the new Articles-based Congress, in 1784.

The leaders in the new states (the traditional conservative Tory/ Whig plutocrats and evangelical religious cult operators), adopted conservative state charters to facilitate the accumulation of wealth by the wealthy model and the reconciliation with Great Britain.

The liberal plutocrats responded to the conservative nation-state initiatives, in 1788, with a new "Constitutional Convention" proposing a second Constitution.

The second Constitution was sent to the Articles of Confederation-based Congress by the representatives serving in the Constitutional Convention that was created to amend the Articles Constitution. Thirty-nine of the 55 appointed representatives in Philadelphia Convention voted for and signed the proposed second Constitution. Sixteen rejected it or opted not to sign it.

The new Constitution proposed a new way of sharing power between the nation-state plutocrats and the people, through a representative-based federal republic and social contract model that had evolved from John Locke's liberal theories of government.

The conservative state plutocrats, favoring the traditional nation-state model and confederation, became the Anti-Federalists, opposed to the new Constitution and model.

Eventually, 1,648 of the United States' elitist plutocrats were wealthy enough to qualify as voters on the constitutional question. The Federalists (a coalition of liberal Whigs, Federalists, and liberal Tory plutocrats) won the constitutional vote by a 1,071 to 577 count in 1788, according to Wikipedia.

The new "for the people" representative-based "meritocracy" model of self-rule held its first elections and began operation in

1789, with 9 of the original 13 states. All 13 original colonies/states eventually voted to join the new nation by 1791.

The defeated Anti-Federalists became the Anti-Administration Party in the 1792 election, before transforming themselves into the conservative Democratic-Republican Party by 1794 (led by Slaveholder Jefferson and Big Business owner Madison).

Many of the conservative plutocrats also developed a cult-like anti-liberal movement to disrupt the new federal law model and to promote the failed nation-state model. The Anti-Federalist plutocrat-based cult has lived alongside the Constitution and has intervened in government's performance through both political parties. Asimov, in 1980, adroitly named the basic long-lived conservative group, the Cult of Ignorance.

The plutocratic Cult, while intervening via the political party system, has also spawned a variety of new secret anti-government societies in addition to the conservative wings of the political parties and a variety of new evangelical "Christian" denominations.

The new "rule of law" government model and its pro-plutocrat political party system that began in 1789 embraced the older secret societies (the Sons of Liberty, the Freemasons, the Rosicrucians, the Illuminati, and knighthood orders) with ties to Europe and the new voting and appointing processes created by the Constitution.

It is obvious today that the initial plutocrat-based political party process was a watershed event in history.

The number of House of Representatives members awarded to each state under the new Constitution was based on congressional districts (land mass and not people).

The newly created House institution was granted sole power to pass laws and fund the operation of government. Plutocrats in the land districts received seats based on population and were awarded 3/5 of a male person vote for each slave to give slavers numeric control over the Congress (8 Slave States and 5 Free States) and the Electoral College that selected the presidency. Each state also retained the right to determine who could vote in the federal elections.

The new Senate was granted oversight authorities and the authority to approve the House legislation and funding appropriations. The Senate, or upper chamber, was staffed with 2 state-appointed members (equal plutocrat representation from 8 Slave States and 5 Free States), with the authority to veto the House legislation.

The president and vice president, were also appointed positions, chosen after a referendum vote. The appointing body consisted of the Electoral College (a state-based plutocratic body consisting of people with no direct role in the federal government). Seats in the College were generally awarded to the political party that won the presidential vote.

The Anti-Federalist and Anti-Administration conservatives that became the Democratic-Republican Party took over most representative roles from the Federalists with the election of Thomas Jefferson in 1800. The Republican, Whig, and Federalist Parties virtually disappeared with the election of Democrat Andrew Jackson in 1828.

The conservative agrarian slavery plutocrats (the Democratic Party) and the national land-grab coalition of the rich Republican plutocrats was eventually displaced in 1854 by the liberal Federalist Whigs and Tories operating under the banner of the new Republican Party (the Grand Old Party and GOP relabeling by the Federalist liberals).

The "all men created equal" restrictions inhibiting the slavery-based economy in new states, the transfer of public land to private ownership, the anti-Indian/Mexico land grab and the abolitionist movement were all hot political issues by the 1850s.

The "for the people" versus the "for the accumulation of wealth" conflict over the first 50 years of the new century had produced ups and downs in terms of its governance performance. Clearly, the conservative ideological principles bloomed during the national land-grab era (Manifest Destiny). The land grab reached the Pacific west coast by 1850, when California became the 31st state.

On the other hand, the liberal goals of forming "a more perfect Union" and establishing "justice to insure Domestic Tranquility" had not done well. By 1850, Slave States were threatening to secede and by 1861, 11 of the states were in open rebellion against the union with a stated goal to preserve and extend the slavery-based economies.

The failure to avoid the Civil War and the post-war Reconstruction produced the "If voting made any difference, they wouldn't let us do it" quote opening this chapter.

To clarify, it should be recognized that there is no record of Mark Twain (or Samuel Clemens, his real name) ever saying, writing, or posting on Facebook or Twitter that "If voting made any difference, they wouldn't let us do it."

The controversial commentator who made up this quote probably just wanted to borrow Twain's credibility while pointing out a perceived weakness in the plutocrat-controlled meritocracy model of representative governance and government.

The quote, like the other information discussed in this book was not intended to produce patriotism or criticism of the country.

The quote's goal back then was probably to generate new thought and insight into ways to improve the political party processes and governance performance for the people results during the Reconstruction Era.

While it seems that Mr. Twain was not the actual source, the critical witticism does reflect a major concern about giving ex-slaves the right to vote in the US political party system used to elect plutocratic representatives to run the federal government.

The fictitious quote gets to the heart of the issues of voting and governance for the people. It suggests that the votes of the people (white or black males only), did not make any difference to the rich plutocrats operating the political party system.

The quote also indirectly implies that the plutocrats who fund, manage, and operate the political party system, effectively control the candidates and ultimately, the actions of the representatives during their service in the "political party" controlled Congress.

Obviously, the conservative plutocratic orders to "representatives" and the "party over country" behavior had already produced the withdrawal of the Slave States from the Union over the election of Abraham Lincoln and the liberal Republican Congress in 1860. An estimated 700,000 Americans were killed in the four-year fight over slavery and the granting of liberty and voting rights to slaves without payment to slave-owners or slaves.

The new "freedom" and "liberty" for slaves (constitutional amendments), the liberal Homestead Act giving away free land for anybody who would farm it (1.6 million claims covering about 10% of the United States were given away) and the radical Republican Reconstruction Act (Reconstruction of the South and restoral of the Federalist principles) were all fresh in the mind of whoever asked the question on whether voting matters.

Despite the Civil War and post-war disaster, the political party and federal republic voting processes and meritocracy operations seemingly produced a viable way for the voters to directly influence and manage the never-ending ideological conflict between the liberal candidates and their "for the people political ideology" versus the conservative candidates, with their "for the accumulation of wealth by the wealthy" political ideology.

Global indicators also suggest the political party and federal republic voting model was also beginning to appear in other parts of the world late in the 1800s.

Today, (242 years since the inception of a voter-based republic), 180 of the 220 nations and territories on the planet use a plutocrat-funded political party system and federal republic voting processes for *de jure* (legal) governance in one form or another.

The traditional birthright and anointed plutocracies (kings, monarchs, etc.) have virtually all lost governance control, although *de facto* (in actual fact) dictatorships for the accumulation of wealth remain operational in many *de jure* republics.

Both sides of the US political dichotomy (for the people liberals versus for the accumulation of wealth by the wealthy conservatives) have demonstrated an ability to pass controversial legislation in the US over the objections of the opposing party.

Extending healthcare to 19 million people with a tax increase and a deficit reduction military spending plan like the Obama era Sequester versus the recent tax cuts for the rich, a military spending binge and the massive deficit increase plan from the Office of Management and Budget are two modern-day examples of the liberal versus conservative dichotomy.

The diverse legislation also shows that voting for representatives and the voting in Congress is risky, but the process of assessing candidates and electing representatives does make a difference to the quality of life of the people in the nation.

Various chapters in the Voter Guide will explore the competing state plutocrat operations and the "party over country" national risks. We will also examine the historical events and voting anomalies leading up to the current candidate assessment and "voting risk" in terms of the liberal government ideology model (for the people) versus the conservative government ideology model (for the accumulation of wealth by the wealthy).

The two conflicting governance models were an obvious threat at the founding of the new nation. Many safeguards were built into the Constitution to provide checks and balances and avoid the concentration of power by plutocrats favoring one over the other.

Although the development a two-party political system was considered anathema by Washington and Adams (the first two Federalist presidents) in terms of the new nation that they were trying to build, the embedded anomalies in the federal voting processes produced today's *de facto* two-party political system in spite of their concerns.

In fact, by 1800, the liberal administration was pitted directly against the conservative Democratic-Republican Party. Jefferson and the conservative political party won and inadvertently set the nation on its path to the Civil War.

The guide will examine the nation's evolution over the 240-plus years and will in some ways suggest that the last 50 years of congressional and executive branch performance have proven to be as divisive as the fifty years following that 1800 election of Jefferson.

Hopefully, the current VEP will develop their candidate assessment and voting skills and avoid another shooting war within in the United States, trying to resolve the "for the people" versus the "for the accumulation of wealth by the wealthy" governance issue.

Our current social and economic environment does demonstrate that Washington and Adams were also prophetic in addition to being Founding Fathers. They foresaw the risk of a two-party political system where the political ideologies of both parties become the accumulation of wealth by the wealthy model, just to fund the election campaign cost.

The next chapter will explore the role of government and civics, the role of the people and how they interact with the economic and social system of a nation.

Enjoy the rest of the guide.

CHAPTER 2

The Role of Government, Civics, Economics, and Social Order

"Remember, democracy never lasts long. It soon wastes, exhausts, and murders itself. There never was a democracy yet that did not commit suicide."
—JOHN ADAMS

The institution of our government is a mixture of local, regional and national controls over the land, the resources and the people living on the land. The output of the political government institution is law and order, the social-economic environment of the nation and the economic/cultural operating milieu within the nation and between nations.

Our Federal government's legal rights, authority and role are summarized in the Preamble of the Constitution. "We the People of the United States: 1. in Order to form a more perfect Union, 2. establish Justice, 3. insure domestic Tranquility, 4. provide for the common defence, 5. promote the general Welfare, and 6. secure the Blessings of Liberty to ourselves and our Posterity, do ordain and establish this Constitution for the United States of America."

Notice it was the people of the nation and not the states looking for a more perfect union, justice and domestic Tranquility. It was also not clear which states wanted a common defence, while promoting the general Welfare, to secure the Blessing of Liberty...

As implied by the direct quote from Mr. Adams, the America he helped create was not a Democracy (derived from the Greek word demos meaning people and kraytos meaning rule). The Constitution that the founding fathers installed is a Representative Republic meritocracy, empowered by the eligible voters and operated by the representatives of the voters. Every State and territory have voted to accept the constitution and pledged to support it. Thirteen (13) states have formally violated their pledge to the for the people constitution, in pursuit of the accumulation of wealth by the wealthy model.

The Constitution that specifies the Federal government authority and roll also spells out the privileges and obligations of its citizens, their representatives and the states. The science behind the citizen's responsibilities and rights are called civics.

The combination of the rule of law and civics interacting with the economy, the social environment, and the various layers of government, generates and produces the economic, legal, religious, and social environment of the nation. Many people refer to the general environment as the eco-system while others use the term social milieu to describe where and how they live.

The historical overview in this chapter is intended to provide you with facts and insights into the history of other government models and how government processes ultimately evolved over time. This information should help voters identify and select better candidates and avoid re-electing representatives based on their personal behaviors and patterns that produce government "for the accumulation of wealth by the wealthy" versus government "for the benefit of the governed people."

In the same way that historical records do not show exactly

who learned how to control fire, make a wheel, or plow a field (The Neolithic Revolution), we do not currently know exactly who first learned how to convert governance into the economic engine for powering the development of the various societies and the various national economies.

Early artifacts and ancient history credit Mesopotamia and the Babylonian monarchy as having inspired some of the most important developments in human history, including the invention of the wheel, the planting of the first cereal crops, the development of cursive script, the development of mathematics, the development of distillation, the development of astronomy, the development of agriculture, and the development of civics, with written laws and behavioral expectations and punishments for anti-social behavior.

The Babylonian monarchy is also recognized for the introduction of the Nation-State Government (NSG) model and the implementation of the Monetary Sovereignty banking model that facilitated fiat money to drive the exchange of goods and services in ways that produced the notions of income, expenses, and profits, with fiat money as the value medium, replacing simple barter and trade value exchanges between people and tribes.

The Monetary Sovereignty and NSG model were initially very successful ways for governments to manage multiple cultures and large land masses for the accumulation of wealth by the royal family, the appointed aristocracy and the other plutocrats.

The 282 written laws and the scaled punishments for freemen and slaves in "The Code of Hammurabi" dates to about 1750 BC. These early records of law and order, civics, and banking all helped earn the Euphrates River area the title as the "cradle of civilization" (Iran, Iraq, Syria, Turkey, Egypt area today).

Other pockets of advanced cultures clearly existed around the world. Most of them did not develop a recording system showing how the sustaining governments created civics, banking, law and order, and an economic model for producing wealth.

What is obvious from history is that over the centuries, various nations developed their own unique eco-systems and social/cultural/political milieu.

What is also obvious is that "gods" and the aristocracy were typically the primary force of government, not people.

Today's religious training materials, such as the Bible, Torah, and Koran all provide insights into the development of many unique government models. The Genesis story in both the Bible and Torah, for example, presents a unified description of the creation of the universe, governance, government, civics, and their economy.

In the book of Genesis, on the sixth day, for example, God became the first lawgiver, lawmaker, and government service provider, creating law and order and civics, along with Adam and Eve. According to Genesis, the new government also created the unalienable rights and granted them to mankind, along with human rights, human frailties, free will to decide based on personal self-interest, and dominion over the land and sea.

In the Genesis story, the initial role of the people seems to have been the pursuit of happiness. Their civic responsibility, in the story was to simply obey the laws of God. For the government's reasons, God mandated that people leave the tree of knowledge alone. You probably know the outcome. The law was broken, and the tenants got evicted.

The Cain and Abel murder story later in Genesis and the Moses commandment narrative in the Bible and Torah both demonstrate the need for governance, government, and laws to regulate human behavior, while Leviticus helped define civics and other personal behaviors.

The political implications are clear in the religious documentation. God typically granted the authority to pass laws and govern to the local leaders, who were selected by God.

This theocracy government model, in which a **deity is the source from which government authority is derived,** dominates the Bible, the Torah, and the Koran. In fact, whenever you see the terms "master," "ruler," or "government" in these books, you also get the message to obey the laws of God, passed down to the people via the government.

Secular government models (non-religious based authority to govern) also evolved. Artifacts and records suggest that a secular group of people (tribal elders, village leaders, military leaders, witch doctors, and plutocrats) either voted for a leader to be the government service provider, or the leader voted to take over the nation.

In these early secular government models, **people are the source from which government authority is derived. Civics emanated from the same sources.**

The theocratic-secular history records produced many government and civics models, ranging from simple autocracy (dictators and self-proclaimed gods of Egypt) to plutocracy (government controlled by a small minority of the wealthiest citizens).

The Mongolian-style **democracy** of Genghis Khan, the Athenian democracy of Greece, and the Harappan and Aryan dynasties in India and Pakistan all have a place in the historical evolution of government models and civics.

The centralized national government model (called the unitary model, covered in Chapter 3) operated from a relatively weak centralized base (the monarchy) that developed political ties to the local area plutocrats and the theocratic local ministry.

The political ties were typically based on grants of nobility, fiefdoms, and close ties with the religious establishment and military enforcement resources.

The monarchy and locally appointed aristocracy/ministry <u>focused on the "accumulation of wealth by the wealthy" plutocrats, the religious leaders and the hierarchical aristocracy, nobility and plutocrat landowners and trader-merchants that operated in the unitary model.</u>

Figure 3 is an example of the unitary government model and civics structure using the Great Britain terminology and model that produced the liberal revolution for the people in America.

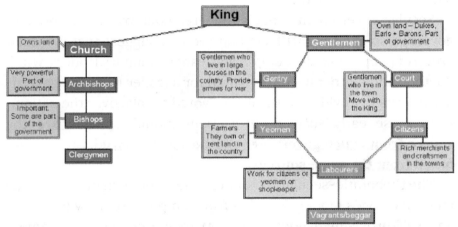

Figure 6 *The Traditional King Church Unitary Model of Plutocrat Government and Society*

The unitary model is based on a weak centralized government organized into a hierarchy, with political power and authority emanating from the top (the strongman patriarch) and distributed downward via the appointed and titled local government service operators. Many of today's conservatives incorrectly suggest the federal republic meritocracy model was intended to replicate this hierarchy model of wealth creation.

For most of recorded history (as mentioned recording of history began around 5000 BC), the national government generally consisted of a deity-enabled leader and an appointed aristocracy. The patriarch/king could be a God (Egypt), the religious patriarch leader (Israel/Judah), and was often the strongman leader (Roman Emperor).

In most cases, the leader was ordained king/emperor by the priests and granted the divine right of sovereignty over the land and dominion over the people by the local gods.

There were over 100,000 formalized unitary national "governments" that operated various national models in pre-recorded and recorded history, before the new rule of law, federal self-rule processes and the new representative based meritocracy staffing model of the United States was adopted in 1789.

The early unitary nations ranged in size from the city-state of Athens (small area) to the multiple-state nations (multi-cultural area such as Great Britain) and ultimately, the empire (massive geographic areas like multi-continent Russia). Clearly, these 100,000 national governments had a positive impact on the population growth.

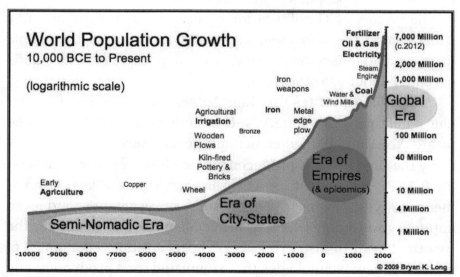

Figure 7 *Government, Population Growth and Civilization Milestones from BC to The Global Impact AD Era of Today.*

Whether the force of the national government and the impact of religious controls were solely responsible for the population growth is debatable. Any number of factors other than law and order, civics, and a stable economic, legal, social, and political government environment are possible causes of the extensive population growth.

For example, the invention of the wheel, the development of agriculture, the ability to master the plumbing of water, and even the scientific discovery of fermentation and distillation processes could be other possible root causes for all those new people showing up on the planet.

While other factors could be the cause of the population explosion, there is virtually no debate that the unitary Nation State Government (NSG) model was generally responsible for the development of national economies, the social structure, and the quality of life of the people within its borders.

The unitary NSG political force began replacing the nomadic tribal elders, the holy men, the local warlords, and the simple metes and bounds notion of land ownership with a national political entity about 5,000 years ago.

Wikipedia postulates that King Menes was operating a hierarchical multiple-state unitary NSG as far back as 3150 BC when he formed the United Kingdom national government of Egypt.

By the time humans produced written history records (around 3500 BC?), the multi-tribe governments, urban village governments, city-state governments, state governments, and even national governments seeking the accumulation of wealth for the wealthy began to also produce job specialization, economies of scale, and new technologies that stimulated food production and population growth.

These technological and economic advances produced more

exchanges of goods and services, a better understanding of natural resources, and increased knowledge of how to use resources and technologies.

As shown in the previous population trend line, the technology, knowledge, and government process hit major inflection points about 5000 BC and again at 1500 AD.

The process of learning from history and using the knowledge of predecessors to create new knowledge seems to have produce these spikes in the population trend line.

The population spikes also reflect certain groups creating an economic advantage over other tribes and other groups for the collection of taxes and tribute.

Conservatism, the political ideology generally defined as the desire to avoid change and maintain the status quo, became the political ideology of choice, regardless of size, model, and religious persuasion of the unitary government.

By 500 AD, royal family notions of inheritance rights and government hierarchy had become the economic mainstay supporting the conservative ideology.

Conservatism remained the political ideology of choice for most of recorded history.

The desire and need to avoid change and maintain the status quo monarchy, dynasty, patriarchy, or theocracy for the accumulation of wealth by the wealthy also became intertwined with newer religious belief systems (Christianity and Islam).

Nation-states, kingdoms and empires (under a single unitary government) became the cornerstone of economic growth (accumulation of wealth by the wealthy) and the subtle driving force behind the population growth.

The development of the Roman Empire signaled the high point of the ancient civilizations. Notice the national extent of Roman

Empire government that had evolved by the time of Christ. Also notice the massive unitary nations outside of Rome's control.

Figure 8 *Europe, Northern Africa, Middle East and the Unitary Government Model*

The separation of the Roman Empire into the Eastern and Western Empires about 300 AD and the eventual "Fall of Rome" to barbarians from Germania in 476 AD signaled the end of the ancient unitary civilizations and the start of the Middle Ages unitary model.

The deity-enabled royal family and king/priest strongman unitary model transitioned to the inheritance and royal family rights model during the Middle Ages. The family inheritance of authority to rule extended the government's leadership role and institutional power through generations of the same family, although new theocracy-based nations also appeared via the Islamic cultures in the East.

The political government and religious confrontations of the Middle Ages were enormous. Changes in the Middle Ages began with the rise of Islam (900 AD), the Great Catholic Schisms (1080 AD), the Protestant Revolution (1200 AD), the Renaissance (1300 AD), the Enlightenment (1500 AD), the introduction of liberalism (1600 AD) and the development of capitalism (1700 AD).

The unitary plutocracy model of government for the accumulation of wealth by the wealthy was virtually unchanged by these massive intellectual, ideological and political developments.

Liberalism and its acceptance of change for the benefit of the people became the heretical antithesis of the resistance-to-change conservativism, much as capitalism and prosperity for everyone in the nation would become the heretical antithesis of mercantilism, for the accumulation of wealth by the wealthy.

The Humanistic movement within the Renaissance Period (1300-1700) and the Enlightenment that followed produced the philosophers, theorists, and truth-seekers like John Locke (Father of liberalism) and Adam Smith (Father of capitalism).

Locke, a physician, questioned the legitimacy of conservative government with inherited divine rights. Smith, an economist, questioned the legitimacy of mercantilism for the accumulation of wealth by the government and its hierarchy instead of the people.

Locke claimed that men are by nature free and equal and born with the same inalienable rights. Conservative governance models were at the other end of the rights spectrum. The conservative model claimed that God had made all people naturally subject to a monarch (chosen government leader enabled by God). Moreover, the chosen ones were also divinely empowered with sovereign rights to the land and dominion over the people. People in general were considered sinful (the fall of Adam and Eve) and in need of governance and ultimately salvation.

Locke went further with the liberal claim that political power is the natural power of each man collectively given up into the hands of a designated person (representative). In this model, a community, state, or nation of people surrenders some degree of their natural rights to a selected representative-based government, which is better able to protect those individual rights in comparison to what any man or small collective could do alone.

From Locke's liberalism and the social contract of people with government perspective, the people empowered government. In this social contract context, the government exists solely for the well-being of the people and the communities. Government for the accumulation of wealth by the government (mercantilism was the term used in the day), its nobility, and its appointed aristocracy were simply not in the best interest of the people, according to the liberal revolutionaries.

From Locke's treatise, any government representative that would break the contract for the benefit of the people can and should be replaced. In fact, according to Locke, the community has a moral obligation to revolt against or otherwise replace any government that forgets that it exists only for the people's benefit and to "promote the general Welfare" as the constitution describes one of the key roles of the government.

Liberal plutocrats like John Stuart Mill espoused these political ideologies about people-empowered government for the benefit of people, as an alternative to the tax- and tribute-based mercantile model for the accumulation of wealth by the wealthy.

Likewise, the notion of a moral obligation to revolt against or replace a bad government model struck a chord with certain people outside of the aristocracy, ministry, and nobility circle in Great Britain and the colonies.

History clearly suggests that taxes for the accumulation of wealth by the wealthy, living in Great Britain, and placed on the plutocrats, living in the Crown Colonies in North America, transformed a small number of the liberal plutocrats in the colonies into traitors to the Crown, the King of England, and the religious head of the Anglican church.

The transformation of colonists into traitors and scoundrels began the day plutocrat John Hancock hired George Washington (the richest plutocrat in the colonies), to create a Continental Army and lead an uprising against the British government (June 19, 1775).

The threat of a plutocrat army turned into the shootouts in Concord, Lexington, and Boston. The following year, 1776, the threat of liberalism and voters became obvious. Fifty-six liberal plutocrat voters approved the Declaration of Independence.

The new liberal political ideology and the civics model was clearly at the opposite end of the political ideology continuum with respect to conservatism. Instead of maintaining the status quo and divine rights of the royal family, the liberals were open to creating a new government process, driven by elected and appointed representatives.

This new government behavior model included the willingness to discard the conservative values of the national government for the accumulation of wealth by the wealthy and replace it with a government for the benefit of the people.

The July 4, 1776 document was released by Congress explaining their rejection of the royalty, aristocracy and nobility government model and their proposed new model of voter empowered government representatives working for the benefit of the people.

In 1788, the threat of liberalism and voters formally began to change the course of unitary government history, with the second Constitution proposal.

The first Constitutional Convention in 1787 was convened to amend the first national Constitution. Instead, the liberals proposed a radically different federal government and civics model for sharing governance with the individual NSG (nation-state governments). The liberal representative-based plutocracy model was formally adopted by the 9th State in 1788. With the adoption, the new law of the land went into effect in 1789. The final 4 NSG plutocracies joined the original 9 nation-states by 1791.

As the nation developed, expanded, and grew in population, land mass, and importance, it became apparent to history that the second Constitution for the benefit of the people had been a watershed event in both government and civics.

The civics idea that House members would earn their position (meritocracy) via a popular vote was an unprecedented break with the past. The number of House seats were determined by land area boundaries and not just the local population counts.

The new House members were granted a two-year term of office and the sole source of power to adopt laws and fund the federal government, while serving in a congressional session. The short-term cycle (2 years) and sole authority to fund the government operations ensured representatives would "merit" a re-election, based on their actual performance.

The Senate members (2 per state) of the new Congress were to be appointed by the state plutocrats. The appointed plutocrats served for a six-year period.

The Senate was granted approval authority over the laws from the representatives. The Senate representatives were also granted oversight authority on treaties and the hiring of key federal employees and Supreme Court judges. Senators were granted the unique authority to convert legislation from the House of Representatives into the all-powerful Acts of Congress.

The executive branch (president and vice president) was to be evaluated through a popular vote referendum. The executive branch was elected, though, by a vote of state plutocrats serving in the Electoral College. Plutocrats in each state could appoint or elect members to the Electoral College. The number of state votes in the College was equal to the total number of House and Senate seats. Each College member initially had two votes, one vote for president and one for vice president.

The 1790 census shows there were about 2.4 million freemen and 600,000 slaves in the nation. Based on records, 38,818 votes were cast in the first election (1788).

George Washington ran unopposed as an independent liberal (not as a Federalist or an Anti-Federalist). He got all the votes from the 38,000 plutocrats in the first election. He also received all 69 Electoral College votes. Adams was elected as vice president with no popular votes and only 34 Electoral College votes.

The new executive branch would serve a four-year term of office and have the authority to appoint Supreme Court justices with advice and consent from the Senate. The justices were granted the authority to adjudicate conflicts and be the final decision point on any disagreements with the States.

The unique new meritocracy model (representative based government) sharing various authorities with the nation-states, effectively granted the representatives some of the nation-state's sovereign rights.

In this sovereign power context, states cannot coin money, grant titles of nobility, or regulate commerce with foreign countries or other states. States are also not authorized to naturalize citizens, fix standards of weights and measures, declare war, or support an army or navy.

The new republic model has become relatively successful over the centuries. The green areas of the map reflect the various federal republic government models, versus the blue areas where unitary forms of government still operate.

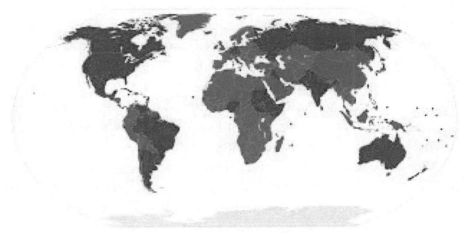

Figure 9 *Federal Republics*

The federal republic meritocracy and governance model has also been adapted by the unitary governments in ways never conceived of by the founding fathers. The following chart reflects how the new model has permeated the unitary structure as well.

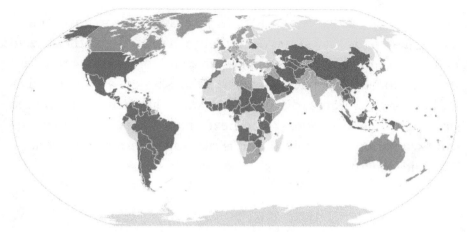

Figure 10 *Federal Adaptions to the Unitary Model*

Legend[edit]

- ▋ Presidential republics with a full legislative Congress and presidential system
- ▯ Presidential republics with a semi-presidential system
- ▮ Parliamentary republics with an executive presidency dependent on the legislature
- ▯ Parliamentary republics with a ceremonial/non-executive president, where a separate head of government leads the executive
- ▮ Constitutional monarchy with a ceremonial monarch, where a separate head of government leads the executive
- ▮ Constitutional monarchy which have with a separate head of government, but where royalty still hold significant executive and/or legislative power
- ▮ Absolute monarchy
- ▮ Countries where the dominant role of political party is codified in the constitution
- ▮ Countries in which constitutional provisions for government have been suspended (e.g. military dictatorship)
- ▯ Countries which do not fit any of the above systems (e.g. transitional government or unclear political situations)
- ▯ No government

Note: this chart represents *de jure* systems of government (according to their laws). It is not directly correlated with the *de facto* degree of representative democracy in a nation. Several nations are constitutionally republics on paper, although they are operated as authoritarian plutocrat driven Fascist states like Venezuela and the privatized Russia of today. The next chapter describes how well our own nation ran, evolved, and is running in terms of our federal republic Constitution and its mandates for the people.

CHAPTER 3

The New "For the People" Federal Government Process and Performance

"... that the nation, shall have a new birth of freedom, and that government of the people, by the people, for the people, shall not perish from the earth."
—ABRAHAM LINCOLN

The liberal political ideology to improve the quality of life of the general population ("promote the general Welfare") instead of just the wealthy grew out of the Renaissance, the Enlightenment, the new thoughts about the nature of man, the massive religious conflicts (Catholics, Protestants, Evangelicals and Muslims), the new capitalist ideas about the wealth of nations being the wealth of the people in the nation, and the advances in science and technology (1350-1800 AD) late in the middle ages.

The new theories about the nature of man and government from John Locke and his followers fundamentally changed the role of national government by rejecting the unitary hierarchical government model (aristocracy/plutocracy) of the nation-state government mandate for the accumulation of wealth by the wealthy.

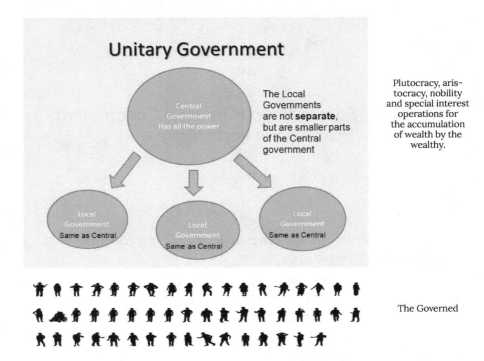

Figure 11 *The Plutocrat-Based Unitary Model of Government*

The new federal model of the United States proposed in 1788 rejected the Confederation model of independent nation-states (NSG) that the conservatives had adopted in 1781.

The new national governance for the people in the hands of voters, appointers, and their selected representatives, hit upon the idea of sharing local, state and regional governance authority and power with a new centralized government, chartered to perform national tasks of justices, security and a mandate to promote the General Welfare for the people in the multiple states.

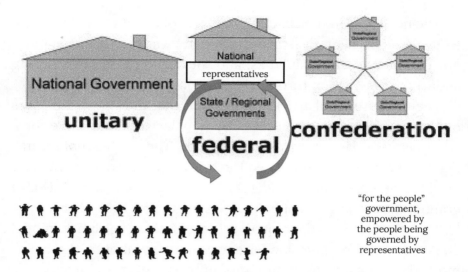

Figure 12 *The Voter-Representative Based Federal Model of government*

The federal republic constitutional model of the United States delineated the national shared governance framework that would become a *de jure* (legal) template.

The Constitution's first three articles define the three new branches of the federal government (Congress, the executive branch and the Supreme Court), the powers of each new institution, and the separation of powers between the three entities. The new law also outlawed the granting of nobility and the acceptance of emoluments.

Articles IV through VI (four through six) entrench the basic liberal concepts of federalism and how national laws were to be made and adopted. These sections also include the description of the rights and responsibilities of state governments, the oaths of the adopting states, the commerce rules, the supremacy definitions, the state relationship to the federal government, and the ways to amend the Constitution.

The newly created bicameral Congress of the United States (the House of Representatives and the Senate) was granted legal powers, commerce responsibilities, and the authority to effect (bring about) the new nation through legislation.

The Constitutional articles spelled out that the House members of Congress were to be selected by popular vote and serve for a two-year period in a congressional session. The elected representatives of the voters were granted the sole authority to pass laws and fund the operation of the federal government. Each state was also granted the authority to appoint two senators for a six-year term.

The elected and appointed representative legislative model changed the economic model and ultimately altered the social model by stopping the granting of nobility rights and mandating House elections based on popular vote and head counts.

Initially, the appointed and elected representatives and the voters themselves all came from the plutocracy. As individuals, the representatives had little personal power in Congress. On the other hand, as a group, Congress had and still has virtually unlimited power and authority to effect (bring about) the development of the nation.

The new representative-based national Federal Government model (NFG) distributed political power between wealthy liberal plutocrats and conservative plutocrats from multiple states and territory regions of the county. The new government model centralized our national economy (commerce clause), the national military, and the national monetary system, while making the national government the only source of national banking, governance, protection, and legislation.

It should be noted that the new NFG model did not replace the "for the accumulation of wealth by the wealthy" economic role of the Nation-State Governments running the states. States were left to their own devices, at least until George Washington marched 14,000 soldiers into Pennsylvania to put down the tax-avoidance

Whiskey Rebellion claim that the federal government could not levy taxes on their state.

The new federal Constitution model and the voting processes indirectly facilitated the rapid adoption of a new "for the people" economic system called capitalism.

The new economic and social ideas of capitalism and federalism put into motion a new political process that would stimulate the development of "for the people" rights and the notion of a non-plutocrat voter enabled governance model, in the new republic.

The heretical "for the people" notions of capitalism had been introduced to the world by Adam Smith (the Father of Capitalism) in 1776, just 90 days or so before the heretical Declaration of Independence introduced the new political governance model.

Adam Smith's *Wealth of Nations* opus in 1776 was an economic review and survey of human social psychology about life, welfare, political institutions, the law, and morality.

The then-new economic social model of capitalism, like the new liberal political model of meritocracy-based government (voters and representatives) were both focused on the people in the nation and not just the aristocracy/plutocrat accumulation of wealth.

In general, Adam Smith's ideas of capitalism directly attacked and ultimately altered the mercantile supply-side economic system of the conservative plutocrat government models that were in place for the accumulation of wealth by the wealthy.

According to Adam Smith and his *Wealth of Nations* theories, national wealth was not to be measured by the amount of precious minerals, pretty stones, buildings, and artwork accumulated and locked up in castles, estates, summer homes, church ministries and the plantation mansions owned by the aristocracy, church, and nobility.

Mr. Smith suggested the accumulated wealth of the wealthy produced virtually nothing of real intrinsic value for the nation or the people in the nation. Moreover, Smith suggested that the government's focus on the accumulation of land, minerals, and raw resources (mercantilism), inhibited the creation of prosperity for the people in the nation.

National prosperity in the industrializing economy, envisioned by Smith, required the consumption of goods and services (commerce) by the people in the marketplace.

This exchange of goods and services by the people in the market is based on their own self-interests in making the exchange. The best interest of the people in an exchange does not often correlate well with the best interests of the rich in the acquisition of wealth.

The personal self-interest exchange model of commerce would produce income for owners and wages for the people. The wages would produce more "exchanges," ultimately producing prosperity for the nation and the people, according to the principles of capitalism.

The new government role in the capitalism-based market economy was to **effect** (bring about) private property, ensure justice, protect its citizens and provide the government services that the markets needed to ensure justice, produce prosperity for the people, and provide the domestic tranquility to **effect** their safety and happiness.

As mentioned earlier, the equality, the unalienable rights, the written Constitution, and the representative meritocracy model of the new federal government for the people was not an evolutionary governance development, flowing from the conservative-based unitary nation-state government model for the accumulation of wealth by the wealthy.

In fact, the new liberal political ideology of equality, unalienable rights of men, and the representative-based government for the benefit of the people was and is in direct conflict with the unitary NSG model and economic/political conservatism plan for the accumulation of wealth by the wealthy.

Although the liberals were successful in getting the new Constitution adopted, their efforts also created what would become the Cult of Ignorance. This chapter's opening words from the Gettysburg Address, recommitting our nation to the unique United States model of "by and for the people" is testimony from our history to the ongoing conflict with the conservative Cult of Ignorance support for the NSG model.

Although the Civil War shooting and secession of states ended a long time ago, the war between the liberal federal republic model for the people and nation-state government model for the accumulation of wealth by the wealthy continues.

Amending the Constitution is the legal way authorized by the Constitution to change the role of government. Both Congress and the nation-state governments have the right to propose amendments. The Constitution has been amended, <u>by the representatives in Congress</u>, 27 times over the years since its initial adoption in 1788.

Most of these amendments and changes were designed to confer, clarify, and define the legal rights of people associated with the "for the people" role of government. Several amendments deal with the way elections and voting processes are handled.

As an example, the first ten amendments, often called the Bill of Rights, were prepared by Congress in 1789 (its first year of operation) and adopted by the states, in 1791. The original Federalists did not want these rights spelled out. Liberals wanted them spelled out before their states would take a final vote on entering the union. Conservatives wanted what would become the tenth amendment, in hopes of using its words to block the scope and scale of the new federal government.

These first ten amendments clarified the authorities of the federal government, the state government and the civil rights of the people. It should be noted there were 12 proposed amendments in the original package. One of the originally rejected two amendments were adopted nearly two hundred years later. As of 2018, only one of the original twelve amendments has not yet been adopted by enough states.

Clearly, the "for the people" political processes and the voting, appointing, and approval processes have produced significant economic and societal changes.

Many of the economic changes were driven by new thoughts about capitalism.

The social change, though, was driven by the liberal idea of voting power, elected representatives and the process for passing laws and legislation for the benefit of the people, instead of the accumulation of wealth.

The idea of voting was not a new liberal idea. Voting was a method, developed by people, to enable people to decide or express an opinion about a course of action.

The new representative-based republic operation, for the benefit of the people and posterity, coupled with the defined national shared governance framework of government authorities, produced a unique new way to control the behavior of people, the development of the economy, and the social environment.

The new, unique NSG-NFG (State-Federal) relationship has produced an ongoing transformation, as the federal representatives tested and developed new economic theories, new plans, new markets, and new government practices and processes.

Today, after several hundred years of constitutional operations, the actual enacted laws, amendments, and the funding of the federal government operations has produced the current economic, political, social, and cultural milieu of the United States. In short, the past produced the present, and solving today's problems requires insight into the past.

In the current environment, for example, the United States is now the third most populous country (340 million people) on the planet. In addition to the massive growth in populations, the US has also become the richest country in the world, in terms of income, profits, Gross Domestic Product (GDP), and the sale of goods and services.

While it certainly seems rational to hold our federal republic out as a national success, it should also be recognized all is not well. The Cult of Ignorance and radical right-wing conservatives have induced 28 state legislatures to call for a Constitutional Convention to amend the Constitution in ways that have never been used before.

Moreover, radical leftists in California and radical right-wing conservatives in Texas are calling for the two states with the largest economies and populations to secede from the union. What could go wrong, with a Constitutional convention and the two states seceding from the Union, given our current opinion base of government leadership skills?

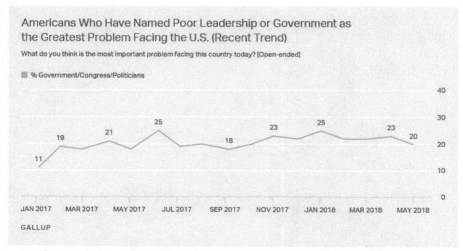

Figure 13 *The Latest Figures from Gallup's Values and Beliefs poll, Conducted May 1-10, 2017.*

The next chapter will explore the transition of the original plutocrat republic (only the rich landowners could vote) to today's democratic republic, where 240 million of the nation's 320 million adults (18 and older) are part of the Voter Eligible Population (VEP).

CHAPTER 4

Transforming the Original Plutocrat Republic into a Democratic Republic

"When people find out they can vote themselves money, that will herald the end of our Republic."
—BENJAMIN FRANKLIN

Sarcastic conjecture has it that the Americans for Prosperity got this quote from Franklin's personal email to the Koch brothers, thanking them for their support of the Cult of Ignorance and their personal effort to reboot the conservative republic model.

Many readers probably determined that the quote is phony and that the sarcastic conjecture is also fake by deducing the information, thinking carefully about the known facts, and drawing a logical and rational conclusion.

Logical reasoning is not an art form. It is a thinking process to figure out the truth (or facts) based on what you already know and then deciding what to do. All software programming relies on this simple concept; whether you use inductive reasoning, where the information gives you the evidence to draw a logical conclusion, or deductive reasoning, where general knowledge can be applied to the specific instance under examination.

Could the first Postmaster of the United States, who was appointed in 1775, have sent an email over a system that was not created until 1972? Would the author of *Poor Richard's Almanack* and the *Dogwood Letters* ever have said something that inane about the voters and representatives, he helped create, via the federal republic model?

To deduce something through logical reasoning is a mental process used to arrive at a fact or a logical conclusion by reasoning. Reasoning requires some level of previous personal knowledge about the subject. This knowledge can only be acquired through learning and practicing.

How much knowledge you need to deduce something correctly depends on the subject at hand. Misinformation, personal misperceptions, and the very lack of basic knowledge about the subject do not help people correctly deduce something.

For example, how many people have read the phony Franklin quote and assumed it was probably true? How many dismissed it as an absurdity and ignored it since it was not an important fact that might influence their future decision-making? How many knew it was bold-faced propaganda, designed to influence people negatively and persuade some of them to consider the illogical implications of this phony quote?

Think about it. Somehow voters and their elected plutocrat representatives will loot the rich Plutocrats and destroy the Republic, according to Benjamin Franklin.

A cursory knowledge of historical facts and how events occurred in ways that would impact the outcome of future events is often important in reaching a logical conclusion. People without facts and those with embedded misinformation and illogical interpretations have an advantage (and a disadvantage) in today's information-age and misinformation-age society.

As an example, the nation seems to be caught up in an extraordinary number of voter, voting, gerrymandering, voter interference and ballot box stuffing controversies. Who can vote? What is an acceptable form of voter ID proving you are who you say you are for voting purposes? Clearly, the illegal voting and interfering with elections by a foreign power were headline news in the 2016 federal elections, while voter suppression, gerrymandering of voting districts, and the rigging of elections controversies dominated 2018.

Moreover, the then president-elect claimed during the White House race in 2016, and even after his election, that the presidential elections were rigged by the Democrats and the secret deep state Republicans being operated by the Justice Department and the intelligence agencies. The president also claimed there were at least 3,000,000 illegal voters who caused his loss of the popular vote. As you probably know, he won the Electoral College vote despite the rigging, deep state conspiracy, and illegal voters.

Based on Trump's political conjectures, conspiracy theories and deep state babble about the Justice Department working against him, one can only deduce that voter interference, propaganda, and gerrymandering are the most effective ways to win presidential elections, compared to the rigging, ballot-box stuffing, and the ineffective, anti-American, deep state processes.

In any case, this chapter covers the underpinnings of the evolution to the current democratic republic voting rights and the liberal transformation of the original plutocratic republic that came into existence via the liberal votes from some of the richest plutocrats living in the United States, in 1788.

Although liberal plutocrats outnumbered the conservative plutocrats in the initial constitutional vote (1788-1791), the vote did not put an end to the ideological conflict of equality and promoting the "general Welfare" of the United States model, versus the aristocracy/plutocrat class and the "for the accumulation of wealth by the wealthy" government model.

The journey of the initial plutocratic republic to the current democratic republic form, began in Vermont (a non-colony territory). The territory entered the new Union of States in 1794, based on a white-adult-male-only popular vote. Most of the states joining the union after 1794 used a similar model between 1795 and 1860.

While some of the original 13 nation-states expanded their voting populations by granting suffrage rights to non-landowners and non-plutocrats, this was not a popular nation-state action. In fact, it was the newly created federal government and the various acts of the Congress of the United States that ultimately changed the Voter Eligible Population (VEP), over a 170-year period, to produce the current democratic federal republic representative model of today.

The federal government, for example, added the male adult ex-slaves to the citizen and voter rolls in 1867, with several amendments to the Constitution.

The amendments also extended the constitutional protection of rights and the delivery of justice to the all the male citizens living in the nation.

In this same vein of adding voters and extending constitutional protection to people living in the states and territories, the Federal Bureau of Immigration was empowered by Congress and began setting national standard for naturalized citizens born out of the country in 1882. Various federal laws and treaties eventually added male Native Americans and males in various territories, like Hawaii, Puerto Rico, American Samoa, and Guam to the Voter Eligible Population (VEP) of the United States.

Several additional constitutional amendments were passed in the last 100 years. Two liberal federal efforts have dramatically altered the VEP. Adult women were added to the VEP roll in 1920, making them the largest group of voters in the VEP. Another constitutional amendment in 1972 added young adults between the ages of 18-21.

The addition of these two large non-plutocrat groups to the voter rolls was also coupled with a massive population and economic explosion over the last century. To put the VEP growth and economy in perspective, there were approximately 77 million people with an average life expectancy of 58 years living in the US, according to the 1900 census.

Approximately 12 million people (20%) were in the VEP at the turn of the century. The nation was a middling country economically at the time and a relatively minor player on the world stage. Voter turnout rates in national elections were in the 70 to 80% range, at the beginning of the 20th century. Many historians suggest these high turnout rates were a result of voters casting multiple ballots in the same federal election cycle.

The population of the United States grew to a little over 282 million people with a life expectancy of 78, according to the 2000 census.

Approximately 170 million people (70%) and five separate generations of adults (GI Generation, the Greatest Generation, the Boomers, the Generation Xers and the Millennials) cycled in and out of the VEP over the century. In 2000, the nation was the undisputed world leader in terms of its economy and its military might, as the world's surviving superpower. Approximately 190 of the 282 million people were part of the VEP.

In general terms, 45 to 50% of the modern day VEP vote in federal elections. These lower turnout rates are probably the result of better security, personal apathy, and the voter registration/interference processes that became available in the century.

The four factors (voting rights, life expectancy, voter interference, and population growth) transformed the nation and its economy. Chapter 5 and 6 will explore the economic and cultural impact of these issues in more depth.

On a governance level, the original liberal (for the people) and conservative (for the accumulation of wealth by the wealthy) ideology conflict morphed into a more diverse "political issues" conflict between millions of people and the various generations, rather than the original liberal versus conservative Plutocrat conflict between the richest plutocrats in the nation.

As mentioned in Chapter 1, the economic and social issues surrounding "equality" and the liberal idea of government "for the people" versus for the conservative consensus to maintain the aristocracy ultimately caused the Federalists, the Washington Administration, and the liberal Whigs to fall out of political favor, among the conservative plutocrat voters.

The decline in these political forces came along with the rise of the conservative Anti-Administration Party and its successor, the Democratic-Republican Party (1794), supporting the slavery economy and the robber baron land-grab economic system.

The initial Republican portion of the conservative Democrat-Republican coalition soon disintegrated. The election of Democrat Andrew Jackson in 1828 signaled the Democratic-Republican political party coalition's formal demise.

The Liberal Whigs and Republicans in the northern states created a lot of political party confusion over the next two decades, through various single-issue political parties (Anti-Masons, Free-Soilers, Know-Nothings), and various party propaganda occurred before the northern liberal Whigs revived the Republican Party in the 1850s.

The new "for the people" Republican platform in the 1850s included handing out land free to sodbusters (Homestead Act) and the railroads. The party also supported actions to restrict the expansion of the slave-based economy of the South, the coolie/migrant slave labor camps in the West, and the company towns in of the North.

The new liberals also provoked the conservatives in the South and the robber barons in the North through the anti-slavery abolitionist movement. The economic, political, and social conflict produced Abraham Lincoln and the Civil War (1861-1865).

Today, both major political parties tout the acceptance of equality and the governance mandate "for the people" with "political party issues" now being the primary difference between the two major political parties.

While such claims are well worded, the actual actions of the political parties and their plutocratic patrons (funders), suggest that the core issues remain the same.

What is different is that the battle lines are among the Independent voters that outnumber the party specific registered voters in any single political party. Moreover, you should also be aware that most voters do not act like political party partisans at least until they step into the voting booth to select representatives from candidates. In today's environment, most voters know little about the candidates or their potential future voting proclivities.

Worse yet, the marketing and promotional skills of the political parties and their respective candidates have reached a level of Promotor sophistication and investment that overwhelms the deductive reasoning and logic skills of many voters.

Recognizing the name (incumbent or common name) and the desired political party is often enough to receive the confirming vote for a representative.

In most elections, most of the votes will be cast for incumbents, regardless of their job performance.

As a point of reference, there are now approximately 235 million age-eligible people in the federal Voter Eligible Population. Approximately 70% of these are registered to vote (145 million).

Eighty to 85% of the registered voters typically show up to vote (100 to 125 million). The 80% typically show up in off-year or midterm years, while the 85% show up during presidential election years.

The implications of our federal republic, with respect to our population, voter turnout and voting percentages are demonstrated in the following presidential chart.

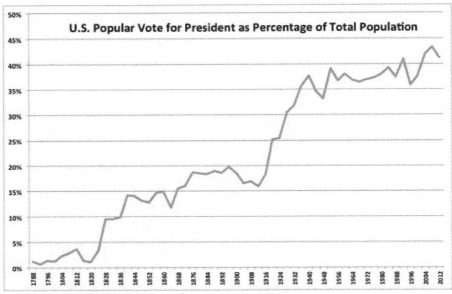

Figure 14 *Voter Turnout – Popular Vote for the President*

In addition to the peaks, rapidly expanding periods, and vastly higher numbers of people in the VEP, the voters in elections have also become more politically diversified.

Today, there are 28 federal-ballot-qualified political parties and their candidates vying for votes. Some candidates are more successful than others at attracting a constituency. The five largest ballot-qualified political parties with registered political affiliations (Constitutional, Green, Libertarians, Democrats, and Republicans) typically represent 55 to 60% of the votes that are cast in a federal election. The rest of the votes come from independent voters who have not registered as a member of a political party.

The political party voting tendencies makes the issues separating the parties complicated. The following political party comparison chart tries to summarize several of the complex political issues, in terms of political party comparisons.

Modern political party comparisons					
Issues	Green	Democratic	Libertarian	Republican	Constitution
Primary related subjects	• Green politics • Eco-socialism • Left-wing populism	• Modern liberalism • Progressivism • Social liberalism	• Libertarianism • Classical liberalism • Economic liberalism	• Neo-conservatism • Economic liberalism • Social conservatism	• Paleo conservatism • Fiscal conservatism • Social conservatism
Universal healthcare	Yes[35]	Yes[36]	No[37]	No[38]	No[39]
Redistribution of income and wealth	Yes[35]	Yes[36]	No[37]	No[40]	No[41]
Open borders	Yes[35]	No[36]	Yes[42]	No[43]	No[44]
Drug liberalization	Yes[45]	Yes[46]	Yes[47]	No[48]	No[49]
Non-interventionism	Yes[35]	No[36]	Yes[37]	No[50]	Yes[51]
Gun control	Yes[45]	Yes[36]	No[37]	No[52]	No[53]
End capital punishment	Yes[35]	Yes[36]	Yes[37]	No[54]	No[55]

Figure 15 Political Party Comparison (Wikipedia)

The political party voting percentages fluctuate during election seasons. In a typical federal election, the minor parties typically represent 6% of the actual votes, the Democratic Party represents 30% of the votes, and the Republican Party represents 25%. Independent voters (those with no registered political party affiliations) typically represent 35 to 40% of the votes in a federal election.

The liberal (left) versus conservative (right) ideological and economic dichotomy on the distribution of income and wealth continues. The political party voter constituencies, the voter ambiguity and the voter apathy also come into play.

The following chart reflects the actual voting results by political party in terms of the House, Senate, and the presidency over the last 150 years or so. Later chapters will explore general political party behavior patterns and the economic and social results achieved during these blue and red cycles of political party governance.

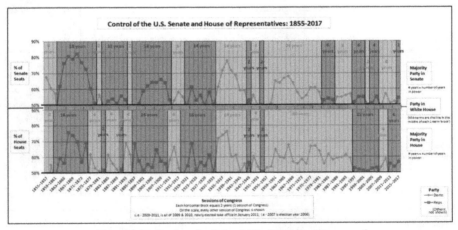

Figure 16 *Control of the U.S. Senate, House of Representatives, and Presidency 1855 to 2017.*

It should be clear from the chart that we the people in the VEP did, in fact, operate the federal government through a *de facto* two-party political system, with significant Ideological and political constituency differences.

Based on the registered voter makeup, it should also be clear that the Independents today are now the largest actual voting bloc and their votes determine the outcome of most elections, based on their evaluation of Party promoted candidates.

While not as clear and as conclusive as Independent voters, key voter attributes (the makeup of the VEP in terms of age, race, and education) and their respective voting rates also contributes directly to the outcome of most elections.

The following demographic charts from Michael P. McDonald, Associate Professor, University of Florida Department of Political Science, reflects the respective voting turnout rates by general attribute.

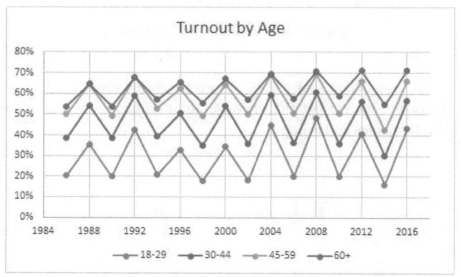

Figure 17 *Voter turn-out by age group by age group*

The conclusion that can be drawn from this chart is that the younger you are, the less aware you are with respect to the value of your vote or its potential impact.

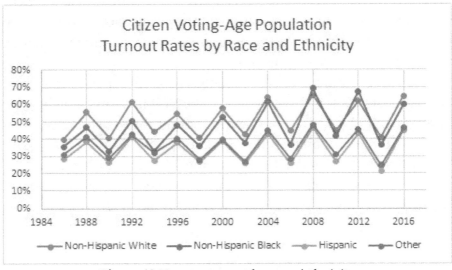

Figure 18 *Voter turn-out by race/ethnicity*

The conclusion that can be drawn from this chart is that the blacks and whites get the message about voting value, more so than Hispanics and other.

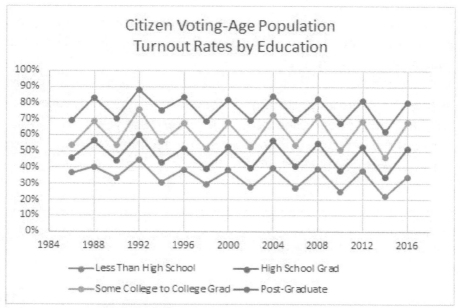

Figure 19 *Voter turn-out by education*

The conclusion that can be drawn from this chart is that the more educated you are, the more likely you are to vote, based on the quality of our educational system.

The Voter's Guide will also examine other relevant information, historical events, facts and provide helpful insights into the events created by the red and blue governance model. This information is intended to help you develop your personal political ideology and knowledge of candidate behaviors reflecting for the people, for the wealthy or just their party loyalty. This improvement of your assessment skills should help improve your selections and the actual performance and rating of Congress.

In the world of today, you, as a member of the VEP, need to understand that you elect representatives to Congress, whether you vote blue, red, or even if you do not cast a vote at all. The

winning candidates are your representatives in the federal government and you, as a member of the VEP are jointly liable for the
quality of their performance.

The confidence voters have in our Congress is a clear measure
of the VEP election performance. According to Gallup, voters do
not have much confidence in their representatives. Even worse,
our confidence in the Congress is clearly declining, in response to
the poor voting skills in the VEP.

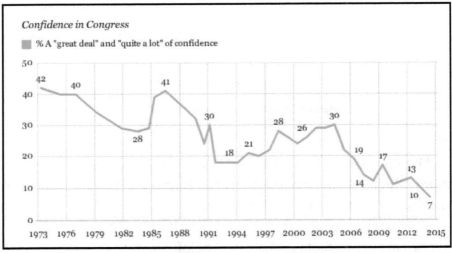

Figure 20 *Confidence in the Congress of the United States*

The confusing part of the voting selections and the lack of confidence in the Congress you elected is that the liberal "funded government programs" and free for the people stuff, the conservative
"trickle-down tax programs" for the accumulation of wealth by
the wealthy, and even the small, limited government ideas are all
passed on by Congress as being for the people, though actual economic results show they are not.

Obviously, historical events, facts, evidence, economic results of legislation, and economic results of governance and government suggest the elected representatives and their legislative actions are the root cause of the increasing lack of confidence in Congress and the previous generations of the VEP.

In addition to general historical information and facts, the Guide will examine the economic dichotomy of liberalism versus conservatism, in terms of skills and hopefully motivate you to become a better capitalist. This notion of political capitalism suggests that you need to vote for your own best interests and the best interests of the people in future federal elections.

This new capitalist motivation should generally help millennials to select better legislators who can produce higher quality legislation and hopefully restore the people's confidence in the Congress of the United States. Moreover, your improved voting skills will also help solve what seems to be the most important problem that the nation faces, according to Gallup Poll voters: The Baby-Boomer-created dysfunctional government.

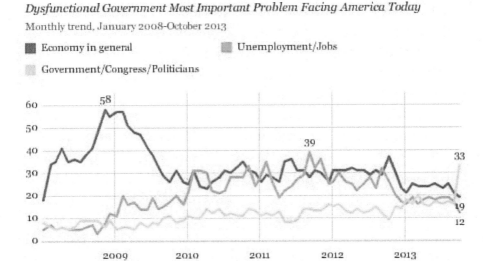

Dysfunctional Government Most Important Problem Facing America Today
Monthly trend, January 2008-October 2013

■ Economy in general   ■ Unemployment/Jobs

■ Government/Congress/Politicians

GALLUP

Figure 21 *Most important Problem facing America – Dysfunctional Government*

The Millennial Voter Guide itself is just a book, prepared in 2018-2019, at the end of a conservative Republican Congress and Republican presidential demonstration of dysfunctional government, via a tax cut for the accumulation of wealth by the wealthy and a 35-day federal government shutdown that ended the 115th Congressional Session of Congress and delayed the start of the 116th session by almost a month.

The year 2018 was also a transition year in the development of the workforce and the VEP of the United States. Millennials (those born between 1982 and 1997) became the single largest generation of people in the US workforce and the largest age block of voters in the US VEP.

With these two unique societal roles in place, Millennials now lead the older generations and have the generational leverage to protect the nation from the conservative threat to the republic and the people. In fact, the 2018 federal election results suggest the Millennials have already started resolving the dysfunctional problem, with votes that produced the election of a Democratic House for the first time eight years.

The conservative plutocrat dysfunctional government and its threat to the nation was initially produced by the Generation X parents (born 1965 to 1981) of the Millennials, in cooperation with the Baby Boomer generation (born 1946 to 1964). The older generation's evangelical survivors (born 1907 to 1945) also joined in the fray.

Together these generations have virtually disgraced the GI Generation (born 1880-1920) and the Greatest Generation (born 1921-1945), by electing and re-electing conservative congressional representatives who have failed the people of the United States for the last 50 years, based on the Gallup Job Approval Opinion Polls.

The following job approval chart puts the congressional rating in historical context. Although more will be said about this chart in later chapters of the guide, notice how the mislabeled 10-20-30% line has been displayed, so that 9 and 17 ratings of Congress look like they are near a 40% approval. Was the optical illusion manipulated to confuse the reader or mis-convey the information about another terrible Congress?

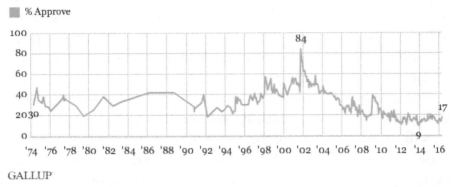

Congressional Job Approval Ratings Trend (1974-Present)

GALLUP

Figure 22 Congressional Job Approval Ratings retrieved via Google images

In any case, the general low opinion of the performance by one of the most important institutions in the world are just recent data points in an ongoing history of mediocrity from the previous generations of voters and representatives. The almost laughable opinion of the congressional performance is no longer news or a new opinion.

The mathematical average approval rating of the Congress of the United States, since the first Gallup Poll in 1974 up to the start of this century in 2001, was in the 30 to 40% favorable range, versus 60% or so unfavorable.

The average legislative performance rating since the 2000 elections that seated the Republican-led Congress in 2001 has been 20% favorable 80% unfavorable. Obviously, the VEP needs to improve their selection skills just to get Congress from their current poor performance to the 40% level.

The Guide will be providing you with opinion polls, graphs, charts, historic analysis, and reliable information sources to help you develop a better grasp of how personal theocratic and political party beliefs are interrelated with the liberal versus conservative ideology dichotomy and conflict.

After reading the Guide, you may still believe that tax cuts for the rich, deficit and debt increases, and increasing the wealth of the wealthy is good for the economy and the people. You may also believe that small government is good government for the economy and the people.

What you do or do not believe about the economy, equality, and government performance is relatively unimportant. Intentional ignorance (the absence of valid information) is a well understood phenomenon that was first described by the Thomas Gray theory that "Ignorance is Bliss."

Understanding that the Congress of the United States is in a constant state of battle between the liberal ideology for the people and the conservative ideology for the accumulation of wealth by the wealthy is what is important to learn from the Guide.

Applying this new knowledge and understanding of the political conflict during federal elections will hopefully make a difference in your evaluation of the candidates' qualities and their future voting patterns, either for the people or for the wealthy.

The new knowledge might also help you grasp the fact that you, as a VEP group member, are jointly responsible for converting federal candidates into representatives. Moreover, It is up to you to assess the facts and ideas presented by the candidates.

You personally must evaluate and decide whether you believe the candidate plans to represent the people of the United States, their own political party dogma, their own local constituencies that voted for them, or the plutocrats who funded the primary race and actual campaign.

Whether you cast a ballot or not, your vote counts, and you are partially responsible and liable for the outcomes and results.

The good news is that most facts show the purported Chapter 1 quote that "votes do not matter" is not true. Voters do have the opportunity to make a difference in the direction of government and its ability to bring about improvements in the quality of life of the people and their posterity. The bad news is that, based on the Gallup Poll ratings of the elected Congresses over the last fifty years, there does not seem to be any valid information that disproves the phony Ben Franklin quote about the Voter Eligible Population (VEP) and their representatives destroying the republic.

In fact, the Gallup Opinion polls and the voting results seems to imply that the VEP knew that the Congress had performed poorly but does not seem to realize that their elected representatives over the last 50 years or so were, in fact, effectively destroying the republic and its liberal contributions for the people and posterity.

Ask yourself if the candidates you voted for would vote for or against the nation's welfare state legislation that was produced by Congress while fulfilling the constitutional charter to "promote the general Welfare" of the people.

Women's Suffrage Amendment ■ Social Security
Minimum wage law ■ 40-hour work week ■ Overtime pay
Civilian Conservation Corps ■ Works Progress Administration
Workers Compensation Act ■ National Labor Relations Act
Unemployment Compensation Act ■ Clayton Antitrust Act
Agricultural Extension Service ■ Soil Conservation Service
Rural Electrification Act ■ Federal Housing Administration
Feral Deposit Insurance Corp. ■ Securities & Exchange Act
G.I. Bill of Rights ■ Marshall Plan ■ NATO ■ Pell Grants
School Lunch Program ■ Occupational Safety & Health Act
Operation Head Start ■ Peace Corps ■ VISTA ■ AmeriCorps
Civil Rights Act of 1964 ■ Voting Rights Act of 1965
Medicare ■ Medicaid ■ Equal Pay Act ■ Older Americans Act
Guaranteed Student Loans ■ Freedom of Information Act
Corporation for Public Broadcasting ■ PBS ■ NPR
National Science Foundation ■ Apollo moon program
National Endowments for the Arts and the Humanities
Clean Water Act ■ Clean Air Act ■ Food Stamps ■ WIC
Centers for Disease Control & Prevention ■ Motor Voter Act
Family & Medical Leave Act ■ Balanced federal budget

Figure 23 *Sample Acts of Congress promoting the General Welfare*

Now ask yourself if you would vote for these Acts of Congress and support the representatives who voted for them?

Votes, and a voter's personal beliefs, have consequences, and your voting actions impact the eco-system and the quality of life of the people, whether you are a liberal voting for the benefit of the people or a conservative voting for the accumulation of wealth by the wealthy. You have the responsibility to evaluate the candidates based on your own criteria and your expectations of their future behavior while serving as a representative of the people.

PART 2

HOW ARE WE DOING AT PROMOTING THE GENERAL WELFARE AND IMPROVING THE QUALITY OF LIFE FOR OURSELVES AND POSTERITY?

Claim

> "Our representative democracy is not working because the
> Congress that is supposed to represent the voters does not
> respond to their needs. I believe the chief reason for this is
> that it is ruled by a small group of old men."
> —SHIRLEY CHISHOLM

Rating

Mostly true. The actions of the VEP, their voting record, and the selection of representatives who produced the poor ratings have generated the present economic and social reality, including today's dysfunctional government. Even conservatives are wearing hats looking to Make America Great Again, in their misguided effort to direct the conservative model away from the accumulation of wealth by the wealthy model.

I am not sure where or when Chisholm made this statement about representative democracy. I am also not sure whether she is referring to the elected representatives, the plutocrats who financed their campaigns or the conservative Cult of Ignorance that captured the Republican Party in 1980. What is obvious, however, is she was not talking about the disastrous 115th Congress or the recently elected 116th. She passed away in 2005, long before dysfunctional government hit the top line on the Gallop Chart.

In any case, Shirley clearly perceived the same dysfunctional governance problem as the voters in the Gallup Polls. Was her belief true when she spoke, and is it still true today? I personally disagree with her limited chief reason being a small group of old men. I think representative democracy is not working well because of the ill-informed portion of VEP supporting the Cult of Ignorance candidates representing the plutocrats "for the accumulation of wealth by the wealthy" versus the plutocrats "for the people."

The question of whether our representative democracy is working well for the people or not working very well for the people is shown in the Gallup Opinion polls. This section covers how the federal governance model works, while the next chapters will cover our economic performance as a nation in terms of wealth, income, life expectancy of the population, and poverty reduction, in comparison with other nations.

As stated in previous chapters, the second Constitution of the United States pitted the liberal plutocrats who were pursuing the development of a unique, strong central government for the benefit of the people, against the conservative plutocrats who favored the unitary nation-state government model for maintaining the status quo focus on the accumulation of wealth by the wealthy.

The unique, new representative government model that was adopted in 1788 surely fulfilled the initial liberal promise that was first articulated in the Declaration of Independence in 1776.

"We hold these truths to be self-evident, that all men are created equal, that they are endowed by their Creator with certain unalienable rights, that among these are life, liberty and the pursuit of happiness. <u>That to secure these rights, governments are instituted among men, deriving their just powers from the consent of the governed.</u>"

The new elected and appointed federal government in 1788 was instituted among men by the richest white male plutocrats in the country.

The liberal "for the people" plutocrats clearly focused on capturing the "consent of the governed" plutocrats in each state.

The new nation overrode the nation-state government model with the Privileges and Immunity Clause of the Constitution: "the citizens of each state shall be entitled to all privileges and immunities of citizens in the several states."

Congress went further with the 14th amendment to the Constitution in 1867. This amendment clarified citizenship and the rights, privileges, and immunities of citizenship.

"All persons born or naturalized in the United States, and subject to the jurisdiction thereof, are citizens of the United States and of the state wherein they reside.

"<u>No state shall make or enforce any law which shall abridge the privileges or immunities of citizens of the United States; nor shall any state deprive any person of life, liberty, or property, without due process of law; nor deny to any person within its jurisdiction the equal protection of the laws.</u>"

This citizenship equality, the rule of law governance model itself, and the civic responsibility of the people became the common thread of life that now connects all Americans with all other Americans in securing the blessings of liberty to ourselves and our prosperity.

Although it took another 150 years after the 14th amendment, the 13 additional amendments and thousands of Acts of Congress, the VEP has produced today's social, economic, and political environment.

The Acts of Congress reflects a clear pattern of growth after the Civil War, as Congress generated the American powerhouse, on the way to creating the greatest nation on the earth. The declining rates of Congressional Act, since 1980, are just as clear.

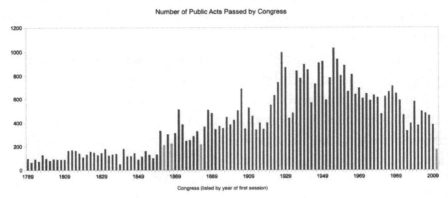

Figure 24 *Public Acts of Congress (legislative contributions to governance) since 1789*

Although we will discuss this chart in more detail in a later chapter, it seems safe to suggests that the decline in legislation prowess over the last 50 years is certainly related to the decline in the economic growth and quality of life in the nation.

In this vein of Congressional observation, notice the declining volume of legislation since 1980. This transition reflects the liberal-conservative political conflict and the resultant dysfunctional governance that is driving new income inequality, reducing life expectancy, and producing a decline in the quality of life in the United States.

The Acts of Congress have also produced a unique culture, economy, and society that is bound together, not by gender, politics, race, birthplace, the accumulated wealth of the wealthy, or even the conservative stand-bye, religion.

What bound Americans together over most of the period was the liberal drive for equality coupled with the liberal drive to promote the "general Welfare" and improve the standard of living of the people, with a shared understanding of our impact on posterity.

The nation's governance direction and its voting and civics processes were initially adopted by the male only liberal plutocrat voters of the day. Their newly adopted governance model included electoral districts, one vote for each seat and a winner-take-all outcome (simple majority popular vote).

In addition to specifying the popular vote processes (House of Representatives and executive office), the Constitution also spelled out the Electoral College process for selecting the president and vice president and the House tie-breaker vote process, to distribute political power among the plutocrats, and the Senate appointment procedures.

<u>Although both Washington and Adams</u> (the first two Federalist presidents) hoped to avoid the liberal versus conservative two party-conflict of the new liberals versus the evangelical conservatives, the new voting processes that were put in place, by the Constitution had anomalies that favored the development of the two-party system. The anomalies also produced other unexpected consequences, as non-plutocrats, non-whites, women, native Americans and young adults joined the expanded VEP.

The first flaw built into the initial voting system became apparent by 1796. The one vote for one seat idea gave each member of the Electoral College two votes.

The candidate with the most votes became president, while the second-place vote getter became vice president. Simple majority rule concept. Based on this process, the Electoral College in

1796 elected a liberal president (John Adams) and a conservative vice president (Thomas Jefferson, representing the Democrat-Republican Party and the Anti-Federalist Cult of Ignorance). This anomaly is like the pending 2019 governance problem, with a liberal House, a conservative Senate and a reality-TV actor as president.

In 1800, the party politics was as bad as they are today for the then-new nation. The liberal administration was officially voted out of office by the Cult of Ignorance and the coalition of plutocrat slavers (Democrats) and big business (Republicans). This transfer of power to the conservative Anti-Federalists became the first peaceful government transition ever, as the conservatives displaced the liberals, without a shot being fired, at the time.

Thomas Jefferson won the popular vote over John Adams. Aaron Burr (the conservative provocateur remembered for shooting liberal Alexander Hamilton and creating the sinister role in a great musical) tied with Jefferson in the Electoral College. Under the new constitutional process, the outgoing Congress ultimately appointed Jefferson president and Burr vice president, <u>after 35 failed congressional ballots</u>.

Although a constitutional amendment in 1804 fixed that problem, other political party voting anomalies have come up over the years. The winner of an election, for example, only needs to get the most votes in the election zone.

This allows a minority candidate (the one without a majority of all votes) to be declared a winner, depending on where and how the votes were cast, instead of how many were cast.

The minority anomaly led to voting multiple times, importing voters, not counting votes, creating fictitious voters and spurious third-party candidates to split the votes.

When people and the national political parties scam the voting process, it is called voter fraud. When the nation-state political party system scams the voting process, it is called gerrymandering and voter suppression.

Many (most) states have worked to limit fraud, gerrymandering, and suppression. More recently, some states seem to have also tried to specialize in the processes, in order to control and directly impact election results.

Some states have also attempted to resolve the minority winning and lack of a majority conflict in their state and local jurisdictions. These states require a post-election runoff between the two largest vote-getters, if neither one has a majority. Others require recounts if the vote total was very close (0.5 to 1% of the votes is a tie in many states).

All states have also strengthened their voter registration and control processes, while trying to reduce voter fraud and in some cases voter turnout. Constitutional amendments were also passed to limit the state gerrymandering and voter suppression actions, although the Congress has generally chosen to ignore the minority winning issue and the problems created by the voter anomalies.

Although minority wins happen, it is difficult for the VEP to grasp how the Electoral College "elected" presidential ticket does not have to win the popular vote to be elected.

Electoral College votes are awarded by state congressional seats. Congressional seats are not based on population or voters. Losing the most populous states and winning enough low population density states enables a "winner" to be elected with fewer popular votes than the loser. If you can read these words, you have lived through a presidential election and midterm election in which the most votes did not achieve victory.

The minority anomaly also happens in the political party-based House and Senate races, where seats are based on land boundaries (place where you vote) and not population or vote counts. For example, winning by a small margin in an electoral voting region with a small population captures a seat for the political party. Losing by a big margin in a highly populous voting area only produces one competing seat.

The minority victory model impact is subtle. As an example, of the 45 elected presidents, only 15 did not win the majority of the popular vote. While 33% minority wins seems like a reasonable number of minority wins (15/45), it should be noted that every Republican President starting with Ronald Reagan in 1980 has lost the popular vote, except for George Bush, in his re-election campaign in 2004. In fact, since Reagan's inability to win the majority of the popular vote, only President Obama has won the majority of the popular vote, in both of his election efforts.

The minority victory model is also prevalent in the low population density congressional seats sector. Low density areas in the nation outnumber the high population density by an 8:1 margin while only holding 40% of the voting population.

In the 2016 Senate races, for example, one party captured 53% of the votes cast by voters for Senate seats but only won 49% of the seats awarded to representatives. The same voting anomaly occurred again in 2018.

The ongoing popular vote anomalies have also fostered and sustained the two-party political system feared by Washington and Adams. Although third-party candidates often exist, they hardly ever win and, as a point of fact, the Congress and presidency have been generally staffed by one of the two major parties since, the 1850s.

While the voting anomalies have unintended consequences, the lack of knowledge and understanding about the nation's liberal versus conservative governance history and the ongoing government direction conflict between the "for the people" and "for the accumulation of wealth" forces has also impacted voting results.

The initial ideological struggle between "for the people" and "the accumulation of wealth" principles of governance was transformed into the political party struggle to leverage voters to acquire control over the power of government, as the VEP expanded from the small number of rich plutocrats in the VEP to today's massive adult VEP.

The ongoing conflict between the liberal "for the people" principles of governance versus the conservative "for the accumulation of wealth by the wealthy" principles of governance is economically measurable. The facts are also easy to summarize and can be clearly described via charts and graphs that convey the information to people in a way that can reduce their lack of knowledge and improve their voting skills.

The implications of the charts and the scientific principles supporting its shape and form, though, are sometimes problematic for providing information to the uninformed or misinformed and those who might not believe in the concepts of science and math.

As an example, earlier charts in the guide used simple line graphs. These are relatively easy to read and interpret from the direction of the line, its label and the distance between the lines. Understanding what a mathematical distribution implies is a slightly more complex issue involving attributes, variables, and relationships in the chart and the shape of the curves.

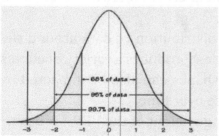

Figure 25 *Normal Curve and Distribution*

The normal distribution curve, for example, has an average (the mathematical mean or the average of all members divided by the number of members). The number 0 in this chart reflects this central tendency average or middle on the chart. The line height displays how much or how many members are near this average. There is also a median (the central tendency point where there are as many members above as below the point (see the blue line). The normal curve also has standard deviations, that mathematically show how far away members are from the average (see green lines).

The standard deviation lines are calculated to describe the distance from the average and the relationship of data points in the observations. In a normal curve, for example, 68% of the members are within 1 standard deviation of the average. 95% are within 2 standard deviations, and 99.7% are within 3. The remaining 0.3% are quirks of mathematic approximations and probabilities created by outlier data points.

If the standard deviation is small, the peak of the curve at the average is higher. The median can be on either side of the average and the curves do not have to look peaked or normal. Moreover, attributes like height and weight may have different looking distributions.

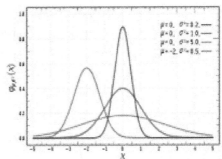

Figure 26 *Normal Curve Shapes*

The areas under the curves, the skewed left and right peaks also help create knowledge deduced from the presentation of the facts.

The plotting of frequency and distribution of data around the mean and median (central tendencies) produces a variety of curves describing the observations. The shapes can also be impacted by changes in attitude or performance over time.

If you wanted to know the average height of the VEP, for example, you could mark down all the actual voter heights from their driver's licenses, add them up, and divide the total by the number of voters. Would this complete count of all voters and their curve also be a pretty good representation of the height of both voters and the non-voters?

The answer is probably. And, I can even tell you mathematically how confident I am or explain the degree of potential error in the calculations of a sample.

The amount of potential error rate between the actual recorded observations and the real values of the non-counted portion of the VEP is controlled by the mathematical relationships. Understanding the magnitude of the probable measurement error (95% accuracy or confidence level, leaves a chance of error at 5%).

Understanding binomial curves also helps in the interpretation of the charted information. A normal distribution, for example, can be used to approximate a binomial probability like yes versus no (binomials can only be one or the other). This probability of accuracy estimate is relevant to the deducing of facts from the observations.

Heads and tails and the flipping of a coin may help in the understanding of error rates from measurements. The general coin flip is a binomial. There are only 2 outcomes. There is a 50% chance of either answer (heads or tails) on every flip.

How many heads and how many tails can be expected from a sample of 10-coin-flip test?

The mathematical laws of probability suggest there is only a 24.6% chance of 5 heads and 5 tails in a ten-coin flip test. That means that if you did the test 4 times, it might occur once. What if it appeared twice, or not at all? It means you need to do more tests to get a valid sample and a relatively normal looking binomial distribution.

For simplicity, you would also find that 68% of the flips had a result between 3 and 7 heads. 95% of the experiments will reflect a number between 2 and 8 heads. 97.7% of the results would be 1 and 9 heads and 0.3% of time you would get between 0 and 10 heads. If we applied these binomial principles to socialist political tendencies versus fascist political tendencies, you should find 68% of people are socialists and fascists with a high peak.

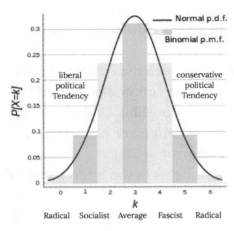

Figure 28 *Binomial Distributions*

The distribution and shape of the curve can also be used to display information in term of quartiles and percentiles. The quartile form of display is often used when the curve is distorted by the preponderance of the measured data point located at one end of the curve.

The use of the quartile and percentile delineation also helps explain the distribution of the observed facts. A quartile is simply dividing the observed results into four equal groups (1st, 2nd, 3rd, and 4th). A percentile converts the number into a percentage. Review the following chart. Notice how the 10th, 50th, 90th, and 99th percentiles changed during the failure of the Congress for 50% of the people over the last 50 years versus their economic success for the people in the first 20 years.

Percentiles of Family Wealth, 1963–2013

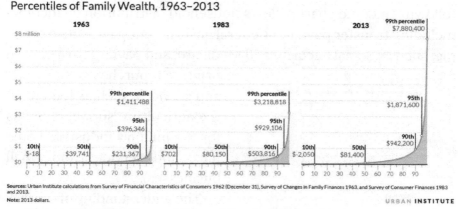

Sources: Urban Institute calculations from Survey of Financial Characteristics of Consumers 1962 (December 31), Survey of Changes in Family Finances 1963, and Survey of Consumer Finances 1983 and 2013.

Note: 2013 dollars.

URBAN **INSTITUTE**

Figure 28a *Quartiles and Percentiles describing the accumulation of Wealth by the Wealthy*

Also notice that the shape of the three curves. It has not changed over time, although the percentile values have been changing and the peak percentile tripled while 50% of the people were worse off or stagnant. The results displayed for 1963, 1983, and 2013 were achieved though the VEP and their representatives' congressional actions for the people (Great Society '63-'83 results), versus "for the accumulation of wealth by the wealthy" (tax cuts for the rich 1981, 2001 and debt spending impacted '83-2013 results).

View 2013 by the percentile method of conveying information. Notice the percentile and absolute value changes on chart 28A in terms of direction and magnitude. The decline in the first 10th, the relative lack of change in the 50th, and the change in 90th, 95th, and 99th percentiles, also reflects congressional actions to facilitate the accumulation of wealth by the wealthy over the period. Likewise, the decline in the 10th and lack of change in the 50th percentiles in 2013, reflect the congressional failure for the people.

Percentile analysis also help understand the relationship between curves with interrelated attributes and shapes. The following income chart reflects household distribution by income, including transfer payment (federal government payments to people, such as Social Security and Medicare, and payments to private firms via purchases of goods and services, such as food from the agriculture suppliers, tanks for the military industrial complex, and service from small businesses).

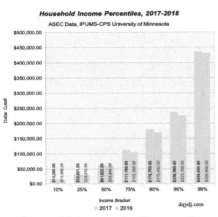

Figure 29 *Income by Percentiles*

The understanding of the distribution of household income by percentile helps visualize and explain the income inequality and the skewed averages underlying the previous chart and the change in government treatments sending more income to the top 25% (increasing income inequality) over the last 50 years.

The VEP members became the focal point of a Psychological Warfare attack, from the Cult of Ignorance members and their conservative followers. The initial communist conspiracy theory propaganda and red scare began early in the 1950s with McCarthyism. The initial attack expanded to include a form of Pavlovian bell training, targeted at the Baby Boomers and all future VEP members. The Pavlovian training process was initially produced by the Dixiecrats (Southern Manifesto in 1956) and expanded upon by the John Birch Society, Hinsdale College, and similar institutionalized conservative machinery. Over the 1960s and 1970s, attack and bell training expanded to general mass media programming via Evangelical TV shows, the conservative talk radio shows and ultimately modern-day conspiracy theory entertainment and training programming.

The Pavlovian training message from the conservatives was clear. Democrats were Liberals. More importantly, Liberals were socialists and socialists were communists.

By 1954, the boomers were also being introduced to the basic concepts of Nation-State duplicity (deceitfulness; double-dealing) through the Dixiecrat-Democrat hypocrisy and real inequality program. The Boomers were just starting to learn about American history, civics, and how to use their school desks as protection during a nuclear attack, while also learning about the conservative hypocritical underbelly of the Southern Democrat Party members.

The *Brown vs. Board of Education of Topeka* Supreme Court ruling in 1954, suggested that "separate but equal" schools was a bold-face nation-state lie and that the very principle of segregation and the systemic inequality of treatment based on skin color was illegal under the Constitution of the United States.

The Baby Boomers got another dose of the inequality issues from the Rosa Parks bus trip, the Montgomery March, the 2,500 union strikes affecting 1,000 or more workers demanding a living wage in 1955 and then again, the 3,600 strikes in 1956.

The young Boomers, and those who would follow them, also had the opportunity to observe the federal government and the Democratic and Republican representatives in action, for the people and equality, versus for the accumulation of wealth by the wealthy and inequality model.

Radical liberal Republican President Eisenhower and the Democratic-Party-led Congress, expanded social security, sent troops to the Democratic-Party held statehouses and schools, and passed the Civil Rights Act of 1957, right in front of our eyes.

Republican President Eisenhower was also turning bayonets and bombers into new cars and the new highway system to drive on. The federal government also came up with a massive increase in low income housing to go along with support of unions, higher wages, and even a higher minimum wage rate in search of a living wage for all employees in America.

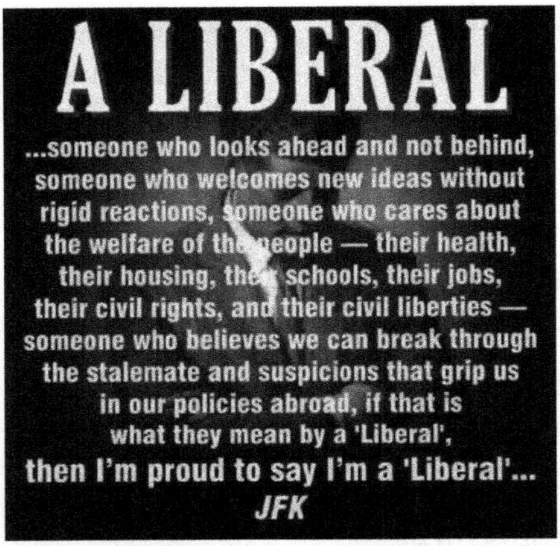

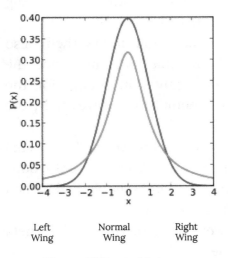

Figure 30 *The Open Definition of a Liberal*

Figure 31 *Party Makeup*

Left Wing   Normal Wing   Right Wing

Republican President Eisenhower also personally refused to send troops to disburse striking Teamsters while also leading the Democratic Congress to establish the new Department of Health, Education, and Welfare and the new NASA for the people.

Over the next 20 years, the Boomers also experienced how the liberal plutocrats in the Democrat Party and the Republican Party kept embracing the equality versus inequality issues for the people.

The Kennedy and Johnson messages were clear to us and the world. Both Political Parties were in synch. Civil Rights, Voter Rights, Women's Rights, Union Rights, Senior Healthcare Rights to Medicare, the Right to Medicaid, and the Great Society initiative with clean air, water, new educational opportunities, and the elimination of poverty and disease in the United States, marked the equality in the Will Of Congress expressed as the congressional activities in the 60s and 70s.

Elvis, the Beatles, Vietnam, Kent, and Woodstock all came about as the Greatest Generation was developing the post-World War II nation through the Congress, and both political parties were deploying the wisdom of Aristotle and the Golden Mean—where moral behavior is the **mean** between the two extremes: at one end is excess, at the other is deficiency.

The moderate centrist political party positions between the two radical extremes (right wing fascism and left wing communism based socialism) shown graphically in Figure 31 reflect a political tendency chart, with a massive amount of overlap between the two parties. This post-Civil War party cohesiveness came together after Reconstruction, as the political parties searched for constituencies in the rapidly expanding and urbanizing nation.

The original Washington and Adams concern with the two-party system generating the liberal versus conservative dichotomy was also becoming a reality though, as promoting the "general Welfare" for the people came into ever more conflict with the accumulation of wealth by the wealthy mandate of conservatives.

The first signs that the "for the people" process was generating conflict began with Teddy Roosevelt's Square Deal plan, promoting "the general Welfare." His "welfare state activities" included the creation of national Parks, arboretums, clean water legislation, child labor laws, politically forcing corporations to raise wage and reduce the workweek, trustbusting, and drug safety were all new breakthroughs for the people.

The income tax on corporations (1909), Woodrow Wilson's election (1912), the Federal Reserve (1913), the income tax on the richest families (1916), and the Estate Tax (1916) provided the federal government with a new funding processes "to promote the general Welfare" at the expense of the accumulation of wealth by the wealthy. The fundamental change in the funding of the government moved from taxes on consumers (tariffs) to taxes on income, wages and accumulated wealth. The new taxes brought the liberal versus conservative conflict to the forefront of politics as the nation prospered.

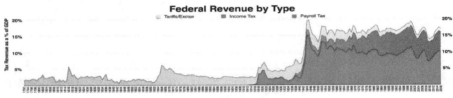

Figure 32 *Federal Funding Sources*

The Republican "Return to Normalcy" campaign in 1920, (anti-welfare-state evangelical conservatives), swept the hardline conservatives into political power, at the start of the Roaring 1920's. Tax cuts for the rich, looting of the farmers, the Teapot Dome scandal and the deregulation of Wall Street, produced the Great Depression, by 1927.

The promotion of the "general Welfare" processes, stalled by the conservative Roaring 20s and the Great Depression, was restarted in 1933, with the New Deal eventually proposing a modern day, economic Bill of Rights for citizens along with a myriad of post-WWII actions including the GI Bill, the Fair Deal, and the development of civil rights, voting rights, human rights, Social Security expansion to cover senior and poor healthcare, and the Great Society legislation, by the 1960's.

The "for the people" versus "for the accumulation of wealth by the wealthy" conflict exploded into the face of the young adult Baby Boomers via the Equal Rights Act demanding desegregation and the following Equal Rights Act for Women eliminating sexual inequality. The Equal Rights Act for Women was passed by

Congress in 1972 and sent to the states for ratification, 52 years after it first came before Congress, in 1923.

The equality and Great Society "welfare state" conflict produced a political turn toward conservatism, with the election of Richard Nixon in 1968. His re-election, coupled with the Watergate political cancer and *Roe vs. Wade*, metastasized into the expanded evangelical conservative cult movement, epitomized by Senator Barry Goldwater at the time and ultimately, the Reagan election to the presidency, in 1980.

The Democratic Congress and conservative Republican president produced a tax cut for the rich in 1981. They also deregulated Wall Street (1984 junk bond) and (1987 hedge funds). The deregulation led to the collapse of the Savings & Loan industry (1988) and the housing market, three recessions, new offshore tax loopholes and doubling of the deficit run rate. Although both political parties seemed to be operating for the accumulation of wealth by the wealthy, the average political attitudes of the voters were initially unaffected, as shown in the following chart from Pew Research.

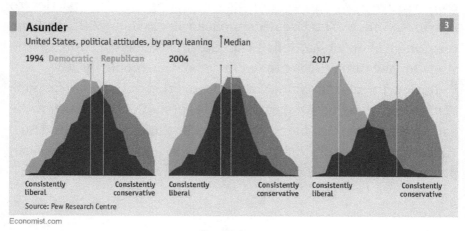

Figure 33 *Political Attributes by Party*

The conservative Republican takeover of the entire Congress in 1994, reinforced the process of legislation for the accumulation of wealth by the wealthy, replacing "for the general Welfare" legislation of the past. Instead of taking kids out of the factories like the Square Deal, Government produced the Raw Deal, with tax loopholes and Treaties that took the factories offshore and stagnated wages in the United States.

The tax cut for the rich (2001), the Unfunded Drug Plan for Big Pharma (2004), two regional wars and the new massive deficit, replacing surpluses were changing the shape of the political attitude curves. By 2004, the number of Democrats overlapping with Republicans had shrunk. The 1994 to 2004 transition altered the number of conservatives in the right wing of the Republican Party, while reducing them in the Democratic Party, as the plutocrats promoting the "general Welfare" model for the people lost political power to the "for the accumulation of wealth by the wealthy" conservative forces.

While the charts reflect the change in the political attitudes of the people, many incumbent Political Party officeholders in the conservative red states were also changing political parties to remain in office. The Great Republican Recession (2007) and the resulting trillion-dollar deficit run rate it produced in 2008, set the stage for the dramatic attitude change of the people by 2017

Review the charts again. Notice the overlap of the political population between the two parties in 1994 versus 2017. Also review the earlier fiscal funding charts and the decline in income tax (red line) collections that were driving the average and median American political attitudes to divisive change, as the overlap shrank.

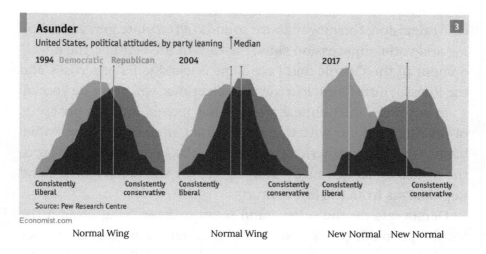

Asunder
United States, political attitudes, by party leaning ⏐Median

1994 Democratic Republican   2004   2017

Consistently   Consistently   Consistently   Consistently   Consistently   Consistently
liberal   conservative   liberal   conservative   liberal   conservative
Source: Pew Research Centre
Economist.com

Normal Wing   Normal Wing   New Normal   New Normal

Figure 34 Political Party Attitudes

Based on the personal Political attitude shifts of the VEP, the Pavlovian bell ringing had worked with a large number of Baby Boomers and their Generation X children.

Politically, the conservatives and most Republicans are now radically conservative fascist supporters when viewed by the average Democratic Party Member. In the same vein, the conservative and Republicans have all moved to right toward fascism and most Republicans are now considered radically conservative facist supporters of the accumulation of wealth by the wealthy" role of government, by the average and median Democrat Party Member. In the same vein, the average and medium Democrat is perceived as a radical socialist, by most of the conservatives and Republican Party supporters.

How much of this dramatic shift in political attitude and voting behavior was a result of conservative talk radio shows, the fiscal and regulatory failures over the last 50 years that ultimately produced the Great Recession, the plutocrat patron dark money campaign funding and propaganda unleashed by the Citizens United

court decision, the new massive rounds of red state gerrymandering and voter suppression since the turn of the century, the development of the Google and Face Time Social Media processes and
the Russian interference in the 2016 elections, will never be known.

In any case, the political attitude has moved into the positions
of warring fiefdoms with one side running under the conservative
banner of Making America Great Again (MAGA) message, similar to
the a "Return to Normalcy" rallying cry for the conservatives and
Republicans from the last century.

Democrats on the other hand seem to be rallying around the
for the people legislative actions ($15 minimum wage, health care
for all, humane treatment of asylum seekers and illegal immigrants,
government subsidized higher education, legislation to reduce gun
related deaths, and taxes to offset the Republican deficit build-up...).

The liberal Democratic Party proposals for the people are all
falling on the deaf ears of Republican supports, as evidenced by
Republican legislative behaviors before they lost the House of
Representatives in 2018

There were over 60 failed Congressional votes (2011-2016)
to repeal the Patient Protection and Affordable Healthcare Act
(PPAHCA), that had extended healthcare, for the first time ever,
to 19 million sick (preexisting conditions) and poor, in 2008. The
Republican Congress also reversed directions of the deficit management processes, the moment they had the opportunity to cut
taxes for the rich, expand payments to the military industrial complex and the return to trillion-dollar deficit run rate, by 2019.

Today, a 'centrist' Republican political attitude "for the people" and
virtually any moderate behaviors by candidates or Representatives
are shamed and shunned and tagged as RINO's (Republican in Name
Only) by the Cult of Ignorance Party Plutocrats and Patrons, running
the Republican Party, for the accumulation of wealth by the wealthy.

The Republican president and Senate leadership have continued to foster the "government for the rich" model in in a variety of forms and non-legislative actions deregulating big business, new massive tariffs on consumer imports, the withdrawal from the Paris Climate Accords, the withdrawal from signed nuclear treaties, the rollback of EPA regulations and a variety of new Neocon warmongering efforts around the world.

Sadly, the liberal versus conservative political ideologies and attitudes, reflected by the charts is also being exacerbated by the general dysfunctional government performance created, by the elected representatives over the last 50 years.

The dichotomy shown in the figure 34 places a new burden on the VEP and the candidate assessment and selection processes for staffing Representatives.

The Millennials need to move both political parties to a renewed focus on the people, versus the current focus on Party Politics, if millennials are going to fix the dysfunctional government performance, before the federal republic collapses into chaos.

Clearly, maintaining the current plutocrat patron driven Political model for the accumulation of wealth by the wealthy can only lead to an environment much like the privatized Russia, via cuts of social welfare spending and increased military spending, as proposed in the recent presidential budget (2018).

The current obvious political polarization initially began, as the Baby Boomers responded to the Pavlovian training and embraced the post-Vietnam conservative worldview, in the mid to late 1970s. Many of their children, the Generation X, entered the conflicted political arena with similar conservative views. Over time, many of the traditional voters from the two generations chose to be independent of the warring Party fiefdom battle, going on over the Congress.

Newly independent voters (unaffiliated and potentially closet partisans), joining with traditional independent voters in the VEP. From their perspective, they, the Independents, select from the candidates, based on the issues rather than the political party ideology.

Although they are ultimately the deciding vote in most federal elections, studies have failed to find any high correlations with the political parties or the new conservative ideologies versus liberal Ideologies.

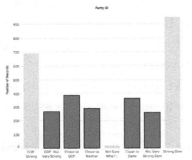

Figure 35 *Independent* Voter *Attitudes*

Figure 35 is an example of independent political party preference results, from 2016 exit poll surveys. The analysis of self-identified Independents seems as conflicted and as extreme as the Parties. The next chapter will explore the economic evaluation of capitalism and the income inequality results from the political party problems.

CHAPTER 5

The Economic Evaluation of capitalism, liberalism and our Legislators.

"We can have democracy in this country, or we can have great wealth concentrated in the hands of a few, but we can't have both."
—LOUIS D. BRANDEIS

The success of capitalism as an economic model, supporting the representative-based federal republic meritocracy model of government can be measured and assessed in comparison to the unitary plutocracy nation-state model, for the accumulation of wealth by the wealthy. As Mr. Brandeis suggests, you cannot have both, although we did have a 60-year economic run, in which there was at least a happy balance between them, while following the "for the people" model to "promote the general Welfare" of the people.

Adam Smith's *Wealth of nations*, published in 1776, twelve years before the adoption of the second United States Constitution, introduced the economic theory of <u>private ownership of the means of production, for a profit, versus the traditional government, church, aristocracy, and nobility ownership, for the accumulation of wealth by the wealthy.</u> Smith began his work with a clear new definition of national wealth.

According to Smith's heretical theory, national wealth included the people and was not just the amount of gold, silver, and property hoarded and protected by the rich (plutocrats). The new wealth of a nation model of capitalism defined <u>national wealth as the value of its production output of goods and services acquired by consumers</u>. The value is expressed in terms of the marketplace exchanges, between buyers and sellers.

The novel new capitalistic idea of wealth being the production and exchanges of goods and services and the acquisition of them, by the people, slowly augmented the traditional accumulation of wealth by the nobility, aristocracy and church based tax, tithe tribute, and looting model. It stood out then (1776) and still stands, in clear contrast to the conservative concept of wealth being the value of the gold, silver, pretty stones, land, buildings, stock certificates, bonds, and property owned and operated by and for the rich.

For a nation to prosper or even survive in the capitalistic economic environment envisioned by Smith, governments needed to increase the production of goods, services, and the consumption of them, by the people. Government achieved their new capitalistic purpose through the facilitating of the markets via the provision of infrastructure, justice, and law, order plus <u>the provision of a path to the economy, for the people</u> ("promote the general Welfare"), and the general protection of the people from economic, social and military based disasters.

The very idea of the prosperity of the nation being created through the buyer and seller exchanges of people, operating in their own self-interest was the economic opposite of the conservative mercantile economic theories of nations, at the time.

Mercantilism focused on the accumulation of wealth by the wealthy and maintaining the inequality between prosperity and poverty, through slavery, low wages, taxes on the people, tribute to facilitate commerce, and the exploitation of farmers, laborers, yeomen, vagabonds, military and the poor (90% of the population), while using the planet's natural resources to facilitate the wealthy model (10% of the population).

Smith perceived governments <u>facilitating the free market operations by creating pathways for people into the new economy</u>, where "prudent men of property" would provide the capital (accumulated wealth) and balance out the economic forces of supply and demand for the best interest of the people, profits, and the wealth of the nation.

Smith's supply-side analysis also undertook to explain the efficiency process of production along with the division of labor concepts and wage payment processes, to increase marketplace size, scale, and scope.

I can only imagine Smith's elation with the equality promise within the Declaration of Independence in 1776 and the adoption of the "We the people" Constitution, in 1788.

The creation and transfer of income streams and pathways between providers and consumers (farmers, laborers, and business operators) versus the accumulation of wealth by the owner of the land, gold, and silver still seems like some kind of crazy heresy to many conservative plutocrats and Royalty enabled governments around the world.

As discussed in previous chapters, the traitorous, liberal plutocrats in the United States, who had adopted the liberal notions of John Locke, espousing the ideas that all men were created equal and that government was instituted by the people for the benefit of the people, actually became early adopters of the new economic theory of capitalism.

As an example, the Continental Congress formed under the Articles of Confederation, took capitalism out for a test drive with the adoption of the Northwest Ordinances in 1785 and 1787. The 1785 Ordinance established the notion of public domain and outlined the process for how to buy land from the government in future Midwest states (Ohio, Indiana, Michigan, and Wisconsin).

The 1787 Ordinance update provided the settlers with a bill of rights that included voting rights (must own 50 acres or more of land to have a vote). The law outlawed slavery and involuntary servitude and set land prices only the rich could afford. According to history, this law was approved by the existing Slave States, to avoid direct tobacco-growing competition from the Midwest (capitalist concept versus slavery). As a note of interest, Ohio did start growing tobacco after the Civil War and still does. I assume they do it in Ohio for farm income and profits, without involuntary servitude or slavery.

The first Congress, under the second US Constitution, also took capitalism and Civil Rights to heart, with the adoption of the Northwest Ordinance of 1789 with an expanded Bill of Rights (first ten amendments were approved by the states in 1791).

In 1790, Congress passed the world's first Heath Care Act, enabling the federal government to pay for and deal with epidemics. This inauspicious start to creating income streams, protecting people, and transferring income streams to people via government was expanded in 1798, with the first socialized medicine law "An Act for the Relief of Sick and Disabled Seamen."

This early Act of Congress mandated the purchase of insurance for seamen, by the ship's owners, in much the same way as Social Security and Obamacare payroll tax uses transfer payments as a path to the economy today, for the elderly, poor, and sick. The Act of Relief created the Marine Hospital Service (hospitals) that were built and operated by the federal government, to treat injured/ ailing privately employed, seamen.

The passing of laws by a strong centralized government process, especially those protecting the defenseless workers, vagabond settlers, veterans, seamen, and the future farmers and mill workers was not well received by the traditional conservative plutocrats.

In any case, the buying, selling, and granting of federal land, the sale of rights-of-way to private businesses, and the building and use of public facilities would soon produce canals, a railroad system for farmers to reach mills, and factories for farmers to reach markets, on both oceans. By the 1860s, the Homestead Act and its free land would soon create a million new landowning farmers and a railroad from sea to shining sea (1869).

These processes of liberal federal government capitalistic involvement in the picking of winners and subsidizing and controlling the economy, picked up momentum after the Civil War, as part of the Reconstruction of the South's slavery-based economy and the initiation of the new energy production (oil/coal) industrial economy.

The Interstate Commerce Commission, Unions, Strikes, and Reconstruction produced the basic robber-baron era in America and ultimately the Sherman Anti-Trust Act (1890). The Act of Congress was designed to protect the people from capitalism's new private business owners, and the financier plutocrats who did not get the "prudent men of property" message from Smith, as they replaced the aristocracy, nobility, and church plutocrats with industrial Plutocrats, before the turn of the 20th century.

The new century (1901) and Harrison's untimely death, brought Teddy Roosevelt, the Trustbuster, to the presidency and the progressive Republican liberals, to Congress.

Together, they passed even more laws for the benefit of the people. These liberal efforts included child labor laws, protection of unions, regulation of Wall Street, general laws protecting the food and water supplies, and even social laws creating national parks and protecting natural resources.

These liberal actions and the liberal political direction of the government made other significant changes to the laws and the Constitution before being displaced by the conservative "Return to Normalcy" campaign in the 1920 election. For example, Congress passed an amendment ending the "appointment" of Senators via a direct election of Senators process in 1913. Later in 1913, Congress created the Federal Reserve to regulate Wall Street, banking, and the supply of money, to the dismay of many plutocrats. They even passed a law that broke the liberal bank, allowing women to vote in 1920.

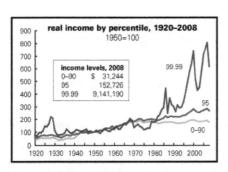

Figure 36 *Real income by percentile 1920-2008*

Mr. Brandeis's quote (Brandeis was a Supreme Court Justice referred to by *The Economist* magazine as "a Robin Hood of the law") introducing this chapter reflected his understanding of economics and the impact of income and wealth on democracy in 1939. The average lifespan of an American in 1920 was 48 and had reached 60, despite the Great Depression. 70 million of the 110 million people in America lived in poverty (65%) in 1920. It had declined to 45% by 1940. The average income estimates by percentile in 1950-dollar values, from 1930 to today are both enlightening and shocking.

The average income of the top 1% and top 0.01% over the last century reflects the initial success and the current failure of the "for the people" economic model.

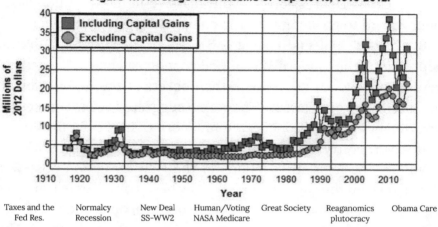

Figure 1.7: Average Real Income of Top 0.01%, 1913-2012.

| Taxes and the Fed Res. | Normalcy Recession | New Deal SS-WW2 | Human/Voting NASA Medicare | Great Society | Reaganomics plutocracy | Obama Care |

Figure 37 Average Real income of top 0.01% 1913-2012

The whirlwind of change in the republic, described earlier (1901-1920) had set in motion a tax base and political and economic partnership between the liberals "for the people" and the conservative Cult of Ignorance plutocrats, for the accumulation of wealth by the wealthy. Clearly, the political partnership for the people ended in 1980, with the introduction of Reaganomics and conservatism for the accumulation of wealth by the wealthy program.

Historically, the Roaring 20s began with the override of President Wilson's veto of Prohibition by the conservative legislators. This was followed by the "Return to Normalcy" Harrison/Coolidge campaign victory, which produced tax cuts for the rich, spending cuts in transfer payments, the Teapot Dome oil scandal, and the stock growth bubble being the high points of the Harrison/Coolidge/Hoover conservative era.

Hoover's Black Tuesday stock market collapse within a year of Coolidge's deciding not to run for re-election was the opening bell for the Great Depression and the massive industrial unemployment record to go along with the collapse of agriculture.

By the mid-1930s (after nearly 5 years of the Great Republican Depression), the modern-day liberal economists began suggesting ways to put money (income) in the pockets of the middle, lower, and even poorest classes. They also suggested these processes would benefit the national economy more than the acquisition of gold, silver, pretty stones, and private homes for the ultra-rich.

Voters, the legislative actions of the New Deal, and post-war efforts revived the capitalistic economy based on income transfers to people, improving the quality of life of the people, and the direct distribution of income to veterans, seniors, and the disabled. The Acts of Congress in the 30s, 40s, 50s, 60s, and 70s, produced an exceptional democratic republic nation, with envious economic results for the people and the nation, before the Reaganomics and the conservative assault on taxes, funding and regulations.

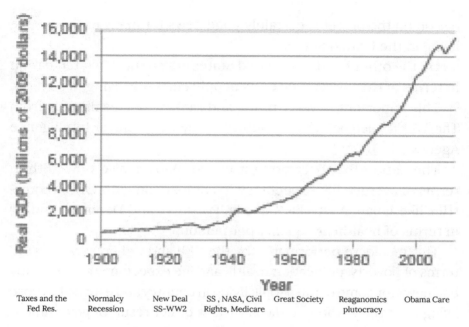

| Taxes and the Fed Res. | Normalcy Recession | New Deal SS-WW2 | SS , NASA, Civil Rights, Medicare | Great Society | Reaganomics plutocracy | Obama Care |

Figure 38 *Real GDP Growth in 2009 Dollars*

The century-long track record enables an economic performance comparison with other nations and a unique way to assess our national voter skills in selecting our government representatives. Clearly, as stated earlier, it is the elected candidates who produce the Acts of Congress that ultimately determines the overall US government performance and the economic fate of the people in the republic.

The following national information is intended to put the modern voting process in the context of the VEP and Congressional results. As mentioned earlier, the United States is currently the 3rd most populous country on the planet. While 3rd in population, we are the wealthiest nation, with the largest economy, the most income, and largest Gross Domestic Product (GDP) output, in the world.

Clearly, being number one economically and the wealthiest

nation on the planet is certainly good news for many of the people living in the United States.

On the other hand, the United States is also the 37th rated nation in terms of the percentage of its people currently living in poverty.

This important poverty rating and ranking comes directly from *The World Factbook* that is published by our Central Intelligence Agency (CIA).

The nation that became first in the 1950s is also now 26th in terms of average life expectancy in comparison with OECD countries like Japan, Australia, Canada, Portugal, and Denmark and 5th in terms of healthcare quality per person.

This mediocre performance by the VEP and Congress, at least in terms of poverty, population health, and life expectancy are certainly bad news for some of the people living in country and especially those living in poverty who also die early as a direct result of government inaction. Worse yet, the poverty legacy of the United States is also bad news for every citizen and every future citizen of the country.

Poverty produces more poverty with devastatingly negative impacts on the economy, the market exchanges between buyers and sellers, and the average life expectancy of its citizens. Moreover, according to capitalism's basic principles, only prosperity from the economy and the market can reduce poverty and its negative impact.

Today, 36 countries are better at reducing the devastating economic, health, and life expectancy impact of poverty in comparison to the United States. Is this important to our economy, our market, and posterity?

Adam Smith answered the economy and market question of national prosperity and the problem of poverty with a simple one liner.

"No society can surely be flourishing and happy of which by far the greater part of the numbers are poor and miserable."
-ADAM SMITH

John Maynard Keynes explained Adam Smith's observation in "aggregate demand" economic terms. Poverty reduces the demand for goods and services and restricts the number of exchanges that produce income and prosperity.

Mr. Keynes also suggested that only the federal government had the economic and political resources necessary to take actions that would stimulate demand and increase exchange transactions.

The US today is the world leader in the development of "aggregate demand" (consumer-driven economy), the production of income, and the accumulation of wealth.

The term "income" is used here to describe the exchange "value storage medium" (money) that facilitates the exchange of goods and services in our economy. These exchanges produce prosperity (more disposable income) while indirectly contributing profits to the accumulated wealth (also called "net worth," defined as acquired assets minus liabilities).

Income from exchanges determines the prosperity-poverty levels among the people. Moreover, income minus expenses also determines the rate of change in net worth or wealth accumulation, over time.

In this context of income and wealth, the lack of income and the underfunding of consumers in our economic system is the root cause of the poverty and the relatively low prosperity-poverty ratio in the United States.

In short, the "promote the general Welfare" role of government for the people and posterity that is spelled out in the

Constitution includes the economic challenge to <u>effect</u> (bring about) an increase in the income of the people.

Moreover, the "promote the general Welfare" role of government for the people has been included in every state constitution and has been the primary challenge for every government representative since 1789, whether they knew it or understood it.

Income prosperity (payments from the exchange of goods and services) and income inequality are also indirectly related to the prosperity-poverty measurements.

Like the prosperity versus poverty numbers, the accumulation of wealth by the wealthy versus general wealth accumulation rates of the people is relatively mediocre in comparison to most countries.

For example, the top 400 richest US families (estimated 0.01% of the population) owns 46% of all the private wealth of the nation. Moreover, the top 10% of the population owns 90% of the private accumulated wealth and as a small group of people, they receive 52% of the national income every year.

On the other end of the US economic spectrum, 80% of the population (240,000,000) receive approximately 38% of the nation's income. Based on the unbalanced split in income, 40% of the population of the United States has a negative net worth (virtually no accumulated wealth) and another 31% have no retirement savings.

Income flows determine prosperity and government actions are the primary contributor to the income flows (economy) of the nation through taxes, government spending to acquire goods and services, transfer payments direct to consumers, and the maintenance of the security and protection of the people (military, fire, police, postal service, medical, healthcare, business infrastructure).

The US federal government directly represents approximately 20% of the US GDP (federal net outlays of nearly $4 trillion versus GDP of about $20 trillion), while state government net outlays account for an additional 18% of the GDP.

As mentioned earlier, 36 other nations are better at managing their flow of income to people in ways that reduce poverty in their nation, versus the poverty rates in the US.

What is even more important to consider is that the United States government and many state governments seem to have been taking legislative actions over the last 40 years to increase poverty and extend its devastating impact onto future generations via poor legislation, deficit spending, and the failure to regulate big business and Wall Street.

The distribution of income graphic, reflecting 1980 to 2000, should help the reader understand the economic inequality problem created by the Congress of the United States and the individual conservative red states, through tax laws, spending patterns, and regulatory actions that create income inequality and expand the imbalance of the income distribution by underfunding consumers.

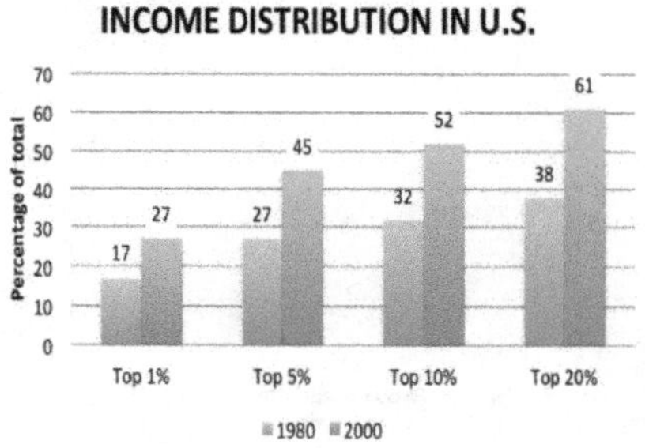

INCOME DISTRIBUTION IN U.S.

Figure 39 *Income Distribution in the US*

In addition to passing legislation to facilitate the accumulation of wealth by the wealthy, Congress has also adopted a financing model to pass their generally disastrous operating performance on to posterity in the form of federal debt.

While the political parties actively discuss the deficit (income minus outflow = deficit), debt is the actual borrowed amount plus interest on the loan. As the debt grows, the interest payments grow, and the outflow of system resources (money) does not produce consumer transactions—just wealth accumulation by the wealthy.

Cutting inflow (reduce taxes on the rich) while increasing outflow and borrowing money to replace the lost inflow increases debt faster than the deficit number implies.

In the last 50 years, Congress has only produced a deficit reduction 3 times. The actual debt grew even with the negative deficit. The loss of income from the three conservative-led tax cuts (1981, 2001, and 2017) is approximately the same amount as the debt expansion since 1980.

The following chart reflects the GDP , the recessions and deficit funding plan over the time period.

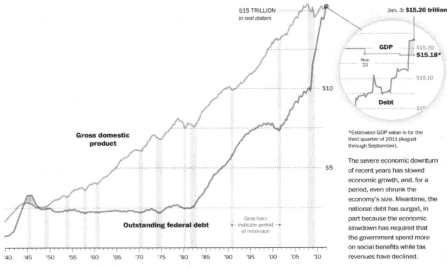

Figure 40 *Deficit Funding the Inequality of Income*

The unbalanced distribution of income, debt financing and underfunding of consumers has retarded the US economy while also impeding the growth of prosperity by the people. The loan balance of the debt also shifts the tax burden to the next generation. As will be discussed in later chapters, laws and taxes that

produced these inequalities have also reduced the economy production rate and expand poverty.

The following 100-year analysis reflects the share of US income
awarded to the top 0.1% and 1%, by legislative actions and the
funding of federal and state operations. The dramatic shifts and
elongated U-shape represent the economic conflict between liberal political ideology for the people and conservative political ideology for the accumulation of wealth by the wealthy.

U.S. Income Shares of Top 1% and Top 0.1% Households – Incl. Capital Gains (1913-2013)

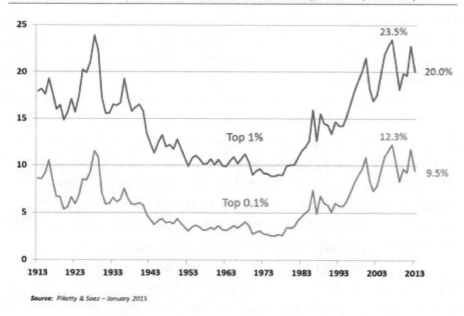

Source: Piketty & Saez – January 2015

Figure 41 *Income Share to top 0.1% and 1% of Households*

The initial decline in the share of plutocrat income from 1913
to 1920 was a result of the liberal Roosevelt/Wilson explosion and
creation of taxes on income and payrolls. The peak and the dramatic increase in share of income in the 1920s was a result of the

tax cuts for the rich and the spending cuts to farmers and the military-industrial complex. The "Return to Normalcy" conservatism created the Great Depression (1928) and the next liberal explosions from the New Deal to the Great Society legislation.

As previously described, the change in the income distribution from the 1930s until 1980 (the Moral Majority Era) that was a result of the regulation of business, the regulation of Wall Street and ultimately the production of the New Deal, the Fair Deal, the Eisenhower Progressive Era, Civil Rights, Voting Rights, and the Great Society legislative Acts (1932 to 1980) for the people. The reversal in the share of income since the 1980s generated the U-shaped curve and the growing inequality of income, beginning with the Republican tax cuts for the rich (1981) and the deregulation of business and Wall Street (1984, 1987).

This government tax and deregulation legislation failure (referred to as the neo-capitalism conservative model) began in 1980s (Reaganomics). The neo-capitalism model initially produced 3 recessions, the collapse of the savings and loan industry, the collapse of the union movement to protect employees, and the building of the deficit, while increasing the number of people living in poverty. The second neo-capitalism tax cut for the rich, in 2001, resulted in the Great Recession and a 16 trillion-dollar net worth loss.

Income redistribution from the people back to the rich to facilitate the accumulation of wealth by the wealthy (neo-capitalism) has also slowed down the economic growth of the country over the period (1980-2017), as would be predicted by the actual capitalism economic theories espoused in the *Wealth of Nations*.

Among the large group of people with virtually no accumulated wealth, 86.5% still enjoy living above the poverty threshold, although many have virtually no retirement savings or pension programs. Approximately 13.5% of the population (46,000,000) live in poverty (defined as an economic condition of lacking both money and necessities needed to live successfully, such as food, water, utilities, and housing).

Obviously, many people with disabilities, seniors, and vets are living in poverty. Moreover, an estimated 32% of the nation's children under the age of 18, live in poverty. This large number of poverty-stricken people and children virtually ensures us that poverty will live on and expand, without national government action to reduce it.

While the US Congress and the states have been inhibiting the growth of the economy, stifling wages, and expanding poverty through the accumulation of wealth by the wealthy legislation, the second largest and fastest growing economy in the world (China) has achieved the seventh lowest poverty rate (2014).

One can only speculate on the amount of economic stimulation Chinese lawmakers created to promote their general welfare and create their new middle class while reducing poverty rolls from 14% to 6% over the last several decades.

Our elected representatives achieved our prosperity and poverty results via legislation. Clearly, the poor results do not suggest or imply that the voters and representatives did not try to improve the quality of life for the people. In fact, the VEP, the actual voters in elections and the congressional lawmakers all get low grades, as discussed in Chapter 3, based on their performance and results, not their effort.

The initial Congress-led poverty reduction and prosperity program began in the US as part of the national land grab and Manifest Destiny (California, the Northwest Territories, Texas, and Florida were acquired by the United States in the 1840s).

The "Free-Soilers" and the eventual Homestead Acts of Congress gave away 270 million acres of farmland (10% of the US land mass) to 1.6 million people against the wishes of the southern plutocrats, who preferred leasing of the land and the operation of the farms via slavery. (Lincoln and the revived Republican Party were in favor of the Homestead Act in the election of 1860, and his election basically kicked off the Civil War).

The second wave of the poverty reduction and prosperity creation process started with the Reconstruction of the South, following the Civil War that had ended slavery as the economic engine of the agrarian South. The Reconstruction effort of Congress also began to facilitate the growth of Unionism, in response to the wage slavery and the "Coolie" labor in the robber baron economic engine of big business.

Our nation's poverty increased in the 1880s as the population grew. Poverty took on a sense of urgency for some with the start of the 20th Century when it became obvious to liberals, progressives, and economists that poor people living in company towns, building products at slave wages, mining coal, servicing oil pipelines, or sharecropping (ex-slave laborers and new farmers growing food and picking cotton) were not good candidates for the consumption-driven prosperity envisioned by Adam Smith.

Trying to fix the "aggregate consumer demand" problem produced a century with massive war casualties, the nearly global collapse of the aristocracy/nobility government model, farm subsidies, healthcare, and a redirection of income from the accumulation of wealth by the wealthy to the development of a higher standard of living for the people.

As shown below, the number of laws and legislative contribution from the US Congress was flat, increased, leveled off and has been declining over the last 40 years.

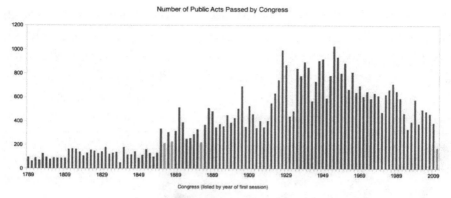

Figure 42 *Public Acts of Congress*

As already mentioned, the federal programs and anti-poverty effort began in earnest early in the 20th century with the Square Deal program of Teddy Roosevelt. The program committed the nation to the conservation of natural resources, the regulation of corporations, the establishment of labor laws protecting children and workers, and consumer protection laws to improve the health of the people in the United States.

The second national poverty reduction program, the New Deal, committed the nation to economic growth, the regulation of Wall Street and business, full employment, and social changes to educate the people and protect union workers, farmers, and seniors from poverty and illness. The

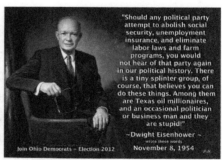

Figure 43 *President Eisenhower on the Cult of Ignorance*

post-World War II legislation, from the GI Bill to minimum wages to the highway system, were all in conflict with the accumulation of wealth by the wealthy proponents and the Cult of Ignorance.

The third major anti-poverty program for the people began with the Fair Deal and the Eisenhower Progressive Era that produced Civil Rights, NASA, public housing, voter rights, healthcare rights, and the Great Society suite that committed the nation to the elimination of poverty, the provision of healthcare for seniors and the poor, and the elimination of institutionalized injustice.

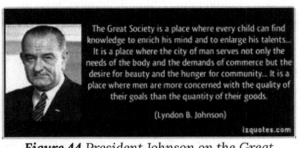

Figure 44 *President Johnson on the Great Society Program*

In terms of voter and congressional results from these ambitious programs, most proved to be relatively successful, based on the GDP, before the 1980 shift back to the accumulation of wealth by the wealthy, neo-capitalist theories, and the Reaganomics model of government.

Today, only India ranks worse than the United States in terms of poverty among the most populous countries on the planet. China, with the largest population, ranks second in prosperity behind the US and seventh in terms of the percentage of its population living in poverty, per *The World Factbook*.

The poverty ranking of China is 30 points better than the United States, ranking 37th of the 180 rated nations. China lags Taiwan (a Chinese island nation of 24,000,000), the world leader in the elimination of poverty, with only 1.5% of its people living in poverty. This poverty rate in Taiwan stands in stark contrast to Mississippi's 24% (state with highest rate of poverty) and Puerto Rico at 44% (island territory of the United States).

China's population is approximately 3 times larger than the United

States population. In this context of size, China has 6.4% of its people living in poverty. To put this in perspective, Taiwan has 240,000 people in living poverty, China has 82 million living in poverty and the richest country has 46 million of its people, living in poverty.

A rational person might wonder if the government representatives in China and Taiwan developed a secret sauce to reduce their poverty rates, versus the United States and India.

If they did have a sauce, they only shared their anti-poverty "secret" with 35 other countries, including Russia, Germany, Great Britain, France, and Canada, where poverty rates are also lower in comparison to the wealthiest country on the planet.

While many people might like to believe a new secret sauce exists, there is none.

The secret to government success, at least since the initial voter rejection of the conservative ideology for the accumulation of wealth by the wealthy in 1788, has been legislation, government spending, and legislative programs.

These government processes and capitalism have demonstrated their ability to drive the economy and stimulate job growth while reducing poverty levels through transfer payments in many countries, including China, Taiwan, and the United States.

On the other hand, it seems obvious that the accumulated wealth locked up in acquired assets, jewels, minerals, foreign banks, and stock buybacks all reduce general consumption levels and consumer demand for goods and services.

The question is how to convert underfunded consumers into funded ones to produce profits and prosperity versus maintaining the poverty. Maintaining poverty also has a downside because the underfunded consumers are also an opportunity cost that ultimately drags down the economy.

Moreover, the poverty "drag" compounds, just like interest. The drag also reduces the growth rate of the economy and even causes the loss of income, as poverty increases.

For example, if the government handed the 46 million people in poverty in 2017 the income equivalents necessary to remove them from the poverty list, the economy would be approximately 10% larger, and that 10% expansion would start growing at least a 2% rate every year (the nation's average economic growth rate during the last 50 years of decline has been at a 2.1% average rate as a result of the state and federal legislation).

The failure to reduce poverty since the 1980s and the misguided laws that stimulated the growth in poverty has had the opposite impact on the economy of the United States.

Based on the federal and state laws that underfund consumers and overfund the wealthy over the last 4 to 5 decades, the United States is destined to see China become the largest and most profitable economy on the planet.

This loss of economic leadership to China over the next several years is a function of the growth rate of their economy. Their accelerated growth compared to the United States is partially driven by their reduction in poverty rates, versus the voter-congressional failure to produce the Great Society results over the last 50 years.

The following figures are an overview of the economic implications of increased poverty caused by voter-congressional failure. It should be noted that the congressional results are time-shifted and skewed by the recessions and tax laws that facilitate the accumulation of wealth by the wealthy and spending plans that underfund the consumers.

Figure 4.
Number in Poverty and Poverty Rate: 1959 to 2012

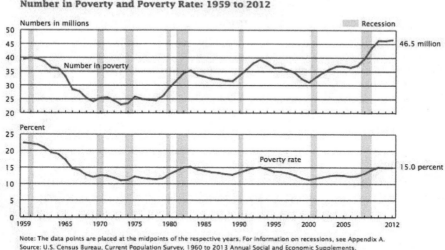

Note: The data points are placed at the midpoints of the respective years. For information on recessions, see Appendix A.
Source: U.S. Census Bureau, Current Population Survey, 1960 to 2013 Annual Social and Economic Supplements.

Figure 45 *Number of People Living in Poverty 1960- 2012*

This chart reflects the impact of voter/congressional failure on the middle class share of income:

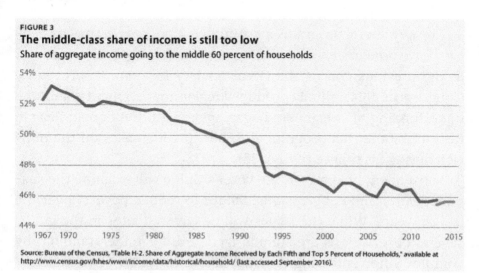

FIGURE 3
The middle-class share of income is still too low
Share of aggregate income going to the middle 60 percent of households

Source: Bureau of the Census, "Table H-2. Share of Aggregate Income Received by Each Fifth and Top 5 Percent of Households," available at
http://www.census.gov/hhes/www/income/data/historical/household/ (last accessed September 2016).

Figure 46 *Middle Class Share of Income in Decline*

The decline in the middle class share of income is also reducing the number of families in the middle class, as shown below:

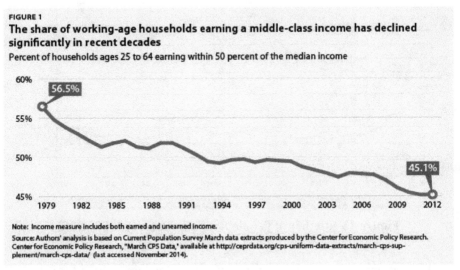

FIGURE 1
The share of working-age households earning a middle-class income has declined significantly in recent decades
Percent of households ages 25 to 64 earning within 50 percent of the median income
60%
55%
50%
45%
56.5%
45.1%
1979
1982
1985
1988
1991
1994
1997
2000
2003
2006
2009
2012
Note: Income measure includes both earned and unearned income.
Source: Authors' analysis is based on Current Population Survey March data extracts produced by the Center for Economic Policy Research. Center for Economic Policy Research, "March CPS Data," available at http://ceprdata.org/cps-uniform-data-extracts/march-cps-supplement/march-cps-data/ (last accessed November 2014).

***Figure* 47** *Number of Families in Middle Class is also Declining*

The key liberal programs instituted by Congress in the last century have done much while failing to achieve their goals. As shown in the previous charts, the Great Society Program, approved by Congress in 1964, initially produced major improvements, until the underfunding of consumers began again, with the Ronald Reagan tax cut for the rich program and the 7 tax increases on the non-rich during his tenure (1981-1988).

Subsequent chapters in the Voter's Guide will examine the sustained voter and congressional failure to reduce poverty over the last 40 years. While the issues will be covered later in the guide, several observations are summarized here for understanding the complex voter and congressional failure in terms of capitalism/liberalism and neo-capitalism/conservatism.

Laws and programs that regulate big business, regulate banking/ Wall Street, support unions, increase wages, and transfer value into the hands of the underfunded working-class and poor consumers have seemed to be more successful at raising the standard of living of people in comparison to deregulation programs, tax cuts for the rich, and downsizing the government transfer payments.

We will also review economic implications in future chapters and blame Congress for the torturous results. Congress, though, is not the whole issue. The officeholders in Congress are representatives. It is the voters who select the representatives who have failed in their execution of congressional mandates for the people. In short, actual voters are the root cause of the congressional problem and its failures.

The failure of actual voters and the representatives they elect is obvious to the poverty-stricken portion of the American population and the 40% of the population without accumulated wealth. It is also obvious to the people who understand that the failure is also restricting profits and inhibiting the growth of the national economy.

While recognizable to some, others seem oblivious to facts and uninformed about the potential power of their votes or the economic benefit that are produced by the reduction in poverty.

As an example, over 50% of the registered federal voters in the United States did not vote in the 2016 or 2018 federal elections. The rate of apathy is typical and worse in years without presidential elections. What is not obvious to many is that given the way we count votes and declare winners; a non-vote is a virtual vote for the declared winner.

Based on the lack of participation, a minority portion of the Voter Eligible Population (VEP) elected the representatives who have put the nation in 37th place in poverty ranking, 1st in debt, 1st in trade deficit, and 1st in profits, while retarding our entire economy, as well.

These voters and the plutocrat patron selected candidates who become representatives that produced the mediocrity also enabled China to be poised to take the economic leadership position in the world.

Economically, the federal government's inaction and poor actions for the people are producing the underfunding of consumers.

These neo-capitalist conservative actions to underfund consumers in a consumer driven economy have also failed to reduce poverty while reducing the average expected life span of an average American for the last three years. In addition to passing laws to increase poverty since 1980s, Congress has also stagnated the US economic growth of the nation, by reducing the production possibility curve, over the same period.

The recent Republican tax plan (passed in 2017) is increasing the deficit today and is expected to produce a trillion and a half deficit run rate every year for the next ten years. The 2018 House-planned budget cuts to consumer spending is forecasted to decrease the potential Gross Domestic Product (GDP) of the United States by six trillion dollars over the same period, according to the Office of Management and Budget analysis.

The combined impact of tax cuts for the rich and spending cuts to Medicaid, Medicare and Social Security exchanges will contribute nothing to the nation's prosperity.

On the other hand, the tax cut and budgeted spending plan will increase the debt load on posterity by nearly $15 trillion, expand the personal debt load on the working poor paying for the higher education of their children and will probably result in another Republican recessionary spiral, a massive recession, and the plundering of another $20 trillion in Net Worth, just like previous Congressional Actions facilitating the accumulation of wealth by the wealthy in the roaring twenties in the last century, and the disastrous Great Recession last decade.

The red and blue lines on the following chart represent the political party holding the majority in the House and Senate. The double lines at some periods in time reflect when a different political party was holding the Senate.

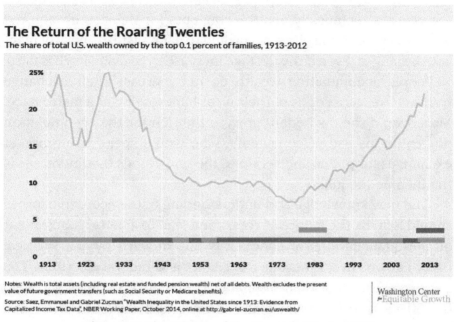

The Return of the Roaring Twenties
The share of total U.S. wealth owned by the top 0.1 percent of families, 1913-2012

Notes: Wealth is total assets (including real estate and funded pension wealth) net of all debts. Wealth excludes the present value of future government transfers (such as Social Security or Medicare benefits).

Source: Saez, Emmanuel and Gabriel Zucman "Wealth Inequality in the United States since 1913: Evidence from Capitalized Income Tax Data", NBER Working Paper, October 2014, online at http://gabriel-zucman.eu/uswealth/

Washington Center
*Equitable Growth

Figure 48 *The Return of the Roaring 20s in 2020*

The graph itself and the U-shaped curve depict the legislative shift from the "accumulation of wealth by the wealthy" income inequality model, to the "for the people" model in the 1930's, and back to income inequality model in the 1980's. The rapid growth in Income Inequality, slowed down the GDP growth rate from the 3% average between 1940 to 1980, to the 2% plus average between 1981 and today.

The information and a better understanding of the historical events and their economic impact should help voter improve their candidate assessment skills and provide them with better tools to assess the plutocrat patron candidate's advertising and promotion plans used in the future election cycles.

The claim that tax cuts can technically pay for themselves, for example, is clearly used to persuade and influence voters. Although the claim is technically possible, tax cuts for the rich do not and cannot pay for themselves, according to capitalism's theory of market exchanges. Even if the tax take increases, the claim itself is false.

People accumulating wealth do not increase their exchange transactions, as a result of their wealth increasing at a faster pace. Moreover, if the tax benefit goes to the rich for the accumulation of wealth, instead of consumers, who would spend it on market exchanges for goods and services, the only things that increases is the Income Inequality.

The new knowledge and understanding of the economic forces should help fix the failure of voters and lead to a better assessment of the qualifications of candidates put forward by the Political Party Patrons in the various local, state and federal elections. The better assessment could dramatically change outcomes and help the 50-year voting malaise and the overall failure of the elected representatives selected by the Baby Boomers and Generation X.

As suggested in the Inequality Chart, the nation is on a path to produce another Roaring 20s decade and it is up to voters whether that includes another Great Depression slamming the people or a new period promoting the "general Welfare."

The voter problem is identifying high quality candidates to be representatives for the people, versus the candidates who intentionally, inadvertently, or mistakenly support the accumulation of wealth by the wealthy and neo-capitalist processes of the conservative plutocrats, patrons, and the Cult of Ignorance model.

Although no candidate for office runs on a platform to stagnate the US economy or increase the wealth of the wealthy, they have done so, while serving in office.

In this context, there are people who really do believe that tax cuts for the rich and the big businesses that are owned by the rich will stimulate capital investment and growth. Likewise, there are others who think cuts to spending that reduce transfer payments and the future GDP will somehow produce positive outcomes for the people of the United States, with fewer exchange transactions creating fewer profits.

Spotting the conservative candidates trying to facilitate the rapture or the misinformed candidates and those holding illogical personal beliefs (like denying climate change, evolution and science) is a challenge and clearly the role of the VEP.

On the positive side, the voting processes today do provide the VEP with the opportunity to evaluate candidates and potential representatives. While there are certainly obstacles in the voting processes, voters do have the opportunity to selecting those candidates that will address the issues of creating prosperity for the people. Voters elect and they can reject the conservative processes, attempting to maintain things as they are with a clear focus on the accumulation of wealth by the wealthy.

I personally hope the information in the Guide will specifically help motivate millennial voters and sway some of the non-participating VEP bystanders, to join with the millennials and vote. This personal contribution to the voting processes could help offset the embedded results of gerrymandering, interference and voter suppression processes.

A positive shift in vote counts could also help guide the elected representatives back to the basic concepts of the republic and its goal to "promote the general Welfare" and help improve the quality of life in America for the people and posterity.

This liberal notion of government for the people and voting for a better quality of life via your representative might become contagious.

Understanding Mr. Brandeis's observation that "We can have democracy in this country, or we can have great wealth concentrated in the hands of a few, but we can't have both" leaves the choice of Representatives, in the hands of voters.

Reconciling the needs of the Forbes 400 and the other 1.4 million other households in the top 10%, with the needs of 240 million people through a tax code is a unique challenge, that Congress, in its history achieved, for nearly 40 years, before failing to do it well, for the last 50 years.

Had the Congress closed the offshore tax loopholes and used a 50% tax rate in the period since the 2001 tax cut, instead of the actual 26.9% effective tax rate, the debt would have been a trillion dollars lower in 2020, the GDP would be approximately 25% larger and the projected number of people living in poverty would have been reduced by 60%, based on math simulations.

While it is hard to assess such "what if" scenarios on historical numbers, it is clear from the tax reports that the Forbes 400 and the other 1.4 million households collected $24.4 trillion in income between 2001 and 2016 and their net worth increased approximately 14% per year over the period. Had the proposed tax burden been implemented, their net worth would have only increased by 6% per year over the period.

While a Political Party is promoting another tax cut for the rich in 2020, if they win the Congress and Presidency and the other Party is calling for things that increase transfer payments and raise taxes, you the member of the VEP have to evaluate the candidates and select Representatives, who will take legislative actions in the future that deal with the same economic reality and democracy.

"We can have democracy in this country, or we can have great wealth concentrated in the hands of a few, but we can't have both" is a never-ending issue, first identified by Mr. Brandeis in 1939, and here again, in 2017.

The next chapter on learning about history, government, and civics might also help stimulate the thought of what voters and the VEP could do for the people and posterity through the improved selection of representatives of the people, instead of being representatives of the plutocrats in search of the accumulation of wealth.

CHAPTER 6

The Conflict of the Liberal "For the People" Political Ideology, versus the Conservative "For the Accumulation of Wealth by the Wealthy" Political ideology.

"Learn from history, or you're doomed to repeat it."
-JESSE VENTURA

Learning, like deducing, logic and reasoning are personal processes. The learning process is used to transform raw data and information received from the environment and senses, into actionable knowledge and personal behavior.

The received raw data and information are categorized, processed, correlated, and stored in the brain for future use in the assessment of situations, the deducing of logical alternatives, and the decision-making processes that produces personal behavior. The concept of learning how to suck a nipple at birth and the learning of the ability to avoid nuclear holocaust, use the same human learning process.

In this chapter, it is important to recognize that history is a compilation of observations and interpretations of circumstances and behaviors that produced memorialized events. Although the historical events no longer exist, according the laws of physics, that does not mean the behavior of people did not produce the events or the results in the past. Learning from that previous reality is what you need to do to avoid reproducing it from your personal lack of knowledge and resultant behavior.

Jessie Ventura's quote introducing this chapter offers people his unique insight and sage advice about learning from history. The ex-Navy Seal, Mongol biker club member, pro-wrestler, author, national political commentator, and governor offered an insight that augmented the older, less poignant, Santayana wisdom of "those who cannot remember the past [being] condemned to repeat it."

Both the failure to remember and, worse yet, not learning from history implies that your behavior can contribute to the re-creation of the economic, political, and societal circumstance that can cause memorialized past events to virtually repeat themselves.

The notion of being condemned to repeat it or doomed to repeat it are both clear warnings that history contains both good and bad results for people and nations. In this context, learning is the force of nature that empowers you to take actions that can help you avoid being condemned or doomed to repeat the bad events from history.

In logical terms, learning from the processed data reflecting today's reality and assessing it with both current knowledge and an adequate understanding of "old" information from history typically enables people to improve their personal skills and enhance their performance over time.

These skill and performance benefits flow from experience, practice, study, and being taught how to interpret information and use the new knowledge in the real world, where your personal behavior contributes to the results and outcomes of current events.

Does your understanding of the events and their causes in history really matter in your decision-making? Can this eclectic "old" knowledge about failed nations, depressions, recessions, and the role of government directly impact what you do to accomplish your goals and avoid potential doom? Logic suggests that it should, at least when you live in a republic that determines the quality of your life through its governance and government actions.

Obviously, you can make good and bad election choices with or without historical knowledge. You can even join the "did not vote" list, although doing nothing also produces certain results, according to history. Moreover, the plutocrats running the political party processes to benefit their party and their investors can certainly negate your vote by manipulating elected representatives to bring about bad legislative actions.

As an example, the 60-plus votes held in the Congress of the United States to take away healthcare from 19 million people and the numerous floor votes to reduce Social Security, Medicare, Medicaid, and unemployment protection for 68 million people is proof enough that Congress can be manipulated into poor legislative action to the detriment of the people, versus fulfilling the constitutional charter to "promote the general Welfare."

Although Congress can and has produced significant benefits for the people, it has also produced the economic disasters, the corruption, the misallocation of resources, and in some cases, the mismanagement of resources to the detriment of the people.

The liberal founding fathers and the writers of the second Constitution took a variety of steps to build in structural protection for the people and the union of people against the conservative actions of plutocrats to accumulate wealth for the wealthy.

The "winner take all" voting process for representatives and new legislation are examples of protections built into the process. The short, 2-year congressional session process for all members in the House of Representatives is an example of trying to protect the people and the union of people from the political forces of the plutocrats.

These operational processes, coupled with the separation of the authorities between the House, the Senate, and the executive branch clearly provides a direct method for voters to quickly address and hopefully correct, poor political actions, adopted by Congress and approved by presidents.

History itself seems to be an opportunistic teacher for voters, especially since history produced today's reality. Failing to learn from the history lessons or misinterpreting the information can still produce disastrous voting results, even with the protections.

As an example, virtually all voters in 2016 remembered the tax cuts for the rich in 2001 and the Great Recession (2007-2010) and seemingly learned nothing from them.

Was there a direct cause and effect relationship between lighting the fuse (tax cut for the rich 2001) and the explosion (deficit and recession 2008), as many believe, or was the disaster a result of the combination of other memorialized events (9-11, Afghanistan and Iraq Wars, deregulation of banking and Wall Street...) that produced the disaster.

Obviously, the 2001 tax cut when combined with the deregulation of Wall Street and banking produced the sub-prime lending market and the junk bond binge-buying.

Likewise, the addition of the unfunded Feature Group D payments to big pharma, coupled with the non-existing weapons of mass destruction debacle generated the seemingly never-ending Middle East war that produced a new massive increase in military spending. Combining these events with the tax cuts obviously produced the new Trillion-dollar annual budget Deficit, replacing the 2000 Federal Surplus, in eight years.

What Jesse Ventura introduced to the VEP at the opening of this chapter is the idea of active learning from the legislative disasters and history, versus simply remembering the timeline of what happened.

Webster defines learning as "the action you must take to gain or acquire information needed to create knowledge or a personal skill in something."

Obviously, voters did not remember much of anything from the 2001 tax cut or its political cycle for the rich. They also did not learn very much from the historical cycle of 2001-2007, nor from the previous tax cut cycle for the rich in, 1981. The evidence of the VEP not remembering and not learning was produced by the VEP in the 2017 tax cut.

The studying and learning processes suggested by Ventura hopes to create the learned knowledge and a better understanding of history to avoid the doom, especially the obvious ones, that inevitably come after lighting the fuse with a tax cut for the rich. The lack of VEP study effort and the failure to learn from the lessons of history makes their poor voting judgment of Representatives worse than the failure to remember events.

Clearly, personal skills and performance improve from practice and being taught how to interpret facts and situations. The failure to understand the facts of the Great Recession, the three Reagan Recessions, and the Great Depression were clearly etched in the failure pattern of the VEP in 2017, and even their more recent mixed success, in 2018, where they cleaned the House but failed to repair the Senate, at the same time.

This chapter is designed to teach and help you learn from history and the facts. These historical review processes can be used to development your own skills to assess the relevance of "old" information and learn from it via your own personal knowledge creation and new understanding of causes and effects.

Briefly, science, economics, and history provide the individual voters and the whole VEP with personal and group evaluating and sorting processes.

These sorting processes use facts, logic, fuzzy statistical measures, word descriptions, personal ideology and mixed with theology principles, to <u>examine the variables</u> (elements, features, or factors that vary in importance and proportions), <u>the attributes</u> (qualities or features regarded as characteristics or inherent parts of someone or something), <u>the causes</u> (persons or things that give rise to an action, phenomenon, or condition) and <u>the effects</u> (changes that are the results or the consequences of actions or other causes).

Seeing and evaluating the conflict between sorting and the interpretation of facts and results is one of the prime advantages of the learning process. In this chapter, for example, the liberal federal government model for the people and the union of the people can be directly evaluated and compared to the conservative unitary government model for the accumulation of wealth by the wealthy.

The following graphic summarizes the last 100 years or so of our federal government's economic actions and contributions to the people, independent of its cultural achievements that produced today's democratic republic by granting women and young adults the right to vote and the creation of the public education system to go along with the failed effort to create the Great Society.

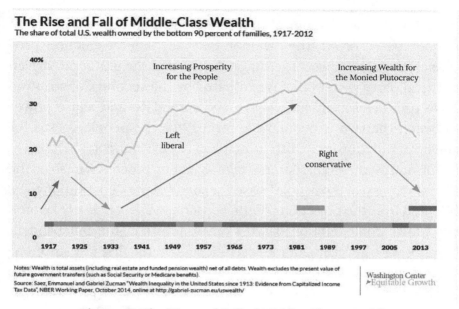

Figure 49 *The Rise and Fall of Middle-Class Wealth*

Congressional political party status enables the application of deductive logic to draw the blue/red arrows to represent the direction of the political party contributions to the "increasing prosperity for the people" over the last century, in direct comparison to the conservative "increasing wealth for the monied plutocracy" economic and governance model over the period. The years with double lines on the chart represent Congress being controlled by different parties.

Without oversimplifying the clear ideological dichotomy between "for the people" and "for the accumulation of wealth by the wealthy" results, it should be noted that there is no way to reconcile the political conflict between the liberal principles of government for a union of the people and the conservative principles of government for the accumulation of wealth by the wealthy in the monied plutocracy.

Although the ideological difference between the left and right cannot be resolved, the "winner take all" federal election processes, the voting processes in Congress, and the plutocrat-driven political party system that was created by the second Constitution have produced a unique way to accommodate and share power between the two irreconcilable forces (for the people versus for the accumulation of wealth principles) of government.

Obviously, the simple "winner take all" voting processes enabled the liberal's "union of the people"-based second federal Constitution to be adopted over the objections of the conservatives that clearly favored the initial Confederation based Constitution and the independent Unitary state government model embedded in the first Constitution.

The Federalist and liberal Whig victory over the conservative Anti-Federalist plutocrats was short lived. The plutocrat landowners operating the slave-based economy of the South formed the Democrat-Republican Party to blunt the liberal threat.

As mentioned in earlier chapters, the first two Federalist presidents (Washington and Adams) feared the development of a two-party political system pitting liberals and conservatives in a political power struggle, vying for the power of government to "insure domestic Tranquility," "promote the general Welfare, and secure the Blessings of Liberty."

The new liberal Federalist principles, the new separation of powers Constitution, and the quickly enacted Bill of Rights addition were all designed to reduce the risk of a conservative insurrection that could destroy the union of the people and the new government that had been empowered, by the people and for the people, to "establish justice" in the new federal republic, the United States of America.

It should also be noted that to get enough "yes" votes to adopt the new Constitution and reduce the possibility of an insurrection, the liberal founding fathers also embraced several compromises to placate the centrist (random mixture of liberal and conservative ideology) plutocrats in the southern Slave States.

According to history, the voting districts for the House of Representatives were set up based on land covered and not just population or population density.

The very nature of the geography, the transportation systems, and the communications processes between these blocks of coverage were viewed as natural obstacles to the accumulation and concentration of political power by the political parties.

Population counts were also arranged to award conservative slaveholders with significant leverage over Congress and the presidency (a black male slave would be counted as 3/5ths of a person in determining House seats and Electoral College seats).

With 8 Slave States and 5 Free States, the 3/5ths slave-counting convention assured the conservative slaveholder states that they would have control of Congress and 40% more seats in the House and the same 40% advantage in the Electoral College.

The 8 to 5 Slave State Senate majority (16 senators to 10) advantage in the new union of people was quickly reduced to an 8 to 6 advantage with the addition of Free-State Vermont, in 1794.

The southern conservative plutocrats responded to the change in power base by creating Tennessee and Kentucky, as new Slave States, out of Virginia and North Carolina. These changes reestablished voting control over the Senate (10-6). With New Jersey and New York voting to end slavery (1799/1804 respectfully), they re-stoked the never-ending battle between the liberals and conservatives, over the slavery issue.

The Louisiana Purchase in 1803 changed the size, scale, and scope of the political battlefield. The purchase itself more than doubled the land mass of the nation. In today's terms, the massive purchase formed the basis for more than 15 new states, stretching from Louisiana to North Dakota. The purchase also added 50% more appointed Senators to Congress. It also fueled the slavery and indentured servant economic conflict facing the evolving new nation.

By 1820, the Louisiana land purchase and the Missouri Compromise had enabled the creation of four new Slave States to offset the liberal non-slave-state growth of five. The new 12 liberal and 12 conservative state standoff in the Senate would last for nearly 20 years, as the nation sought "domestic Tranquility" while avoiding the collapse of the Union from a new war between the liberals and conservatives.

The 1820 population of 9.6 million Americans included 1.6 million slaves and an estimated 400,000 indentured servants.

Because of the 3/5ths counting compromise in the Constitution, the Slave States held 1/3 more seats in the House, and they acquired 1/3 more Electoral College votes.

This simple mathematical advantage ensured the maintenance of the conservative slaveholder plutocrat interests over the interest of the people for most of the first 50 years of the new century (1800 to 1850). The number of Public Acts of Congress chart shown earlier reflects the conservative pre-Civil-War congressional activity on a yearly basis. If you review the chart again, also notice the stark contrast in activity before the Civil War in comparison to the liberal leaning post-Civil War Acts of Congress.

With the addition of Texas, Florida, and California, by 1850, there were 64 appointed plutocrat senators being appointed to Congress by 17 liberal Free States, versus 15 conservative slave states. The nation's population had increased to 21 million people, including 3.2 million slaves and 600,000 indentured servants and "coolies." This shift in population and Free States had reduced the conservative 1/3 House and Electoral College advantage from the 3/5ths slave counting process, to a 1/4 advantage.

By 1860, there were 68 senators being appointed to Congress

by 19 liberal Free States and the same 15 conservative Slave States. The population had reached 27 million people, including 4 million slaves and 700,000 indentured servants and "coolies."

Approximately 4.5 million people out of the 27 million (see presidential chart on page 5) voted in the federal election, with about 40% of them selecting Abraham Lincoln and the reconstituted Republican Party (liberal Federalists' and Whigs' revival campaign).

The Republican Party victory in that year also demonstrated that it was possible for a minor political party to win the most seats in the House, Senate, and the presidency, with just a simple plurality of votes and no majority vote victory.

The minority victory process had already happened in a national election of the executive branch. Andrew Jackson, for example, won the popular vote in 1824 and was not elected president because the Electoral College and House voted against him.

The idea that a minority liberal party candidate could win control of the House, the Senate, and the presidency occurred in 1860 as the nation's unique voter disenfranchisement strategies backfired on the Slave States.

In 1860, for example, the Republican Party candidate, Abraham Lincoln, was not allowed on the ballot in Texas. Texas also did not allow northern Democrat Stephen Douglas on the ballot. The southern Democrat won the state and the Electoral College votes but not enough other slave state votes to win the election.

The voter disenfranchisement processes that began in the 1840 to 1860 era, grew more prevalent after the Civil War and the resulting constitutional amendments freeing the slaves and defining citizenship. The disenfranchisement processes became so pervasive in municipal, regional, state, and federal elections that it generated the "if voting made any difference, they would not let us do it" quote attributed to Mark Twain earlier in the book.

Ballot box stuffing, violence, fraud, poll taxes, literacy tests, and restricted registration blossomed all the way into a pure "White Primary" election process in Texas and 26 years of litigation against the practice, before it finally ended in the 1920s.

Many Americans today think these voting anomalies and practices were virtually ended with the Voting Rights Act of 1965. This law and its amendments over the years corrected many abuses, although new ones took their place to disenfranchise voters.

Gerrymandering, voter suppression, voter intimidation, and various logistical processes have also been added over time as ways to influence and ultimately win elections. Do these processes and the "dark money" of Plutocrats and Corporation influence election results and the performance of the nation?

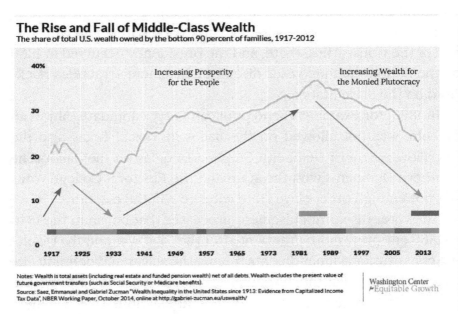

Figure 49 The Rise and Fall of Middle-Class Wealth

While most Americans like to think and believe the voter suppression processes have little to do with the performance of the nation, a quick review of Chart 49 certainly suggests that something has gone wrong with either the theory of capitalism or the voting process for the people versus for the accumulation of wealth by the wealthy.

The increasing prosperity of the people for nearly 50 years prior to 1980 is probably considered a good thing by most people. Explaining away the economic lines and their income direction since 1980 becomes a little harder to reconcile. Some people might suggest it was just bad luck and not indicative of direct intent of the conservative plutocrats' political party or its elected representatives to dismantle the urban industrialized and unionized states in the North and Midwest.

Historically and statistically, the bad luck theories make little logical sense, and they do not explain away the data points nor the direction of the lines. Based on the laws of probability, plutocratic political forces were the underlying cause of the observed economic rise of the rich and the middle-class collapse over the century of results.

Even with the clearly demonstrated "for the people" successes and the current ongoing failure of the Congress of the United States, it was and remains an important contributor to the development of society on this planet.

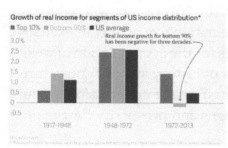

Figure 50 *The Growth of Real income*

While figure 49 clearly displays the failure of Congress, it does not totally covey the magnitude of the problem that the VEP and Congress has created over the period. Congress in the early part of the 20th century (1917-1948) was instrumental in converting a middling nation into the economic and military powerhouse and the most profitable nation on the planet. The 1948-1972 interval reflects how well they balanced the needs of the people with the need for the accumulation of wealth by the wealthy. Likewise, the 1972-2013 period clearly displays the magnitude of the VEP and Congressional failure for the people.

Over the last 40 years, the Voter Eligible Population has also clearly demonstrated a unique inability to learn much from this history. As such, the VEP now faces the same doom as their great-grandparents (living through the Great Depression) and their parents (living through the Great Recession).

Contextually, the 1981 tax cuts for the rich and the use of deficit financing of government to offset the accumulation of wealth by the wealthy and the lost revenues from the tax cuts set in motion three recessions in the Reagan years. Compare those days of yesteryear in the last century to the 2001 tax cuts for the rich and resultant deficit as the accumulation of wealth built up a head of steam and ultimately rocked the nation with the Great Recession.

While charts and graphs display the information, the goal of this chapter is to suggest that you and the rest of VEP need to learn from the actual history, or you are doomed to repeat it.

For these simple learning purposes, you, a member of the VEP, need to grasp and understand that the 2017 tax cut will reduce the production possibility curve of the national economy in exchange for an increase in the flow of profits for the accumulation of wealth by the wealthy. These are the facts of history and not conjecture.

The reduced and lost production from the congressional failure also forgoes the economic exchanges and prosperity for the people, as discussed by Adam Smith.

Hopefully, the failures clearly expose the conservative analogy of trickle-down economic theories and paying for themselves that were created by the Cult of Ignorance and marketed to the VEP, as a rational economic theory that is, in fact, nothing more than mis-information babble to mislead the gullible, within the VEP.

In fact, the lost consumer exchanges from the 2017 tax cut for the rich and 2018 tariffs imposed on the consumers will directly reduce middle class income, as the lost tax revenues are distributed to the wealthy, the number of profitable transaction declines from the higher prices on goods and services, while the Federal debt will be increased in capitalism response to the conservative economic actions from the Republican Party.

Together, these viral economic forces that reduce exchanges and reduce income of the people also produce other economic chaos, according to history and economic theories associated with the new financial uncertainties factored into the stock markets.

In today's environment, the Voter Eligible Population has the sole responsibility for the staffing of Congress and fixing their legislative and economic failures they have been producing while facilitating the accumulation of wealth by the wealthy. With the historical learning and knowledge, you have gained up to this point in the guide, you should certainly have a better grasp of the preposterous claims that fully funded Social Security is somehow related to the disastrous performance. You should also have the better assessment skills to understand the President and

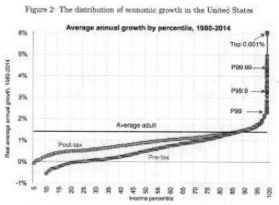

Figure 51 *The Distribution of Economic Growth by Percentile*

Political Party dangling of another tax cut and fix for Social Security, if you elect a Republican President and Congress in 2020.

Figure 51 is another way of displaying the impact of the bad legislation and how it impacts the quality of life for the entire nation.

The obvious question from these percentiles and this chapter is, "what can the current VEP and millennials learn from the economic disaster that was produced by the VEP and Congress after the economic prosperity and liberal democracy binge from 1930 till 1980 that preceded the conservative results from the Nixon to Trump Republican era disaster?"

The most important thing the VEP can learn may be the "throw them out" House success in 2018, especially when they can clearly see with their own eyes that the entire VEP recognizes the failure, at least in terms of the congressional Job Approval Ratings.

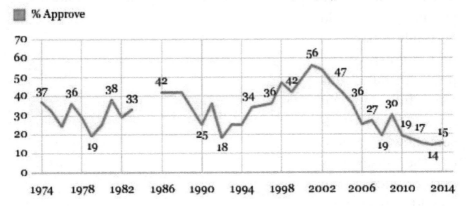

Congress' Job Approval Ratings, Yearly Averages

Do you approve or disapprove of the way Congress is handling its job?

Note: Gallup did not measure congressional job approval in 1984-1985.

Figure 52 *Congress Job Approval Rating Yearly Averages*

In the context of the low opinion of Congress and the general disapproval of the way the elected candidates have been handling the job, it is very clear, well-recognized, and deserved disdain earned by the 112th, 113th, and 114th congressional sessions.

Whether the obvious voter failure to produce an effective Congress was a result of the failure to learn from history or the failure to remember history is a matter of conjecture.

Election year rhetoric, false advertising programs, Plutocrat dark money financing, Russia-derived propaganda efforts, gerrymandering, voter suppression, Corporate manipulation of taxes and the rewriting of history to distort it are facts and not conjecture.

A large conservative voter constituency that believes that untaxed profits flowing to the rich will miraculously trickle down and generate benefits for the rest of the general population and posterity is also not conjecture.

In any case, it should be obvious from this chapter's glimpse of our history that Ventura has provided sage advice about how to avoid the doom as we prepare for the 2020 election. The next chapter will explore the impact from the conservative destruction of the middle class to facilitate the "accumulation of wealth by the wealthy."

CHAPTER 7

Congratulations to the VEP and their Representatives for Your Success at Producing Income Inequality and Losing the War on Poverty Over the Last 40 Years.

"An imbalance between rich and poor is the oldest and most fatal ailment of all republics."
—PLUTARCH, ANCIENT GREEK BIOGRAPHER (C. 46-120 BC)

Under the second Constitution and its amendments, the Voter Eligible Population and the representatives in Congress are jointly responsible for all of the federal laws, the funding of the federal government operations, and the performance of the federal government in terms of its constitutional charter to **"establish Justice, insure domestic Tranquility, provide for the common defence (sic), promote the general Welfare, and secure the Blessings of Liberty to ourselves and our Posterity."**

According to the income inequality problem chart shown on the next page, the VEP and the elected representatives managed to create the richest nation on the planet over the 100 year period, while "promoting the general Welfare" and reducing the income equality problem, by keeping millions of people out of poverty, using tariffs, payroll taxes and Income Taxes.

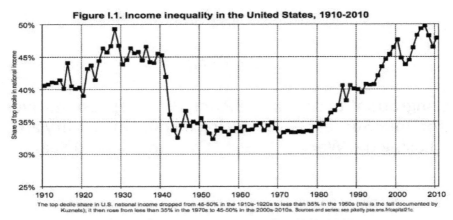

Figure I.1. Income inequality in the United States, 1910-2010
Share of top decile in national income
50%
45%
40%
35%
30%
25%
1910
1920
1930
1940
1950
1960
1970
1980
1990
2000
2010
The top decile share in U.S. national income dropped from 45-50% in the 1910s-1920s to less than 35% in the 1950s (this is the fall documented by Kuznets); it then rose from less than 35% in the 1970s to 45-50% in the 2000s-2010s. Sources and series: see piketty.pse.ens.fr/capital21c

Figure 53 *US Income Inequality* 1910-2010

Congress also achieved the mid-30's Income Inequality results through consumer protection laws and the creation of income transfer payments streams to consumers.

For whatever reason, the VEP re-infected the Congress in the 1980s with the same "accumulation of wealth by the wealthy" virus that had created the Great Depression and the income inequality peak in 1929. The newly infected Congress produced various anti-consumer laws, in cooperation with presidential leadership, to re-create the Income Inequality levels, not seen in the United States, for nearly 100 years.

The anti-consumer laws, included tax cuts for the rich, massive tax loopholes for unearned income and off shore banking, the deregulation of monopolies, and the creation of the Wall Street junk bonds/hedge funds/commodity pools operating as a "Kraken" monster, to plunder "undervalued" companies and maximize capital gains, from flipping assets and draining their treasuries, instead of building companies.

Together, the poor Congressional legislation, the Plutocrat CEOs, and the presidential leadership produced the income inequality growth rate and the collapse of industries along with four (4) recessions, including the Great Recession of 2007.

The mixed results over the century began with a massive change in the VEP in 1920 (women's right to vote) and the Great Depression (1927) that together generated the New Deal and a series of Congresses (24) that reduced the income inequality levels and the massive poverty by creating a new consumer-driven capitalistic economy and a new middle class in America, while also reducing the number of people living in poverty.

The new consumer and union protection laws from the New Deal onward and the transfer payments created along the way, produced the distribution of income to the people (bottom 90% is in blue on the chart below) in ways that also reduced the income inequality, as the nation became the world's largest economy with the most profits for the rich. The unique economic growth from the transfer payments and government funding of transactions for the people shrank the rate of growth of the top 10% of earners slightly, while still increasing their total volume of earnings.

Given the growth of real income in the 1917-1948 and the 1948-1972 period, today's VEP clearly owes a debt of gratitude to the earlier generations and Congresses for the economic and sociological improvements Congress produced through their legislation for the people. Sadly, as you can see on the chart,

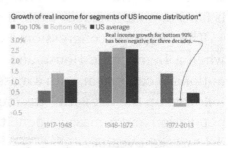

Figure 54 *Growth of Real income*

many of the economic benefits were lost over the last forty years.

The implications of this economic loss for 90% of the people are also reflected in the poverty and life expectancy rates. Both rates improved until the 90s, then went stagnant. Today, poverty rates are higher than they were in 1980 (12% versus 14%), indicating losing the battle in the war on poverty, while life expectancy rates have declined for the last three years, for the first time in over a century of record keeping.

In global terms, the US Human Development Index from the United Nations declined to 25th from 5th over the last twenty years, as a result of so many people earning less in "real income" and dying early.

The quality of life in the US has also declined in various other ways. Higher educational rates stimulated by the GI Bill, the Eisenhower era, and the war on poverty commitments are now producing **school-debt-burdened families that owe the government over a trillion dollars, for the government's failure to fund education.**

Economically and socially, the congressional failure over the last 50 years is inconceivable and nearly defies any rational explanation. The government performance over the period violates capitalist principles and Christian values. Why the VEP supported the conservative movement for the accumulation of wealth, and why they elected and re-elected the underperforming representatives, is hard to understand or explain.

The negative congressional actions formally began, in 1981, when a Democratic House and Republican Senate perverted the notions of capitalism, with a massive tax cut for the rich. Congress followed up the cut with 7 tax increases on the bottom 90% of the population and a massive deficit funding expansion (doubled the debt in eight years).

In the same early period, Congress deregulated Wall Street (Junk Bond, 1984) and banking (Business Development/Hedge Funds, 1987). Together, the deregulations caused the looting of the savings and loan industry by 1990, and over 400,000 firms were acquired and fleeced with junk bonds and Hedge Funds, by 2013.

This disastrous "Reagan Era" conservatism and Cult of Ignorance Plutocrat period that followed, produced four recessions and another tax cut for the rich (2001). That second cut produced the trillion-dollar deficit run rate, the collapse of the housing and auto industries and the Great Recession, by 2008.

The economic aftershock of this disastrous congressional performance between 1972 and 2013 was another deficit-driving tax cut for the rich in 2017 that led to the House-cleaning voter effort in in 2018, while leaving the failed Senate to the conservatives.

Clearly, the nation has lost a portion of the American milieu over the last 50 years as the VEP, the political party duopoly, and the elected representatives subverted the economy, reduced the production possibility curve of the nation, and retarded the economic growth, to facilitate the accumulation of wealth by the wealthy. The expansion of income can also be seen in the average after-tax income distribution results and the neo-capitalist governance operation for the accumulation of wealth by the wealthy.

The nation's legal and economic history with respect to income inequality shows that it was not always this way.

In fact, the uniquely American milieu before the conservative regression once had a Congress that rejected "God's" grant of sovereignty and dominion to the richest plutocrats.

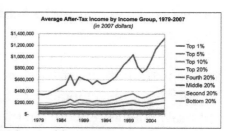

Figure 55 *Average after tax income growth by Group*

The American milieu "for the people" that began in 1789 came from the liberal forces and a purely plutocratic based VEP that rejected the national "for the accumulation of wealth by the wealthy" deal in the Articles of the Confederation.

Moreover, the new "for the people" second Constitution was not imposed as a roadblock to the plutocrats or the creation of wealth. The American milieu embraced the exploitation of natural resources and the theft of land from the Indians and Mexico. The same liberal American human force also ended slavery and produced equal protection for the people under the 13th, 14th, and 15th amendments, in the 1860s.

The "promote the general Welfare" process also created the Square Deal, the child labor laws, the trust-busting laws, the New Deal, the protection of unions, the regulation of business, the protection of the environment, the education of the people, and the protection of civil rights, human rights, economic rights, legal rights, and voting rights on the way to producing the most profits, an improved standard of living and the longer healthier lives for each generation, until now.

Historically, the legal right of seniors to live out their post-working years in dignity instead of poverty, the legal right of the young to an education, the legal right of citizens to earn a living, even when unemployed, and the legal right to healthcare coverage and retirement benifits were created by Congress, before 1980, in spite of the Cult of Ignorance, the big business lobbies, the evangelical conservatives, and the business-friendly states that still inhibit citizens' rights.

The "legal" development of the economic, social, political, and cultural milieu is reflected in the number of the public acts passed by Congress. In the following chart, the blue line segments reflect the general liberal political tendencies ("for the people"). The red line segments reflect those congressional sessions where the conservative political tendencies ("for the accumulation of wealth by the wealthy") overwhelmed any liberal tendencies.

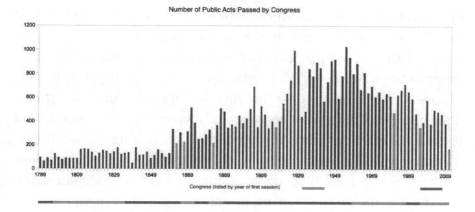

Figure 56 *Acts of Congress and Liberal/Conservative Cycles*

The clearly mediocre performance of the elected federal representatives over the last 50 years (according to the Gallup Polls, the life expectancy, the educational failure, and the poverty results discussed in previous chapters) is

Figure 57 *Income Inequality in the US 1910-2010*

also clearly demonstrated by the inability to maintain economic and social justice, the inability to "insure domestic Tranquility" and the general failure to "promote the general Welfare," as evidenced by the income inequality gap being generated by Congress and the states, over the last 50 years of economic history.

The good news is that the generally mediocre political party and congressional performance over the last 50 years is not an irreversible trend, as evidenced by the post-World War II to Nixon income inequality results. Sadly, the accumulation of wealth, the demonizing of government operations, and the conservative neo-capitalist principles were embraced by a minority of the VEP and the plutocrats operating the political parties.

The 2016 presidential election and the political slogan to "Make America Great Again" certainly reflected the clear recognition by politicians, pundits, and people that America has lost something that it once had. Something was fundamentally wrong in the economic and social justice environment (milieu) of the United States, as of 2016.

While MAGA speaks emotionally to the eco-system problem created by the post 1980 congressional failure, the sloganeering and the mislabeled root causes, intentionally misinformed the people and failed to identify which time periods of history contained greatness. Avoiding this clarity by the MAGA marketing promoters was not accidental.

The dissatisfaction with the country's income inequality performance since 1972 was effectively masked in the political marketing message that parlayed the demonizing anti-government Cult of Ignorance rhetoric with hate speech against Mexicans and illegal immigrants, in 2016.

While the MAGA emotion created by the income inequality is a palpable, legitimate desire for the people, the nation still remains sincerely grateful for the wisdom of the liberal Founding Fathers who wrote the Constitution, the logic of the liberal plutocratic VEP that adopted the new law of the land, and the generally liberal legislative actions displayed in the Acts of Congress over the years. Those Acts of Congress that made us great in the past could someday be tapped again, based on the 2018 House-cleaning results.

The VEP of today certainly needs to be thanked for their voting effort to "clean" the House of Representatives in 2018, while also being chastised for their failure to repair the Senate, at the same time.

Hopefully, a better understanding of the once-proud history of the nation can help the VEP develop their candidate assessment and voting skills to select higher quality representatives who can achieve the nation's aspirations for the people and posterity.

As many of you know, in the current political environment, the VEP elects all 435 representatives to the House and one-third of the representatives to the Senate every two years. The bi-annual election empowers the representatives to act and provides them the opportunity to address national priorities in the two-year congressional session.

The generally adequate-to-good performance by Congress for the first 190 years of its existence (1789 to 1979) is clearly demonstrable in the growth of the nation, its social performance, and its ability to produce the 1917 to 1972 income results.

The following condensed history summarizes the path to "great" success and, sadly, the creation of the doom that was enabled by those not learning from this history.

Figure 58 *A Condensed History of Key Events in the nation's Development, 1789-1979*

The elections in 1980 were a political inflection point that began the re-introduction of the conservative Cult of Ignorance principles for the accumulation of wealth by the wealthy. The tax cut for the rich (1981), seven tax increases on the general population, the unfunded deficits from Reaganomics, the junk bonds on Wall Street, and the Iran-Contra Affair were the opening rounds to the economic and social disaster destined to produce the income inequality trend and the failure to execute the Great Society Program.

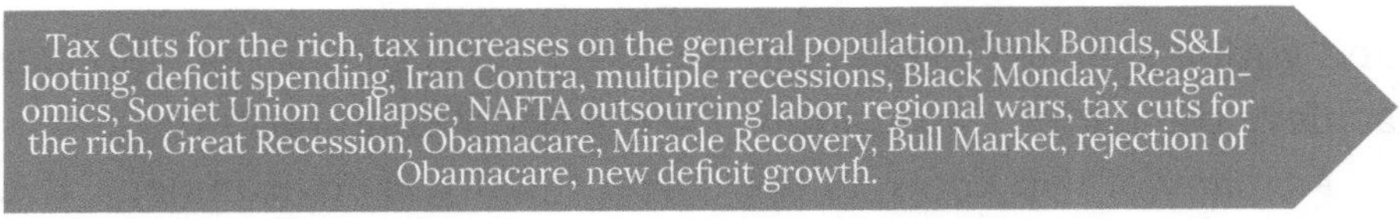

Tax Cuts for the rich, tax increases on the general population, Junk Bonds, S&L looting, deficit spending, Iran Contra, multiple recessions, Black Monday, Reaganomics, Soviet Union collapse, NAFTA outsourcing labor, regional wars, tax cuts for the rich, Great Recession, Obamacare, Miracle Recovery, Bull Market, rejection of Obamacare, new deficit growth.

Figure 59 *Congressional Actions Impacting the Congressional Ratings since 1980*

The Reagan-Bush, the Bush-Cheney, and the Trump-Pence tax cuts for the rich, the ongoing profiteering, the massive deficit, and the Great Recession have produced increased poverty, massive new federal debt, massive student loan debt, and income inequality levels not seen in America since President Harding, President Arthur, and the congressional "Return to Normalcy" government that created the Great Depression.

As reflected by the Acts of Congress chart, the first Great Depression (1927 Wall Street collapse) and the start of the first Great Recession (2007 Wall Street collapse) serve as the conservative Republican bookends on a period of congressional actions that produced high economic growth, massive GDP expansion and the creation of a middle class, before the congressional collapse into 50 years of mediocrity.

By the early 1950s, for example, a new lower level of income inequality had been established via the New Deal, the post-war taxes, and the binding congressional actions. The following economic success also enabled Congress to focus its attention on civil rights, human rights, and voting rights while building a consumer-driven economy through the tax-and-spend processes of capitalism, generating the consumer transactions.

The new government-stimulated economy included the safety net transfer payment expansion for the disabled, veterans, elderly, and unemployed, along with citizens' rights to an education, the safeguarding of rights of minorities, women, and the disadvantaged that served as a prelude to the Great Society plan, to improve education and eliminate poverty.

The economic/social advances of the people also produced the Nixon-Agnew presidency and Watergate in the 1970s and the conservative Cult of Ignorance revival, by the 1980s. The national economic/social/educational upgrade between 1932 and 1980 had been supported by both political parties and only contested by the political power of the Cult of Ignorance and its conservative evangelical following. The results are clear on the growth of income and income distribution chart.

The liberal progress was reversed and stifled over the next 50 years, as shown here, again, for your review and understanding of the impact of income distribution between "for the people" and "for the accumulation of wealth by the wealthy" ideology implementation through the Acts of Congress.

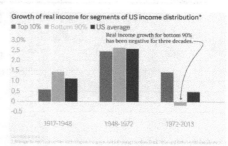

Figure 60 *Growth of Real income and its Distribution*

The scope of the conflict between the opposing political-ideological foundations and the political tendencies of the liberal versus the conservative principles of governance was reviewed earlier in terms of the legislation passed and the events produced.

The legislation can also be visualized as a political tendency continuum between two opposite poles with the tendencies being normally distributed across the population.

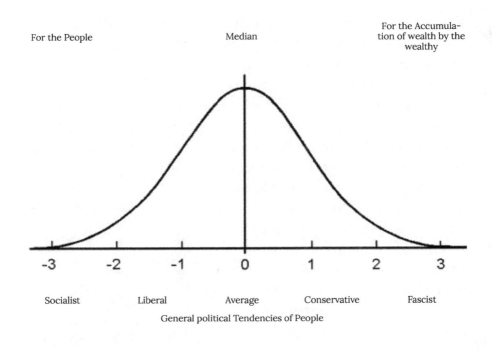

For the People · Median · For the Accumulation of wealth by the wealthy

-3   -2   -1   0   1   2   3

Socialist   Liberal   Average   Conservative   Fascist

General political Tendencies of People

Liberalism

The "for the people" political ideology and liberal bias based on the ideas of individual liberty, individual equality under the law, justice and the general belief that Representative based government is necessary to enhance individual freedom and to protect the individual from harm caused by the environment, big business, the economy, the government itself and other people in the global society.

The Political Ideology Continuum

Conservatism

The "for the accumulation of wealth by the wealthy" political ideology, based on traditional hierarchical plutocratic authority, aristocracy, property rights, the maintenance of the status quo and the general belief that the role of government is to facilitate the accumulation of wealth by the wealthy and provide the resources to protect the economic and social status quo of the conservative model of government operations.

Figure 61 *Political Ideology Continuum*

In the new global economy period following the Second World War (1945 - 1980), the US federal government became the largest single employer in the world, the largest supplier of disposable income to workers and non-employees (income transfers to enti-tled retirees, unemployed, veterans, sick, and disabled) in the world, the largest purchaser of private goods and services, and the largest payer of medical service costs. In aggregate, the states became the second largest economic enabler in the world.

Given the magnitude of the federal tax-and-spend legislation that was driving the economy and the subsequent state spending to sup-port the federal initiatives, it should be obvious to most people that the legislative performance of Congress and the state legislatures is vitally important to the economy of the United States and the people.

On the downside, the two major economic engines of prosper-ity in the United States also have legislators who have produced every downturn in the economy and, at the federal level, are clearly responsible for the most recent 40-year decline in the economic quality of life of 90% of the income earners in the United States.

The poor congressional legislative actions and the flow of events they produced in this period not only disadvantaged 90% of the earners, they also shrank the production possibilities curve of the nation and the economic output of the nation, for years to come.

It should also be noted that the current political rhetoric from the conservative, plutocratic, anti-government evangelicals and the Cult of Ignorance, discounts this assessment of their actions. The conservatives' frame of reference suggests the federal republic's integration with liberalism (for the benefit of the people) is socialism.

While socialism is a bold-faced lie used to attract the misin-formed in the VEP, the inane socialism claim is also being used as a political party propaganda plank by Republicans, in much the same way they politically perverted MAGA.

Clearly, socialists and fascists do exist in the VEP and the political parties. As shown in the earlier political tendencies graph, those VEP members holding socialist and fascist political beliefs represent a small but vocal minority. Clearly, both groups pose political and economic alternatives that are attractive to some members of the VEP.

To help dispel the misinformation and propaganda, readers do need to understand that socialism implies the <u>government ownership</u> of the means of production and that the value of the output (profits) is shared by everyone through government management of the endeavor. This socialist model of government ownership is the opposite of the current model of the United States, where the <u>richest plutocrats own the means of production</u> (stock) using hired plutocrats to operate the production for the benefit of the owners.

The anti-liberal Cult of Ignorance plutocrats, the current Republican Party leadership, and many candidates use the socialism lie intentionally to misinform the public, by suggesting that taxes on the profits of the rich are a secret new electric digital form of socialism. This is pure economic propaganda, but useful political posturing and tax manipulation tactics.

Taxes are, by definition, the involuntary fees levied on individuals and businesses by a government entity—whether local, regional, or national—in order to finance the government activities and pay for the transactions created by the government activity.

The federal republic constitutional government model introduced by the United States in 1789 generated the new role of the government and chartered Congress to produce the functions and fund the federal operations needed to carry out its mandate

As discussed in earlier chapters, the new federal republic model replaced the unitary model that levied taxes on the people, in order to have the people pay for the government activities and facilitate the accumulation of wealth by the wealthy. As mentioned, local liberal plutocrats in the king's personal colonies rejected the unitary model via the American Revolution and the adoption of the second

Constitution, replacing the Articles of Confederation unitary government model that was introduced by the states, in 1781.

Although the liberals threw out the unitary model of government, they maintained the inverted plutocrat funding structure of tariff taxes (fixed taxes on exports and imports) and excise taxes (fixed taxes on manufactured products). Both tax processes ensure that the highest earners with the most wealth and income will pay the lowest effective tax rate.

Moreover, these traditional plutocrat processes, left over from mercantilism, violate the basic principles of capitalism and in many ways, they inhibit the development of the wealth of the nation.

A hundred years of experience and a massive Civil War, killing 700,000 people to end the slavery-based economy of the South, pushed Congress toward the establishment of a new rational and more egalitarian funding model.

The Corporate Income Tax, levied on businesses (1909), the Federal Income Tax, levied on personal income (1913), the Estate Tax, levied on accumulated wealth (1916), and the Gift Tax, levied on the distribution of profits and wealth (1924) shifted a major portion of the cost of government from the consumers, to the wage earners, businesses and unearned Income flows, for the first time in history. The payroll tax (1939) introduced the tax and spend concept of fully funded transfer payments, direct to consumers.

The Federal Revenue model of today and the trend lines reflect the growing use of payroll funding and the stagnant to declining use of Income Taxes collected from the ultra-wealthy, the wealthy, the wage earners and many pensioners.

Figure 61a *Federal Revenue by Type (Source of Funds)*

The liberal egalitarian tax processes pushed through Congress coupled with the Federal Reserve Act in 1913, directly interfered with the accumulation of wealth by the wealthy model favored by the Cult of Ignorance. As shown in the chart, taxing wages, profits, unearned Income and consumers via tariffs are clearly not socialism.

The use of payroll tax legislation for example, to finance transactions for the benefit of the people (Social Security, Unemployment, Medicare, Medicaid, etc.) began in 1939. The fully self-funding of the "for the people" processes also produces income tax revenues, since the Reagan era tax of 1986 and the payment cash flows contributes excess collected cash, interest free, for the Congress to use to fund its other operations (2.5 Trillion dollars of the National Debt is owed to the Payroll Tax based Trust Fund).

Although the tax-and-spend republic model has a dark side called corruption, crony capitalism, collusion, and corporate welfare, the regulation of business activities and the use of taxes to drive the economy and facilitate consumer transactions produced the great economic and societal success story of the last century.

Obviously, legislation mandating clean air, clean water, renewable energy, a living wage, public education, healthcare, the facilitating of private infrastructure investments, funding of research, space exploration, and the protection of the people from enemies, natural disasters, economic disasters, illegal behaviors, the ravages of poverty, and individual exploitation is not only socially responsible, it also proved to be a great way to generate capitalistic transactions, an expanding economy, and a higher quality of life.

Putting the political party rhetoric, bold-faced lies about social-ism, and various conspiracy theories aside, the tax and spend gov-ernment legislation processes have clearly facilitated markets, expanded the economy and generated unique pathways to the econ-omy. Increasing the net income and disposable income of 90% of the population and the top 10% as well, (1917 to 1972) is also documented evidence of the results from the distribution of income challenge.

Although the 1948-1972 income results are entirely consistent with Adam Smith's theories of capitalism, as expressed in *The Wealth of Nations*, the disastrous results for 90% of the people from the conservative Congress's poor legislation between 1972 and 2013 are also consistent with the principles of capitalism.

In retrospect, whether the government is producing roads, infrastructure, bombers, ships, food stamps, social security checks, VA hospitals, Medicaid, a standing military force, NASA, education, national parks, EPA, Fanny May, Freddie Mac, firefight-ers, HUD, or FEMA, such efforts all grow the consumer-based economy of the United States.

Some federal expenditures, like military spending, contribute both transactions and the accumulation of wealth by the wealthy. Other social welfare spending, like the post office, unemployment, and Social Security contribute increasing transactions and profits, but they result in a lower rate of contribution to the accumulation of wealth by the wealthy.

A candidate's view toward these "for the people" social welfare activities versus "for the accumulation of wealth" activity should be assessed in the representative selection process by the VEP. Candidates calling for small and limited government are clearly sus-pect of not understanding the role of government, in our economy.

Those Candidates suggesting, they are business-friendly, socially conservative and want to reduce regulations and benefits paid to consumers are just as suspect of not understanding government economics and the charter to promote the general welfare.

In general, candidates suggesting the cutting of federal income transfer payments in future years (reducing income transfer payments to the people by restricting Social Security, Medicare, Medicaid, Unemployment, educational payments, and disability payments) are either unaware of how their misguided economic concepts of cash flow and exchanges violate the principles and tenants of capitalism, or they are intentionally trying to mislead the listener.

Those candidates holding these types of arcane and somewhat inane views and political parties that support such anti-capitalism principles and rhetoric are obviously not very well informed with respect to the economics of transfer payments.

Their lack of understanding of the transactions or desire to restrict them implies that they are probably not generally aware enough to serve as a representative in government or they are intentionally facilitating the accumulation of wealth by the wealthy. It is just that simple.

Likewise, candidates with plans to increase military spending (increasing the accumulation of wealth by the wealthy business owners through purchases), while reducing income transfer payments to pay for the military, as proposed by conservatives, or even shrinking the scope of the government, as proposed by many Libertarians are other poor economic concepts, flowing from the Cult of Ignorance that violate the principles of capitalism and make poor candidates for any public office.

The misguided spending and taxing ideas that facilitate the accumulation of wealth by the wealthy, also generally reduce the future national production possibility curve and the future prosperity of the nation, when they are implemented. While they are clearly economically attractive to those favoring the accumulation of wealth by the wealthy, these conservative models are what produced 4 recession and the 1972-2013 economic results for the people in Figure 60.

The history of Obamacare is a recent current economic case that demonstrates how the liberal versus conservative political ideology is playing out in the economy of the United States, today.

Obamacare (The Patient Protection and Affordable Care Act, or PPACA), is an Act of Congress that restructured a 28-million-person market, consisting of the underinsured, uninsurable, the least healthy, and the poorest people in the country.

The law was passed by Congress to improve the quality of life of the unhealthy (pre-existing conditions), the poor (an entitled defined poverty group), and the general population. The law established the legal and economic processes needed to extend the economy to a class of people, that had been virtually absent and certainly underserved by the health care industry, in the United States.

The PPACA generated a near-universal guarantee of access to affordable healthcare services via private insurance coverage and the extension of government programs. The law now protects the general public (people in the 90%) from the ravages of medical costs from birth through retirement, for the first time in our history.

Approximately 28% of the general public (26 million people) fell into the newly protected class. Approximately 19 million are currently receiving benefits under the law.

The upper 10% of the population needed no such government protection. Based on repeal votes, Republican plutocrats and the conservative supporters would prefer to leave the 26 million exposed to the ravages of healthcare costs and poverty.

The conservative plutocrats had originally mounted a misinformation campaign in the 70s that had successfully blocked the healthcare rights of people for nearly 40 years, before Congress finally passed the law, creating the new market over their objections.

Portions of the VEP and many elected representatives not in the newly protected class have been vocally and politically active against the new protected class rights.

The anti-PPACA conservatives in multiple Congresses have voted over 60 times to repeal the law and eliminate the new health-care market extension that was created by the law. They obviously do not understand economics or the concept of extending pathways to the economy to facilitate transactions.

The market extension of the Act, for example, generated an estimated $80 billion in sales in 2016. Most of sales values were probably not measured directly in the GDP, since they are categorized as transfer payments.

An estimated $36 billion of the new $80 billion in transfer payment transactions went into the earned income of the employees rendering the services, while an estimated $5 billion went into after-tax profits of the companies, rendering the services.

Of the $36 billion that went into earned income (wages), an estimated $6 billion went into payroll tax payments, and another $6 billion went into the GDP, as the employees purchased goods and services, with their earnings.

Although not in the GDP directly, the government transfer payment transactions that were approximately 2.4% of the GDP in size also produced an estimated 1% growth in the GDP. This growth from the new transfer payment transactions would not have occurred had the $80 billion market extension not been created by Congress, in 2010.

To put that number in context, in 2016, the GDP grew a total of 1.9% and more than half of that growth resulted almost directly from congressional action taken in 2010 to improve the quality of life of 19 million people. Repeal would have the opposite impact.

Again, just for contextual understanding, for those less informed, misinformed, and totally ignorant representatives in the 115th Congress, you voted yes to reduce the GDP growth rate by 50%, and you wanted personally to reduce the earned income of American employees by $6 billion, by removing $80 billion in transfer funded transactions from the healthcare market.

While it is hard to intellectually grasp the economic magnitude of the poor voting choice to repeal the law, it is even harder to reconcile the personal actions of elected representatives, to harm and reduce the quality of the life of 19 million people.

I guess, in defense of the callous actions, it is only fair to point out that the federal representatives joined with the eighteen state legislatures that have blocked and impeded the new market in their state, to the detriment of their state's economy and the national GDP, while inhibiting a higher quality of life for their state constituents.

These observations of economics and the impact of conservative behavior are not speculations or party politics. These are the facts of capitalism, in terms of markets, supply and demand, and the creation of transactions between suppliers and consumers that contribute directly to wealth in the nation and the wellbeing of 19 million people.

The observations and the political ideology used by conservatives to demonize the role of government or justify an action to kill the economic transactions should in the future serve as clear warning to the VEP when assessing any congressional candidates.

Likewise, the VEP should also recognize those types of representatives who favored the "do nothing" about the health care problem for 20 years. They were sending a clear warning message that the VEP needs to include when evaluating incumbents.

The Plutarch quote at the opening of this chapter, about the imbalance between the rich and poor being a fatal ailment of all republics was made at a time when only plutocrats could vote. He may have been correct back then and even in the Unitary Model of governments, as well.

The modern history of many Republics today suggest he may be incorrect. In fact, the three samples of the US economy in figure 60, suggests that a modern Federal Republic for the people can fulfill its government mandate and control income inequality well (1917-1948), very well (1948 -1972) and poorly (1972 - 2013) at times, while avoiding the fatal ailment.

Millennials, as the largest bloc of voters in the VEP today. They face a much more complicated Republic than Plutarch ever imagined. I doubt if Republics had mastered the art of gerrymandering and I am sure Corporations did not have the right to free speech and dark money investment strategies to influence elections. In any case, your Representatives will determine if the nation does well, very well or poorly, in the future.

The next chapter deals with the perceptions (the state of becoming aware of something through the senses), beliefs (a statement of something that is true to the best of your knowledge) and postulations (an assumption of the existence, fact, or truth of something as a basis for reasoning, discussion, or belief) and how these terms relate to government and the candidates offering to serve the people of the United States.

CHAPTER 8

You Can Perceive It, but What to Believe is the Real Issue in Time

*"We must guard against the acquisition of unwarranted
influence, whether sought or unsought, by the* **military-
industrial complex.**" *"Should any political party attempt
to abolish social security, unemployment insurance, and
eliminate labor laws and farm programs,* **you would not hear
of that party again in our political history."**
—DWIGHT D. EISENHOWER

Today's political party environment is demonstrating that President Eisenhower had great insights into the problem that would occur when big business and Plutocrats would take control of the elected government. Too bad the VEP did not heed his warning about big business and dark money enabling Corporations and Plutocrats to virtually own the votes of representatives, speakers and even presidents.

On the other hand, Ike's political party logic seems to be fundamentally flawed, at least in terms of one of the Duopoly political parties not being heard from again in our political history, just for attempting to abolish transfer payments to the people.

History tells us that a political party has tried to end and downsize transfer payments and general welfare payments in several ways, over the last fifty years. Maybe shrink them, reform them, tax them, loot their trust funds, and blame the fully funded payroll processes for deficit spending does not mean an attempt to abolish, when it comes in these various guises, used against the transfer payments to the people.

In any case, the Voter Eligible Population (VEP) that produced the current level of income inequalities, the poor Gallup Poll ratings and the lack of confidence in the Congresses they elected have tended to ignore their own culpability, as the nation hears congressional babble on how we need to cut, fix, and reform transfer payments and food stamps, to reduce the future deficits, while ignoring the impact of shrinking the GDP.

The two issues, influence and control by big business (accumulation of wealth by the wealthy) and the transfer payments (for the people) now represent the same left and right dichotomy that produces the VEP confusion at the voting booth. The massive, totally un-funded, Part D drug coverage program that was added to Social Security in 2003 is a prime example of the problem, the dichotomy, and the confusion it causes.

Obviously, a portion of Congress in 2003 was trying to help people get cost-effective medications. Others voted for the law to ensure the 2004 election results and to cover up the growing deficit. Others voted for Part D to put prescription pricing in the hands of the pharmaceutical Industry and take it away from the Social Security Administration. Others had more nefarious reasons, like trying to bankrupt the trust fund. The law passed and accomplished many of thier purposes of Congress.

The dichotomy and confusion between perceptions, reality, and the actions of Congress were not fixed by the Great Recession that followed the massive deficit. Obamacare, for example, in 2010 demonstrates how the "for the people" versus "for the accumulation of wealth by the wealthy" dichotomy still causes confusion and conflict.

Obamacare implemented a tax increase on the high-income earners, to pay for the transfer payments to the lowest paid 90% of income earners. The vitriol and VEP confusion from the "for the people" whammy on the rich (raise taxes and make new transfer payments) continued to flow right up to the Millennial House-cleaning, in 2018.

While the 2018 House-cleaning may be a sign of hope, it may also be a false flag (a covert term describing an operation designed to deceive; the deception creates the appearance of a party, group, or nation being responsible. Whether it is responsible or not does not matter, if the flag plant gets you to perceive it, believe it, and do what they want you to do). The flag is planted, to get you to do what they want you to do.

As an example, Democrat Brian Frosh, the Maryland attorney general, sought a declaratory court judgment, as of September 14, 2018, in the U.S. District Court of Maryland that the ACA is indeed constitutional, and the Trump administration must stop trying to "sabotage" the Affordable Care Act.

The judgement was denied. Moreover, on Monday, September 26, 2019, a year later, the Department of Justice leadership, under the direction of a Republican President announced that it wasn't going to defend the Affordable Care Act in court anymore. A clear brazen move, to forego their responsibility to the Constitution and to plant a false flag to leverage it, to win back the House of Representatives, in the next election.

Historically, in 2018, when the attorney general filed for the judgement request, a single party held the House, Senate, and Presidency. The Republican Party, the evangelical Plutocrat Patrons and all three institutions were all trying to end Obamacare.

When the Republican Party lost the House in the 2018 election, the President and the Republican Party Plutocrats develop a new plan to kill the "for the people" legislation called Obamacare and push the 19 million people off the benefit package for the poor.

Did the House cleaning in 2018 that went into effect in 2019, fix any problem or just modify the conflict, in the ideological war between "for the people" legislators and "for the accumulation of wealth by the wealthy" legislators and the current President.

Only time will tell. And, if we review history, in 1994, the "they" who were cleaned out were the Democrats. In 2006, the "they" that were cleaned out were Republicans. In 2010, the "they" cleaned out were Democrats, once again. These Party transitions are clear signs of voter confusion, long before the millennials ever joined the VEP.

While it may look like the VEP results in the voting booth in the selection of "for the people" candidates versus "for the accumulation of wealth by the wealthy" candidates are simple, the Congressional oscillations themselves may have long term negative ramifications for the people.

Obamacare is a recent example. The Democratic Congress that passed the bill, generated eight years of Republican Congressional votes trying to repeal it, with no considerations of fixing or improving it. The repeated failed Congressional actions clearly served to polarize attitudes and it clearly demonstrated why the people have no confidence in the ability of the Congress to do its job, for the people of the nation. Congressional oscillations and the frequency of the oscillations themselves have long term implications, resulting from what the legislation Sessions produced and did not produce while the winning party served in the Congress of the United States.

As shown in chart form earlier, the cohesive party goals of the Eisenhower era, disappeared as the political power of Corporations and conservative Plutocrat Patrons increased. Each left versus right oscillation eventually produced the current job performance opinions and clearly, they produced the lack of confidence in the Congress.

There are other artifacts as well. The current military-industrial spending by our government, for example, is higher than the next 12 countries combined. The "for the accumulation of wealth by the wealthy" impact from this program is supported from both Parties. A massive budget increase was approved by the House recently, to rebuild the war-torn forces, even though the Republican Party had been voted out of the House leadership.

For perspective, the money spent on the Iraq war alone could have been used to provide free college education for 35 years, yet the Republican party claims that subsidizing higher education would bankrupt America. In this same vein, according to the military assessments and science, $E=mc^2$ works.

Our military has stockpiled enough of the "*mass*" *or* m *stuff*, to destroy the planet and everyone on it, 157 times or more. We also have 9 aircraft carrier fleets, compared to the one fleet per nation plan of the other countries. Each aircraft carrier fleet has the firepower to destroy the planet several times over, on their own.

While military superiority has advantages, the military advantage was created for the protection of nation, while also increasing the wealth of the wealthy. While the military build does grow the economy and produce billions of transactions, there are also other pressing needs to provide the general population with paths to the economy.

Think about taxes and spending for a moment. The year before the 2017 tax cut, the nation's largest 100 military-industrial suppliers paid an average of 8.9% in actual federal taxes (called the effective tax rate), versus the 35% legislative rate in the law and the 21% effective tax actually rate paid by the typical Corporation in the United States.

The 12% excess military-industrial untaxed profits flowed to the business owners in a program for the accumulation of wealth by the wealthy, implemented via tax loopholes and CEO payments that were negotiated by the military-industrial complex suppliers, The Plutocrats and the political parties. Obviously, the military and Corporate owners need the cash more than the kids trying to acquire a higher education.

This process for the accumulation of wealth is often contrasted and compared for budgeting purposes to the 68 million people who are sucking down those "freebie" tax dollars, paid to farmers via subsidies and people without jobs (retirees on Social Security or VA, Medicare, Tri-Care, the disabled, the general unemployed), plus a bunch of the working poor getting Medicaid/Housing/Food and the young (4-18), getting free education, while the older kids were racking up a Trillion dollars in educational debt.

The Republican Party response to the clear "for the People" situation was to rescinded support from the kid's protection from predatory lenders and a proposed plan to cut food stamps in a way that would generate farm foreclosures, farm refinancing and also cut the future GDP, by 2%.

Clearly, one major political party has successfully joined with the Cult of Ignorance to attract evangelical conservatives and the facist members of the VEP into their big business and for the rich constituency. They described their overt actions as ways to reduce the budget deficit created by the tax cuts for the rich, the middle east wars, and the unfunded Feature Group D of Medicare. Their proposal of another tax cut is already on the political table and a Republican Party platform issue for recapturing the House.

Obviously, transfer payments and government programs for the people do not directly facilitate the accumulation of wealth of the wealthy, at the same rate that is produced by the military industrial complex spending or deregulation of Businesses.

By the way, the intended mislabeling and use of the term "freebies" earlier was used here, to demonstrate how emotional terms are intertwined with every day words and used as false flags, to mislead the VEP and help produce incorrect conclusions and help produce VEP actions that facilitate the accumulation of wealth by the wealthy.

Again, as an example, many conservative advocates, plutocrat donors, evangelicals and their candidates begin their assessment of the economic engine issues and role of government from a convoluted and somewhat perverted frame of reference, with respect to the principles of capitalism and our Republic form of national government.

Typically, the conservatives imply and state that the federal government makes nothing and produces nothing. This is another false flag and general piece of propaganda

The advocates of such rhetoric often refer to transfer payments to people as "freebies" because the transfer payment processes are not part of the GDP measurement or after-tax profits from large businesses. Many suggest that they object to having their hard-earned money confiscated by taxes and given to those who did not earn it.

The same advocates and candidates normally intermingle their false flag economic claims about transfer payments with a need for lower taxes and the need to reduce the handouts to control the growing deficit created by tax cuts and military spending.

Many advocates also pose a variety of other specious claims that were discussed in earlier chapters. Rational thinking and logic often expose the false flag plantings, while not being recognized any more so than Eisenhower's warning.

As an example, lower taxes on the rich do not stimulate spending, nor do they expand the economy or ever pay for themselves.

These misguided suppositions simply plant false flags, masking the fact that an increase the rate of accumulation of wealth by the wealthy has virtually no impact on the rate of exchanges, nor their investment strategies or their use of capital (acquired wealth). Although factually untrue, they do help persuade the uninformed into thinking there is a trickle-down advantage, somewhere.

Both ideas, that the government makes nothing and that tax relief for the rich will stimulate economic exchanges in the market, are fundamentally flawed.

The perceptions and beliefs that flow from these misperceptions and false flag impressions of reality, are a form of psychological warfare. Ring a bell, tell a lie three times and it does not become true, but some will think so. Clearly, the Pavlovian training by the Plutocrat Patrons and Political Parties has produced a voting constituency that produced the Income Inequality and disastrous income performance, over the last 50 years.

In this misguided vein of logic though, the basic notion that government makes nothing, displays the core conservative economic fallacy being fed to their constituency.

The US federal government is solely responsible for the purchase of about 20% or so of the national GDP, based on its cash outflow of about $4 trillion and the total GDP valuation of $20 trillion. In this sort of "Kentucky windage" accounting measure, the states, while producing slightly less impact on the economy are also a primary economic driver in the United States, spending about $3.5 trillion or 18% of the national economy as measured by the GDP.

While public (government) transfer payments are not directly counted in the GDP, the actual transfer payments are virtually all spent on consumer food, products, services, and healthcare transactions, by the people receiving transfer payments. The use of these transfer payment to acquire consumer goods and services flows directly into the GDP.

An economic example might help explain how the indirect flow of Transfer Payments into the GDP makes the productive impact of government spending invaluable to the economy and its production. Just for a moment, consider the recent partial shutdown of the federal government, in 2017.

The partial shutdown "cost" the national economy $11 billion in 35 days, according to *Forbes* magazine, quoting the Congressional Budget Office (CBO) assessment of the lost output from federal workers, the delayed government spending, and the reduced demand and consumption, caused by the shutdown.

Again, per the *Forbes* article and the CBO, the partial shutdown will make the U.S. economy 0.02% smaller than it would have been in 2019.

Hopefully, these kinds of clear data points adequately demonstrate that the conservative notion that government does not produce anything is, at best, just misperceptions and false impressions that some people possess, and some people use, to create confusion, misinformation, and propaganda.

Propaganda aside, Adam Smith and modern economists who deal with the wealth of nations and the quality of life of the people in a nation clearly understand that the transactions of government (public spending), the consumer spending via transfer payments and private spending all produce wealth, via transactions.

Moreover, most of them understand that "promote the general Welfare" for the people is a basic tenant of capitalism, that conservatives suggest is somehow socialism.

The only economic difference between public and private transactions is where the money needed to produce the transaction, income, and wealth comes from, and who gets the transaction-created profits and wealth versus the benefits of the consumption of the goods and services.

In the unitary model, the government and its structural hierarchy received all the income and most of the benefits and trickle down was the only for the people economic force. Today, in the US federal republic model, virtual all profits still flow to the plutocrat owners in the private sector, and 56% of the income created, goes directly to the richest 10% of the population.

In the private business sector, the capital and the cash needed to operate the business comes from the accumulated wealth of the business owners. In the case of public funded activities, the money comes from taxes. You can review the chart in the previous chapter for more insight into the actual tax flow processes and how the federal taxing process works to generate cash to pay the bills that Congress authorizes.

The payment of taxes and the subsequent transfer of the receipts, as an income stream to people is a direct conflict point between the liberal political ideology (for the people) embedded in the US federal republic government model, versus the conservative unitary political ideology, for the accumulation of wealth by the wealthy. This conservative political ideology is directly embedded in the plutocracy government model, favored by the Cult of Ignorance, conservatives, and Libertarians.

In the traditional unitary plutocracy government model that preceded the republic model, the rich captured the wealth, horded the wealth, and any new wealth created flowed to the aristocracy, the clergy, and the plutocrats running the government and the new business ventures. This wealth accumulation by the wealthy process, for example is why King Ferdinand and Queen Isabella funded Christopher Columbus's trip to India.

The liberal notion that all men are created equal and that

people empower government for the benefit of the governed has not yet altered that basic conservative governance model notion, for the accumulation of wealth by the wealthy. You cannot blame people that are rich and in the top 10%, for continuing to embrace that model.

Obviously, collecting taxes and spending the tax money for the benefit of the people (education, Social Security, hospitals, VA, FEMA, Obamacare, child labor laws, highways for the workers instead of toll roads for the state, national parks, electricity-generating wind farm co-ops, etc.) reduces the rate of accumulation, by the rich and in many cases actually add new rich people to the traditional pack.

The republic model causing the transfer payment transactions for the people not only impacted the distribution of income and the rate of wealth accumulation, it changed the entire course of the eco-system and social culture, of the nation and the planet.

Clearly, the setting of minimum wages, regulating business with child labor laws and forcing the redistribution of income from some businesses to working individuals does not play well for those desiring to maintain the status quo social environment and the inequality of income producing processes of labor (people) versus capital (the already accumulated wealth).

This conflict between labor and wealth, first exposed by capitalism, helps explain why the wealthy see the liberal government spending and lawmaking, as an evil force.

While it is true that some elected representatives have in fact been corrupted into acting as an evil force, via legislation to benefit people and friendly businesses (crony capitalism) or to directly line their own pockets (emoluments), most get caught, although they might not get punished.

Although such villainy occurs at the Federal, State and Local levels of government, the illegal actions of the people involved may also have a relatively positive upside, since the transactions they do produce are generally designed to facilitate both the accumulation of wealth for plutocrats, while also producing benefits for the people.

Liberals have a somewhat opposite ideological and economic perspective with respect to government itself being an evil force.

Liberals tend to think of government as a liberating and protective force for the people, the environment and the economy. In fact, the liberals think they empower the government, for the best interests of the people.

The transfer of "income" to the people via government transfer programs for the people are perceived as capitalist processes that are fulfilling the promise of the Constitution, to promote the general Welfare, through various process that connect the people directly to the economy and facilitate the accumulation of wealth.

The general process "to **form** a more perfect Union, **establish** Justice, **insure** domestic Tranquility, provide for the common defence, **promote** the general Welfare, and **secure** the Blessings of Liberty to ourselves and our Posterity" cannot be effectively implemented, without the government connections from the people to the economy.

Given this liberating perspective of government for the people, it should be clear to see from the national debt why liberals think the numerous representatives who were elected and chartered to protect the rights of the people from enslavement by the economically powerful forces of the modern-day plutocrats have not done a very good job over the last 50 years. The numbers and the clear shape of the curve speaks directly to the 50-year long Congressional failure for the people, while Wall Street S&P number from the consumer led economy speak to the accumulation of wealth issues.

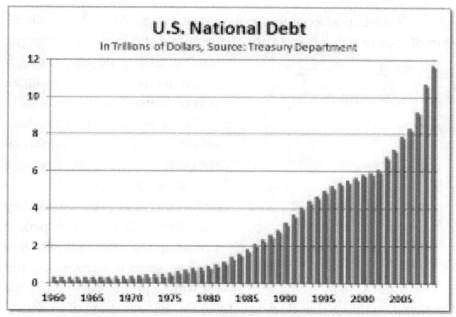

Figure 62 U.S. National Debt 1960-2018

The elected representatives who produced the national deficit that is now larger than the GDP have done a real disservice to the people, as displayed on the National Debt chart.

As shown here and figure 63, Congress chose to fund the current operations of government out of future tax collections, while reducing its investments in the people and the support of the paths to the economy, by generally underfunding transfer payments and limiting their use, except to stimulate recoveries from recessions.

The national debt in lieu of tax revenue and spending over the fifty years shown in Figure 63 is the economic testimony detailing the low-quality of actual performance ratings that are reflected by the Gallup Opinion Poll ratings.

The supply-side economic theories postulated by conservatives, started to be applied after the 1980 election of Mr. Reagan. The neo-capitalist voodoo economics process focused on the accumulation of wealth, via a tax cut for the rich and the transfer of the tax burden to the people, through seven tax increases and stagnation of transfer payments.

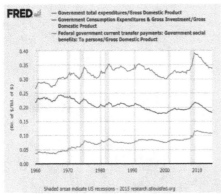

Figure 63 *Federal Government Expenditures 1960-2018*

The grey lines in the chart reflect recessions. Notice how the government transfer payment line goes down before recessions start and goes up as they end. Notice the for the people Consumption Expenditure line decline, since the 1960's and the growing spread between Total Spending on things that flow directly to the accumulation of wealth.

There were two additional tax cuts for the rich, since 1981 (2001, 2017) and the current $22 trillion deficit in chart 62, exposes the unique economic situation facing the current VEP. The obvious question is whether the VEP can muster the political force needed to repair the economic and societal damage inflicted on the nation during the 50-year disaster, produced by the Baby Boomer and Generation X poor voting record.

The growth and development of the middle class and decline of poverty in the 1948 to 1973 period, shown in earlier graphs, demonstrates that it is possible for government to control the forces of the economy for the benefit of the people and the rich, at the same time, without the massive debt financing.

Other nations, from Germany to even Communist China in this century have all demonstrated similar results for their citizens in the distribution of income to the people and not just the rich. And, as mentioned in earlier chapters, some 37 other countries have also demonstrated better results at managing their economy, than the United States.

Each member of the VEP today needs to ask themselves whether 90% of the American citizens have a legal right to expect a living wage, live in decent housing, have adequate food suppliers and enjoy the benefits of the largest and most profitable economy that a political ideology has ever created.

The VEP should also ask themselves and future candidates, whether the government should be driving the economic infrastructure, ensuring the availability of a literate and skilled work force, ensuring the availability of affordable healthcare and protecting people from unemployment and the ravages of poverty, medical bills, recessions, enemies, old age, crime and disabilities.

As federal elections draw near again, the VEP should also ask candidates if they think the government should be operating programs to protect the non-working seniors, the veterans, the retired employees, the unemployed, and the handicapped/disabled.

The answer to these big government questions has been somewhat clear to liberals in the VEP, since the founding of the nation, the drafting of the second Constitution, the Keynesian expansion of demand-side capitalism theories, and the transfer payments that also restored the wealth creation process of the United States faster than the rest of the world. The answers reflected in Chart 49 and 62 do not bode well for the United States and may well prove that Plutarch was correct in his projections.

Voters need to perceive and learn to believe that transfer payments creates consumers and that their consumption is good for the country and the economy.

These tax-based payments to consumers and the exchanges the consumers create have been the primary point of contention between the government political views supporting a liberal versus conservative government payments model. You heard the discussions of the $15 per hour for nearly 10 years. Although implemented by some states and Cities, it is still being discussed at the federal level.

While it could not have been adopted a decade ago, when the country was in the throes of the Great Republican Recession, the choice to not do it and cut taxes on the rich instead, should be fresh in your mind, as the 2020 candidates start coming forward.

The volume, scope, and scale of federal government spending and transfer payments today, come directly from congressional legislation. They appear in several forms, and they represent various portions of the GDP, since their creation in the 1930s.

Review the FRED (chart 63) federal expenditures again. Review the subtle gray bars and notice again how the blue line spending goes down before a recession and up at the end of one.

As a people, we are not smart enough yet to know if this downtown is a signal that a recession is coming, or a flag on how to create a recession. We also do not know if the spike up is the force that ultimately ends the recessions. There are just too many attributes and variables but, still looks to be a good rule of thumb for assessing candidates and projecting their future behaviors.

While the liberal versus conservative conflict has been present since 1776, it was 1932, at the depths of the Great Depression, before Keynesian theorists began to expose the recession and income distribution flaws in the supply-side of the capitalism model.

It slowly become clear to modern day economists that capital, random events driving markets, and the laissez-faire economic policies that were designed to produce wealth for the wealthy did not produce full employment, a living wage for workers and farmers, adequate housing, or protections from the ravages of age, illness, or monopolies.

The pre-Keynesian economic ideas and conservative supply-side economics processes also failed to produce the sustaining banking or national infrastructure necessary to improve the standard of living of the people. In fact, supply-side economics produced the opposite impact on the economy.

The New Deal ideas coming out of America in the 30s, 40s, 50s, and 60s produced massive amounts of legislation that provided insurance and transfer payments to generate disposable income for people.

The liberal new ideas that transfer payments and government investment in infrastructure would generate new transactions that would ultimately drive the nation out of the Great Depression, provide electricity and telephones into rural America, and generate a new sustaining economic environment was tested out and proven to be true.

It should be noted that Germany, Russia, China, Japan, and most other countries in the world were also transforming themselves economically in response to the end of the First World War and the same Great Depression era that followed the end of the war.

Germany and Japan reverted to the traditional conservative economic model for the accumulation of wealth with Germany driven by big business (fascism) and Japan driven by the traditional nobility model (emperor).

Russia replaced its aristocracy with communism, a dictatorship and the government ownership of the means of production in an effort to facilitate the accumulation of wealth by the wealthy plutocrats running the new government. China followed Russia into the communist model, as World War II was coming to an end.

The US on the other hand, began its recovery idea as an experiment with liberal legislation and transfer payments. It began its experiment before World War II with a balanced budget strategy and fifteen major legislative bills from Congress in the first 100 days in office in 1933. Banking regulations and transfer payment projects like the CCC and WPA rolled into the market. The programs spread to infrastructure spending like the TVA and the Hoover Dam while the more progressive states (30 of the 48 existing states at the time) began their own transfer payment programs, that "handed out" approximately $31 million in the year before Social Security was established (1939).

The liberal revolution was truly energized by World War II as innovation and change began to drive the country in response to the demands of the war instead of Wall Street and the accumulation of wealth by the wealthy. As an example, the nation was making virtually no weapons in 1938. By 1943, the nation had become the largest producer of weapons in the world.

The liberal changeover of the country was also evidenced by the Servicemen's Readjustment Act of 1944. The new law, known as the G.I. Bill of Rights, was created by Congress to help the surviving veterans of World War II.

The law established hospitals, made low-interest mortgages available to returning soldiers, and granted financial stipends covering the tuition and expenses for veterans attending college or trade schools.

The expanded economic understanding of demand-side capitalism also produced an Economic Bill of Rights proposal for the general population. The second Bill of Rights was proposed to extend the legal protection of citizens covered by the Constitution to cover their economic protection, as well.

Although not enacted into law directly, the proposed Economic Bill of Rights clearly articulated the new liberal ideas of how to "promote the general Welfare" via economic security and prosperity—regardless of station, race, creed, or even job status.

The following is a seldom discussed summary of Franklin Delano Roosevelt's inauguration speech in 1944. It is reproduced here for a clear understanding of the new "for the people" liberalism based economic ideas, versus "for the traditional accumulation of wealth by the wealthy" ideas and trickle-down theories of conservatives.

According to the liberal ideas, the people of the United States should have constitutional legal rights that would guarantee:

- The right to a useful and remunerative job in the industries, shops, farms, and mines of the nation;
- The right to earn enough to provide adequate food and clothing and recreation;
- The right of every farmer to raise and sell his products at a return that will give him and his family a decent living;
- The right of every businessman, large and small, to trade in an atmosphere of freedom from unfair competition and domination by monopolies;
- The right of every family to a decent home;
- The right to adequate medical care needed to achieve and enjoy good health;
- The right to a good education and adequate protection from the economic fears of old age, sickness, accidents, and unemployment.

Although these liberal ideas were not enacted into law, the various Acts of Congress in the post-World War I era continued the transformation of the American economy and the educational, healthcare, home ownership, and the social/political milieu of the nation, while other nations pursued their own political ideologies.

As history shows, the conflict between liberalism (for the people) and conservatism (for the accumulation of wealth by the wealthy) did not go away after the war.

And, the facts speak for themselves, according to scientific thinking processes. The scientific process also suggests that observed facts, thoughts,

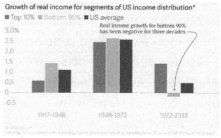

Figure 64 *Growth of Real Income*

and ideas can be converted into understanding and knowledge via inductive logic (conclusions based on selected evidence), abductive logic (conclusions explaining an observation without evidence) and deductive logic (links premises and if premises are true, reach a logical conclusion).

If these scientific principles and processes are applied, it seems easy enough to determine the economic winners and losers over the last 50 years.

The recently elected 116th Congress has been sworn in and was in session for seven weeks as this chapter was going through its last draft. Although the government was effectively shut down for three weeks by the conservatives and the Cult of Ignorance, let's hope the 116th congressional session ultimately signals an end to the congressional mediocrity of the last 50 years.

The next chapter provides additional insights and information to help people understand how easy it is to mislead the VEP and how dangerous they can be when it comes to elections.

As described throughout the guide, and hopefully demonstrated in this chapter, voters are especially dangerous in a federal republic that relies on the VEP for the selection of candidates, the election of lawgivers (Congress), and the election of an executive branch needed to carry out the Will of Congress.

The guide has also hopefully demonstrated that it is the Will of Congress and whether it is dedicated to the "for the people" model or the "for the accumulation of wealth by the wealthy" model that determines the economic and social success of the nation.

In this general context of Congress, the presidency and the Voter Eligible Population, we might be just a congressional election or two and a second term away from being the next Venezuela or a newly revitalized nation, on the way to Making America Great Again.

CHAPTER 9

Introduction to Political Anti-Intellectualism, Ignorance, and Rule of Law

"There is a cult of ignorance in the United States, and there always has been. The strain of anti-intellectualism has been a constant thread winding its way through our political and cultural life, nurtured by the false notion that democracy means that "my ignorance is just as good as your knowledge."
—ISAAC ASIMOV, COLUMN IN NEWSWEEK (21 JANUARY 1980).

Although the voters select the representatives, it is the representatives, operating as a group in a congressional session, who create the Will of Congress. And, it is the Will of Congress that produces the legislation and the funding of government operations.

This chapter's opening quote is from a *Newsweek* article about the voting skills of the American people going awry.

Isaac Asimov was a renowned Boston scientist and world-famous author. He wrote and edited over 500 books before his death in 1992. His works are stored in 9 of the 10 subject matter categories in the Dewey Decimal Library Cataloging System, to give you a feel for the scope of his contribution to knowledge.

He had been observing the decline in the quality of Congress and was one of the first people to point out that the decline was the result of the growth of conservative voters and their false notions of the federal republic democracy.

The quote reflects his precise, if unflattering, words describing the Anti-Federalist plutocrats and patrons, as the source of the evangelical conservative contagion—the Cult of Ignorance. The Cult was originally formed by state plutocrats, to support the new feudalism (neo-feudalism) government model in 1781, with a small, powerless federal government and state control of domestic policies

The establishment of the unitary model with Plutocrats replacing the nobility effectively implemented a unique neo-feudalism social order (the original feudalism was characterized by the church/state integration in a class-based hierarchy, where the plutocratic upper class is conferred by birthright (0.1%) and wealth and supported by the "accumulation of wealth for the wealthy" unitary government model operated by a small upper class (10%). The new feudalism simply rejected the need for the birthrights).

The Cult's unitary political ideology spawned and nurtured the development of the evangelical and conservative right-wing neo-feudalism (agrarian and industrializing) notions of free markets and the distrust of the federal government.

The notions included the idea that states' plutocrats should have the right to nullify domestic polices and the right to secede from the union. These political ideals eventually killed 700,000 Americans in a Civil War, produced segregation after the war, restricted women's rights for 120 years and generated the Robber Baron and "Return to Normalcy" eras, that produced the Great Depression, by 1929.

By the 1950s, the Cult had spawned the New Conservative (Neocon) movement, with McCarthyism and false accusations of subversion and the treason of socialism, being their response to the New Deal (1932) and the Square Deal (1948).

Protecting unions, regulating monopolies, increasing wages, improve working conditions, cleaning up the environment, desegregating schools, providing public education, and creating consumers via transfer payments to the farmers, the unemployed, the retirees, the disabled, and the inner city poor living in public housing on Welfare were the clear signs of socialism and the redistribution of wealth model, according to the fact-free conservative Neocon assessment, that ignored the actual national income results in the 1917 to 1972 intervals (see last chapter figures).

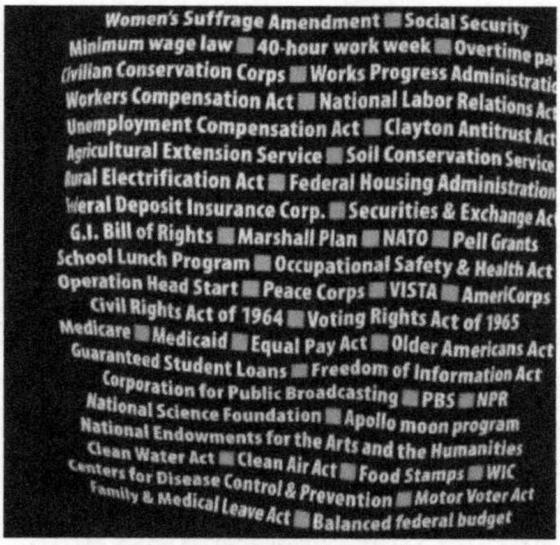

You saw the "promote the general Welfare" actions of the federal government, earlier in the book. The question then and now is this what promote the general Welfare means to the VEP or are these general welfare laws for the people, the slide into socialism and government ownership of profits. The Cult of Ignorance still embrace the inane notion of these action being socialism.

Figure 65 *Sample of "for the people" Acts of Congress*

Although Isaac Asimov was best known for science and science fiction articles and books (like Bill Nye the Science Guy today), his general observation about freedom shocked the *Newsweek* audience. His Op Ed also shocked the political world through the association of anti-intellectualism and its nurtured ignorance with the decades-long conservative groundswell having been accelerated by Watergate, pardons, and the Neocon movement (which included formal liberals turned conservative).

His article, in January of 1980 is considered prophetic today, given that it preceded the election of Ronald Reagan and his anti-government inaugural address by nearly twelve months. According to the Reagan address, "In this present crisis, *government* is *not the solution* to our problem; *government* is the problem."

The Asimov article suggests that some 200 million people had been to school, but must not have learned how to read, understand, or know what was going on in Washington. This educational hypothesis was a unique way to describe the people who objected to the civil rights, the voting rights, Medicare, Medicaid, the Great Society, and expanded education actions from Congress, versus the conservative partisans, who had blocked the Equal Rights for Women amendment (the law passed in 1972, expired in 1979 without becoming a constitutional amendment because it did not receive enough neo-feudal state votes within the authorized period).

His article also postulated that if reading and understanding was not the cause, then the other rational problem source was Neoconservative Anti-Intellectualism (hostility to and the mistrust of the intellect and the intellectuals relying on facts and reasoning).

From this perspective, he was clearly implying the Anti-Intellectual Neocon messaging was being successfully mixed into the political platform of misinformation, creating the neo-feudalistic economic and political ignorance.

The word ignorance that he used covers a wide range of personal behaviors: 1) people who deliberately ignore or disregard important information or facts, 2) individuals who reject the facts for their own economic, political, religious, or social purposes, and 3) those individuals who are unaware of important information or have a misperception of reality and the facts.

This Anti-Intellectualism = Ignorance political paradigm of the Cult plutocrats and the neo-feudalistic political patrons enabled Asimov to establish an intellect-based reference point (the word intellect refers to the faculty of reasoning and understanding objectively, and it is thought to produce the ability to think and behave in a logical way).

From this intellect reference point, he hoped people could better assess and understand the political view and behavior of conservative voters, especially the illogical evangelical conservatives and creationists who embraced the anti-Federalist socialism gambit and the future babble that you cannot trust the elected government, because the "government is the problem."

We have already discussed this conservative absurdity using the economic terms of capitalism in previous chapters. As demonstrated, the federal government is the driving force of our consumer-based post-World War 2 economy, and its legislative actions are the primary social force producing the "for the people" progress in our nation as economically demonstrated in the 1917-1972 results shown in figure 64.

The direct conservative assault on the federal republic and the "for the people" government model simply rejects the constitutional mandate "to promote the general Welfare" in the preamble of the Constitution. The active role of government to promote the "general Welfare" is also embedded within its power to tax and create transactions through military spending (common defense), its regulatory operations, and the volume of transfer payments.

Reagan's ensuing Neocon-based tax cut for the rich (1981), the deregulation of Wall Street (Junk Bonds 1984, Hedge Funds 1987), seven general tax increases on the lower classes (including taxes on social security and unemployment), looting of the S&L industry, and warmongering (Iran-Contra produced more pardons than Watergate). The period also produced 3 recessions and doubled the national debt during the Reagan-Bush tenure. It also caused the Bush "read my lips: no new taxes" tax increase and the rise of a third party conservative candidate (Ross Perot) that cost Bush a second term in office.

The intellect-based point of reference that Mr. Asimov created in 1980 describing the Neocon and Neo-Feudalism class environment is still useful today and clearly helps people understand the "for the people" conflict with the Neocons and the Cult of Ignorance support "for the accumulation of wealth by the wealthy" in today's political environment.

As an example, it is certainly a useful insight with respect to the Flat-Earthers, Anti-Vaxxers, Climate Deniers, Creationists, Libertarians, Trump supporters, and evangelicals embracing an adulterer, and even the illogical Congressmen voting to repeal Obamacare and pre-existing conditions, while lying or misrepresenting facts.

The convoluted Neocon statements implying that the Republican Congress is somehow not repealing the pre-existing condition legal status, while repealing the Affordable Care Act that grants the legal status and its constitutional protection, is amazing hypocrisy and ignorance of the law in action.

Other memorable contributions and takeaways from the Asimov article are the focus on the Cult of Ignorance patrons and the behavior of people, not the political parties. The article never mentions marketing messages expressed by political parties in their quest to influence people and aggregate voters for their political party and candidates.

Isaac also circumvented the political conflict between religious interpretations and science, using the Cult of Ignorance, illiteracy, and the false notion of democracy being a form of ignorance, instead of referencing the evangelicals and conservative religious beliefs or the most recent false Neocon accusations of the day.

The conservative had began an all out psychological warfare attack effort on the public in the 1960's. The John Birch Society (part of the Cult of Ignorance of the day) had laid out the anti-intellectual case against the "promote the general Welfare" of the people mandate, along with William F. Buckley and Hillsdale College regurgitating the Anti-Federalist Cult rhetoric of the day.

An example of their work is hopefully enough to help you grasp their objective.

"Both the U.S. and Soviet governments are controlled by the same furtive conspiratorial cabal of internationalists, greedy bankers, and corrupt politicians," Welch wrote in *The Blue Book* of the John Birch Society in 1961, the year John Kennedy and Lyndon Johnson began their first year in office, with the democratic majority in the 87th congressional session.

The new right-wing Neocon messaging made McCarthyism claims of socialism seem tame. "If left unexposed, the traitors inside the U.S. government would betray the country's sovereignty to the United Nations for a collectivist New World Order, managed by a 'one-world socialist government,'" according to Mr. Welch's misperception of reality.

The myriad of inane words and insane claims from the right-wing conservatives preceded the civil rights laws, the voting rights laws, the public broadcasting era, the environmental protection law, Medicare, Medicaid, the moon technology advances, the Great Society plan to abolish poverty, and the expansion of educa-

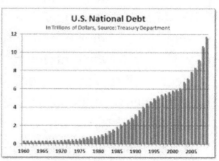

Figure 66 *US national Debt 1960-2018*

tional opportunities and public housing. As shown on the national debt chart, these radical liberal programs, accompanied by the

Kennedy tax cut, the 7 days in May showdown with Russia, and the Vietnam War had virtuallyno impact on our national debt.

The conservative's words from the 60s that produced Nixon, Watergate pardons, Asimov's article about the Cult of Ignorance government agenda, and the Neocon legislation that followed, blossomed into the national debt chart's graphic, detailing the Cult's financial effort to undermine the US Federal Republic government model.

The debt financing of government operations, coupled with the union busting actions, deregulation scams, the revitalization of poverty, and additional tax cuts for the rich produced 7 recessions since the Asimov article and the negative Real Income Growth for 90% of the population (see last chapter), between 1972 and 2013.

This same period (1972-2013) of anti-intellectualism, anti-federal government beliefs and generally conservative legislation, also generated the dramatic increase in income inequality (see previous charts) and the new trillion dollars of student loan debt, hanging over the heads of 90% of the people, as part of the failure to implement the Great Society plans by the Federal Institutions over the period.

Intellectualism (relying on the faculty of reasoning, logic and understanding objectively, at the expense of emotionalism and pre-conceived beliefs), and anti-intellectualism (typically opposed to or hostile toward intellectualism and holding believes that the intellect and reason are less important than actions and emotions in solving practical problems and understanding reality) are the words and terms typically used to describe the diametrically opposed endpoints on the scales of personal behavior patterns.

The terms intellectualism and anti-intellectualism are used, without the intent of denigrating the mental power of the person or the intellect they possess. They are used to describe the actions of those embracing one or the other ends of the behavior patterns. In fact, the power of the intellect itself is intangible (it has no physical presence and cannot be seen or touched), although the actions and events resulting from the actions of people leave behind a historical record that can be evaluated via the intellectualism – anti-Intellectualism scale.

Science generally describes the intellect as the human faculty of reasoning and understanding that produces the ability to come to a correct conclusion about what is true, what are facts, and how to respond to situations, in real time.

Intellect, unlike instincts, personal beliefs, and sentience, relies upon knowledge and the understanding of the information, plus observations received through the senses. This received information gets processed and stored for future use in understanding truths and determining what to do (behavior).

The intellect functions together with instincts, feelings, beliefs, and emotions, as well as outside of them, through the rational thought processes associated with knowledge. In fact, the degree to which a person relies on rationalism (facts, logic, and reasoning) versus instincts, feelings and beliefs, is generally referred to as intellectualism.

Anti-intellectualism is the perceived hostility to, or even mistrust of, intellectualism and the use of logic and reasoning based on facts, truths, and perceptions of reality. The hostility itself, though, is created by the unique functioning of the intellect, within each person. A conspiracy theorist, for example, is not intellectually inferior. They make observations, examine facts, and interpret the facts as part of seeking the truth.

Whether you believe ancient aliens from other planets were the gods that created our society instead of theistic Gods like Atum, who created himself in Egypt, or the Christian God, who created the universe in 6 days and created the role of government on that 6th day, after conjuring up Adam and Eve, is totally up to the individual to decide. They make that decision based on their own intellect and what they learned, since leaving the womb with thier instincts and sentience intact.

Anti-intellectualism is the opposite process, according to Asimov and the dictionary. Anti-intellectualism is directly related to ignorance (lack of knowledge) and the leveraging of the ignorance through the elective use of relatively uniformed and ignorant behaviors, to achieve personal goals and objectives.

This elective use of ignorant behavior patterns enables people to rationalize their behavior, their economic choices, their anti-science rhetoric, the anti-Federalist distrust of government, and even their personal mistrust of their own elected representatives who are attempting, to the best of their ability, to fulfill their constitutional oath of office.

An anti-intellectualism practitioner is not intellectually inferior, any more so than the conspiracy theorist, although they do produce behavior that intellectualism categorizes as illogical or at least inconsistent with what is perceived as logical behavior.

An example of the logical and ignorant concept gap was discussed earlier in the chapter with respect to the ACA. Maybe "those voting for repeal" do not know that the ACA law extends the right of healthcare coverage at affordable rates to an exposed underserved class of citizens, irrespective of their medical condition or history of medical conditions. Maybe "they" did not know that 80% of the nation's people already have those rights, contracted, via their Company insurance plans that cover pre-existing conditions.

While there may be 2,000 other pages in the law, it should be intellectually easy to grasp that Congress cannot repeal it and still have the president enforce the coverage portion of a law that would no longer exist. In any case, the question is how the political party could suggest to the public that the pre-existing conditions would not be impacted by the repeal.

Obviously, there could be many reasons behind the generation of the false information. Whatever the reason though is secondary. The process clearly displays a clear sample of the anti-intellectual thinking, stimulating the illogical behavior pattern that is not perceived as illogical by the party or its leadership.

While such anti-intellectualism is not uncommon in our society, as evidenced by vaxers, creationists, environmental deniers, flat earthers, God's end of time program, for collecting the good boys and girls before starting the apocalypse are samples of the behavior. In fact, people seem to embrace the anti-intellectual processes for any number of personal reasons.

As an example, Richard Thaler recently won a Nobel Prize in economics for his research into the basic psychology of spending.

He documented people's actual behaviors and demonstrated conclusively that people do not always conform to the capitalist economic model or the rational intellectual model that suggests buyers and sellers are rational and logical decision-makers, operating in their own best self-interest.

His research clearly demonstrated what we all subconsciously know about people in general and even ourselves. People are not always rational and logical decision-makers. Sometimes people are irrational, illogical, and even unreasonable.

The integration of this knowledge about people, anti-intellectualism, and a better understanding of the political ideology of the Cult of Ignorance followers of today was the primary purpose of Mr. Asimov's Op Ed and this chapter in this book.

Moreover, both pieces also hope that the information and knowledge will help you improve your skills when selecting candidates for public office of any kind, but especially when selecting representatives to the Congress of the United States, where the Will of Congress determines the success or failure of promoting the "general Welfare."

The conservative anti-intellectual assault on the country and the Constitution emanate directly from the anti-Federalists idea that remain in stark contrast to the "for the people" principles of the nation, as enunciated by John Adams, in 1776.

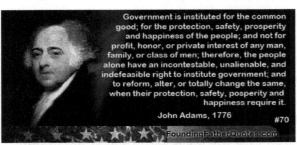

Figure 67 *John Adams on the Role of Government*

The anti-intellectualism forces in Congress and the current presidential behaviors approaching dementia (a decline in mental ability severe enough to interfere with daily life) also reflects the political conflict between "for the people" government and the "for the accumulation of wealth by the wealthy," as much today, as it did when John Adams broached the same two issues in 1776.

The intellectual continuum graphically conveys the voting issue we face in 2020.

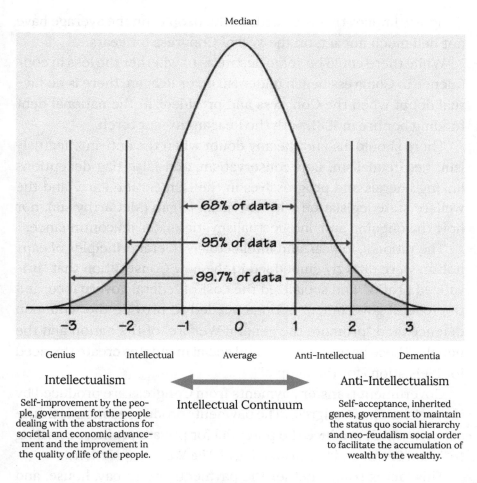

Figure 68 *Intellectual Continuum*

Where a person falls on the intellectual continuum is important to the success or failure of the federal republic model, whether the person is a member of the VEP, an actual voter, or one of the elected representatives, serving in the Federal Government.

Clearly, the early chapters in this book that displayed and discussed the people's opinions and their lack of confidence in

223

Congress implies that the needs of the people, on the average have not had much impact, on the Will of Congress for years.

While there could be some debate as to whether the loss in confidence in Congress began under Nixon or Reagan, there is no factual doubt when the Congress and president lit the national debt funding bonfire in 1981, with the Reagan tax-cut torch.

There should also not be any doubt when the anti-intellectualism, neo-feudalism, neo-conservatism, and false flag deceptions linking liberals and progressives in the Democratic Party and the welfare state legislation with socialism began (McCarthyism), nor how the ongoing anti-intellectualism stimulates its continuance.

The rational, logical, and intellectually liberal principles of capitalism were directly embedded in the new Constitution that "privatized profits" and socialized the cost of federal governance, and the federal government actions needed to provide the "common defence" and "promote the general Welfare" of the nation and the people. These basic economic and social mandates create the need for legislation "for the people."

Government transfer payments from Congress are produced by the legislation of Congress. The payments produce economic transactions, which produce the potential for private profits, according to Adam Smith and the principles of *The Wealth of Nations*.

This fact is true, whether the payments are to pay, house, and feed solders in boot camp, make transfer payments to hire mercenary soldiers like Blackwater, pay service providers like IBM for services, or to keep seniors, unemployed, disabled, and poor from living in poverty.

Privatizing profits from government transactions and socializing their cost drives the economy but does not directly facilitate the accumulation of wealth by the wealthy, unless the legislators pass some mighty bad legislation. And that mighty bad legislative potential was certainly demonstrated by the 1972-2013 economic results.

The next chapter, on privatizing profits and socializing the cost of government via the tax and spend processes remains the Political Party battleground over the role of government "for the people" versus "for the accumulation of wealth by the wealthy" with Socialism and Libertarian false flag masking the never ending conflict.

CHAPTER 10

Privatizing Profits, Socializing Cost, Shifting the Tax Burden to Posterity, and the Anti-Intellectual Inequality Caucus and Party Platforms

"Socialism is a scare word they have hurled at every advance the people have made in the last 20 years. Socialism is what they called public power. Socialism is what they called social security. Socialism is what they called farm price supports. Socialism is what they called bank deposit insurance. Socialism is what they called the growth of free and independent labor organizations. Socialism is their name for almost anything that helps all the people."
—HARRY S. TRUMAN, SPEECH, OCT 10, 1952

As mentioned in earlier chapters, the role of the federal government under the second Constitution was "to form a more perfect union, establish Justice, insure domestic Tranquility, provide for the common defence, promote the general Welfare, and secure the Blessings of Liberty to ourselves and our Posterity."

Article I of the Constitution established the new Congress of the United States. Section 8 of Article I granted the federal representatives in congressional session the authority to tax and pay for federal operations. "The Congress shall have power, to lay and collect taxes, duties, imposts and excises to pay the debts, and provide for the common defence and the general welfare of the United States."

The authority to tax and pay for the federal operation is clear. Moreover, the section clearly privatizes the profits from the government transactions and just as clearly, socializes the cost of the government operations via the taxpayers.

There is no hint of socialism in the Constitutional processes and there certainly was no suggestions that <u>means of production, distribution, and exchange</u> should be owned by the **community, nor is there any suggestion of sharing the benefits and profits from the transactions, with the people.**

Nothing in the remaining seven sections of The Constitution provided any hint of socialism. In fact, the various articles set into motion an abstract Corporation with very little room for discussion except for who pays and how much do they pay.

The new Constitution used words that were a lot like those in the original Articles of Confederation, but written with quite a bit of difference in meanings, scope and implications. In most cases, the changes in government authorities were not subtle. The new words clearly discarded the unitary neo-feudalism government model, in exchange for a new federal republic model.

The operation of Congress in the first Constitution is an example. "All charges of war, and all other expences (sic) that shall be incurred for the common defence (sic) and general welfare, and <u>allowed by the United States in Congress assembled, shall be defrayed out of a common treasury, which shall be supplied by the several states, in proportion to the value of all land within each state</u>, granted to or surveyed for any person, as such land and the buildings and improvements thereon shall be estimated, according to such mode as the United States in Congress assembled, shall from time to time direct and appoint."

In the Articles-based confederation model, the states owned the land and defrayed the Congressional costs, with a common pool of funds from property taxes on the States and plutocrats who owned the land and buildings. Moreover, Congress was not a representative body enabled to pass laws. They were, in effect, employees of the various states. Congress needed to get unanimous approval from the states to pass a law or tax.

In the second Constitution, taxes are collected from the people and used to pay for the specific activities that Congress provides, for the people. "The Congress shall have power, to lay and collect taxes, duties, imposts and excises to pay the debts, and provide for the common defence and the general welfare of the United States."

The liberal shift to the representative model of government for the people, also authorized Congress "To make all laws which shall be necessary and proper for carrying into execution the foregoing powers, and all other powers vested by this Constitution in the government of the United States, or in any department or officer thereof" (Article XVIII). The necessary and proper clause authorized Congress to "effect" or bring about the necessary actions of government needed to achieve the goals of the Preamble.

The unique necessary and proper clause clearly <u>empowered Congress to make the laws that would</u> "form a more perfect union, establish Justice, insure domestic Tranquility, provide for the common defence, promote the general Welfare, and secure the Blessings of Liberty to ourselves and our Posterity" through the laws and legislation reflecting the Will of Congress and not the will of the state landowners or Party Patrons.

The new "privatize the government transaction profits and socialize the cost" model to protect and promote the "general Welfare" is politically, socially, and economically, at the opposite end of socialism's government model, which implies "owned or regulated by the community <u>sharing the benefits and profits of the socialized environment</u>."

The numerous laws passed by Congress over the centuries have all been tested in the Supreme Court, which was also brought into existence, by the same Constitution. 158 of the laws passed by Congress have in fact been ruled unconstitutional. Based on the legal doctrine of *stare decisis*, no unconstitutional laws establishing socialism, or a socialist form of government, exists in the legislation of the United States, as of 2019.

President Truman's observation about socialism being a scare word hurdled at every advance the people have made and being a bogus name used "for almost anything that helps all the people" is as insightful today as it was in 1952.

Moreover, given that the Constitution did not establish socialism, and no law passed by Congress ever established socialism, the Cult of ignorance plutocrats, the patrons, the promoters, the adherents, and the evangelical conservatives making such false flag claims are promoting pure propaganda, while expressing their anti-intellectualism and ignorance.

In the decades since Truman exposed it as a scare word lie, the claim has continued to be used, to nurture the Cult of Ignorance adherents and, as discussed earlier in the book, literally "brainwash" the unsuspecting Baby Boomer population, using well known Pavlovian teaching techniques. The misinformation campaign created by evangelical conservative groups and institutions like the John Birch Society and Hinsdale College was propagated through the new mass market communications processes (TV Evangelist, conservative talk show hosts and conspiracy theory programming). This pragmatic misinformation effort was adopted as a way to cultivate and expand the conservative anti-federalist ideology that still rejects the federal government role as a solutions provider with a mandate to "promote the General Welfare" for the people.

Clearly, the mandate to provide for the common defence (sic) and promote the general Welfare mandate does not directly facilitate the accumulation of wealth by the wealthy, nor help maintain the status quo neo-feudalistic cultural classes and social milieu, waiting for the Rapture.

Based on the real income growth performance reflected in the Chart 69, the Greatest Generation of voters and the Congresses they elected between 1948 and 1972 produced outstanding legislative and economic results. It is also clear from the 1972-2013 numbers that the somewhat confused, misinformed and misled Baby Boomers and Generation X voters contributed virtually nothing to the general population and even a reduced accumulation of wealth rate for the richest 10% of the population..

Many voters and Congress Representatives must have joined the Cult of Ignorance as neo-conservatives over the period. The addle-brained Neocon voters obviously elected addle-brained that passed legislation to reduced the national economic growth rate, the future GDP and the accumulation of wealth by the wealthy rate, while worsening the economic problems for the working class, disabled, seniors unemployed and the poor.

Figure 69 *Growth of Real Income and Income Distribution*

Whether the Congresses were addle-brained or simply led by anti-intellectuals is unclear. It is clear, they passed laws that reduced the national economic growth rate and the future GDP while reducing the accumulation of wealth by the wealthy rate, while and nearly destroying the working class, disabled, seniors, unemployed, and the poor.

Socializing the cost of the Congressional failure, coupled with misguided tax cuts and tax loopholes, also created today's low-wage gig workers and economy, with minimum federal or union protection from the monopolies and junk bond/hedge fund enabled conglomerations. Socializing more of the cost to low-wage workers to facilitate the "accumulation of wealth by the wealthy" (profits/payroll taxes), also created new income inequality results, instead of promoting the "general Welfare."

The following income inequality chart reflects the conservative political caucus leverage on the Republican Party, the rise of anti-intellectualism, economic ignorance, and big business lobbying leverage among the Representatives and Congressional Session leaders that produced Income Inequities not seen in the US, for a hundred years.

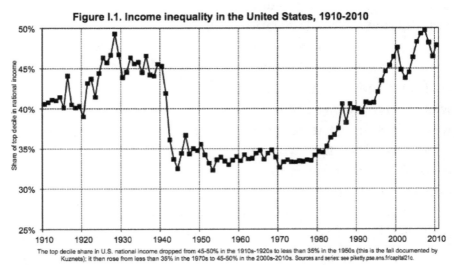

Figure I.1. Income inequality in the United States, 1910-2010
Share of top decile in national income
50%
45%
40%
35%
30%
25%
1910
1920
1930
1940
1950
1960
1970
1980
1990
2000
2010
The top decile share in U.S. national income dropped from 45-50% in the 1910s-1920s to less than 35% in the 1950s (this is the fall documented by Kuznets); it then rose from less than 35% in the 1970s to 45-50% in the 2000s-2010s. Sources and series: see piketty.pse.ens.fr/capital21c.

***Figure* 70** *Income Inequality in the United States 1910–2010*

That transformation in political party objectives and the rise of the conservative caucus pretty well explains the overall job approval rating of Congress (chapters 4-5).

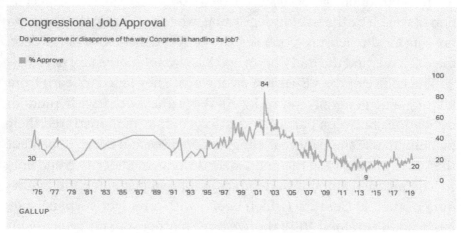

Figure 71 *Congressional Job Approval Rating 1974-2018*

In the context of learning from history, there are many sources. You can even learn, by using the Figure 71 Gallup chart and its false flag posting, drawn to mislead and misinform, via a space where 9 is close to 30, by having 0-29 spacing parameter in the first row of the chart and all other rows being 0-9. Is should also be clear from the Chart that Congress and the elected representatives have generally failed to inspire the people and/or produce high job ratings.

The economic and the job rating failure of Congress also reflects the general failure of the VEP and actual voters to support the "for the people" congressional mandate with the repeated election of the mediocrity to Congress.

The failure of the representatives to get acceptable job approval ratings and the failure of voters to elect better representatives who could earn better ratings, also reflects on the power of the

Cult of Ignorance voting bloc and the stranglehold it has over the evangelical conservative voters and Republican Party candidates.

These Cult-enabled political powers and the propaganda expertise to divert attention via socialism, enabled Congress to mask the facilitation of wealth by the wealthy legislation, while socializing the costs, via tax cuts for the rich, tax loopholes, the budget deficit, the college debt, the toll roads and the Iran Contra and Blackwater mercenary payouts.

The failure of the VEP is just as obvious. They failed to learn from history and generally reproduced the same doom with random oscillations between parties. The also generally demonstrated their inability to use the two-year congressional session cycle, to protect the VEP from creating the multi-decade long, mediocrity trend line.

The massive amount of debt accumulated just since the beginning of the 21st Century (which began with a budget surplus) suggests addle-brained VEP, the wealthy plutocrats and poor result Congresses are drawn together, like moths to flames.

The JP Morgan summary in Figure 72 summarizes the state of our nation in comparison to others. The numbers are a clear indication of what happens when Congress is producing Income Inequalities at record setting rates.

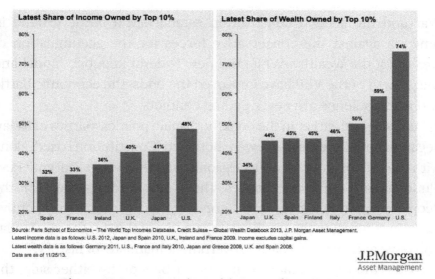

Figure 72 *Income and Wealth Inequality—JP Morgan*

The United States is well stocked with anti-intellectuals, evangelical conservatives, Cult of Ignorance patrons, and conservative caucus adherents who will suggest that the income inequality and the accumulation of wealth by the wealthy reflected on the J.P Morgan charts and income inequality drawings are simply the will of God and the natural byproducts of capitalism, hard work, and rugged individualism.

Intellectuals would disagree, since there are no facts to draw such a conclusion. Most would suggest the charts and graphs are the result of poor legislation and the poor socialization of costs in the taxation/national debt processes used by conservative caucus-based Congresses that favor the distribution of income to the richest 10% of the population in a representative environment, driven by the political party patrons that embrace the accumulation of wealth by the wealthy over the "for the people" mandate.

The liberal forces "for the people" that produced the Revolutionary

War and the second constitution established a battle ground in America against the conservative forces for the accumulation of wealth by the wealthy. While the new Federal Republic model and the growth of the VEP have improved the odds, the economic battle and its turbulence are never ending conflicts.

As discussed earlier in the book, both main political parties of today, began as Anti-Federalist and were both anti-Constitution based, along with the Cult of Ignorance successionist and the evangelical anti-Revolutionaries. Over the centuries, the forces favoring the "For the People" mandate of government grew into an ever more competitive force, in contrast to the traditional strengths of the "for the accumulation of wealth by the wealthy" government mandate, of history.

While the ideological war may never be won by either side, the biannual contest for the Congress and the four-year cycle for the Presidency presents the VEP and the millennial voting block the opportunity to assess candidates and select the one they feel will represent them, their family and their nation and turn back the fascist Plutocrat Patron horde, controlling the political parties.

The economic results over the last 50 years is a clear example with documented proof that the dichotomy and conflict continue relatively unabated. Likewise, the gerrymandering, voter suppression claims and even the treatment of Dreamers, illegals and asylum seekers at the southern border demonstrate the existence of the liberal versus fascist conflict, on a daily basis.

On the upside, the House-cleaning in 2018 shows the VEP that they do have the power to change the legislative branch that is performing poorly. Hopefully, the VEP and the new millennial block will leverage their initial step and repair the congressional branch of government in 2020 and return it to a political environment without fascism in our midst.

CHAPTER 11

Privatizing Profits and Socializing the Cost of Government and the their impact on the Eco-System

"Whenever the people are well informed, they can be trusted with their own government"
—THOMAS JEFFERSON

Privatizing business profits and socializing the cost of national government are the core economic and social attributes of the people-empowered, representative-based federal government model, created by the second Constitution. This economic and social model is the reason the conservative claims about socialism and the government ownership of the means of production and sharing of profits are bold-faced lies.

As discussed in the previous chapters, the role of Congress is to pay the debts, to "provide for the common defence (sic)" and to "promote the general Welfare." Congress achieves its purposes through legislative actions and payment actions that socialize the government costs through taxes and debt instruments that create, facilitate, and regulate the economy and markets in ways that protect property rights, human rights and "promote the general Welfare" of the people.

Socializing the cost of governance in ways that facilitate the accumulation of wealth by the wealthy and actions that work to the detriment of the people or the economy are not the role of the government. Clearly, bad legislation, the failure to "provide for the common defence" and the failure to "promote the general Welfare" can all produce disastrous results for the people, as well.

The following chart (you have seen it before) demonstrates examples of good results (1917-1948 and 1948-1972) and the failure of voters and Congress.

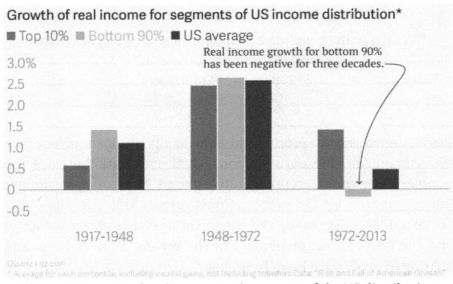

Figure 73 *Growth of real income and segments of the US distribution*

Many of the events that produced the disastrous results have already been examined. Hopefully, you are better informed now, and you can be trusted with your own government, as Jefferson hoped, in his quote opening this chapter.

Being informed implies you are now aware that the "Nixon/ Watergate" attack on democracy and the "government is the problem" attack on the nation were both a result of the Anti-Federalist beliefs and behaviors embraced by conservative constituencies.

The successful conservative attack on the Congress and Legislative branches fundamentally altered the nature of the Federal Government. The representative's behaviors shifted away from the "for the People" mandate to the "accumulation of wealth by the wealthy" mandate.

This chapter provides additional background, examples, and insights into the behavior patterns and the faulty voter and Representative thinking that caused the poor congressional results for the people.

The information and insights will help you understand and recognize the behavior patterns of candidates and help you develop voting skills that you can use to help the electorate avoid the election of addle-brained (muddled or confused mind resulting from 50-year-long Pavlov based propaganda attack) representatives. It is also hoped that the information and insights will also give you a better understanding of their pattern of thoughts and misguided beliefs. They are not bad people. They are your friends, relatives, and work associates that have picked up some misperceptions and embraced them.

As mentioned early in the book, 577 Anti-Federalist plutocrats initially rejected the new federal Constitution. They voted no on the proposal because they favored the traditional unitary nation-state model of government and the feudal class-based society with states' rights in control, versus the new "federal republic" model.

All the qualified voters on the Constitutional question were at the top of the Plutocrat hierarchy in the new nation states. Clearly, the losing Anti-Federalists preferred the hierarchical church/state model and class-based feudalistic economic and social system model. The model had been successful for the accumulation of wealth by the wealthy for centuries and both the feudal and the new industrializing neo-feudal nations were using it.

Although they lost the Constitutional vote, the foundational beliefs of the Cult of Ignorance did not go away. In fact, they survived and have changed very little over the centuries. Moreover, the economic aristocracy (the ultra-rich 1%-ers) and the owner, operator professionals (the 10%-ers) viewed the yeoman, seamen. vagabonds, peasants, labor and poor (90%) as sinful people that needed to be saved and rewarded, in the afterlife, not this one. The slaves, the native Americans and even the indentured servants were viewed down at least a peg or two on the economic scale. Many were even considered as a as a sub-species at best and chattel at worst. And, many of these perceptions are ingrained in the learned behavior patterns of conservatives, even today.

As an example, there are 19 states in which elected representatives are demonstrating modern neo-feudalism behavior today. They are failing to give their state citizenry the benefits of the Affordable Care Act, because the elected state representatives decided to not socialize the cost of improved healthcare benefits for the 90% class. The failure to grant constitutional protection to women via the Constitutional Amendment is another example of traditional conservative, state oriented, neo-feudalism.

Other, more cynical federal examples exist. The Freedom Caucus (consisting of conservative and libertarian Republican House members, Cult plutocrats, patrons, advocates, and other Republicans) have voted numerous times to un-promote the "general Welfare," with the repeal of the healthcare protection for 19 or 20 million people.

I personally cannot comprehend the nature of a person that could take away the benefit, although I can certainly appreciate their 20-year personal efforts to block the health care benefit for the people. The recent tax cut and budget deficit/debt expansion program is another feudal Cult-based example, that is nearly incomprehensible.

Historically, many of the original naysayers on the Constitutional question, and even some of those who had voted yes, maintained the plantation/slavery based neo-feudal market and economic model in-state, even after the Constitution was adopted. Many, like Thomas Jefferson, thought the liberal government experiment would fail. Many took actions to try to make it fail. Some attempted to limit the federal government scope through strict interpretation of the Constitution, while others tried to block any "general Welfare" legislation via the 10[Th] Amendment to the Constitution.

Moreover, many of the early neo-feudalist conservative members embraced the new government ideology that they interpreted as advocating corporatism (the political model to control a state by small interest groups), while controlling the people via the neo-feudal model–with the indentured servants, coolies, and factory town replacing plantation life

The unitary church/state and the special interest corporate-based neo-feudalism model of state government quickly came into conflict with the federal model of national legislation and the socializing of cost to promote the "general Welfare" for the benefit of the people, instead of the local special interest groups and the wealthy at the state level.

The first Congress of the United States, for example, passed a whiskey tax in 1791 (socializing the cost of the government and paying the debts via federal taxes).

The new whiskey tax was supposedly pre-approved by the plantation owners supporting Washington, but not by every one of the various state plutocrats, legislators and special interest groups. Although the tax was well received by the evangelical community, it was not well received or supported by the evangelicals in Pennsylvania.

According to history, the farmers and small distillers were upset with the tax format favoring big distillers over small ones. Many refused to pay the tax, and they started to run off federal collectors and even threatened them with physical harm if they came back.

Protests broke out. Farmers, distillers, and probably some whiskey consumers took to the streets, and violence erupted (the Whiskey Rebellion). George Washington marched 14,000 men (militia) into Pennsylvania in 1794, to end the violence, protests, and tax rebellion. Although no shots were fired, the point about federal taxes was made, and the protests and violence ended. Washington and the army left, the republic was saved, and some of the taxes were even collected, before the law got repealed in 1802.

The conflicts between the states, the evangelical conservatives, the abolitionist reformers, and state special interest groups was exacerbated by the Bill of Rights (1791).

On the political front, the initial Anti-Federalist coalition formed in 1788 (Thomas Jefferson and James Madison) evolved into the Anti-Administration coalition and ultimately, they combined the two Anti-Federalist forces into the Democrat-Republican Party, by 1794.

The Democrat portion of the new Anti-Federalist Party consisted of the conservative plantation-owners (slavers and the traditional feudal class-based agrarian state-based social system) who rejected the union, equality, equal justice for all, liberal abolitionist reformers, and any federalism-based policies promoting the "general Welfare" of the people.

The Republican side of the new Anti-Federalist Party consisted of a portion of the ultra-rich big business owners (plutocrats and the political patrons favoring corporatism and neo-feudalism) who were involved in banking, the exploiting of natural resources, and the importing of indentured servants and "coolies" rejected most of the ideas being put forward by the Federalists/ Whigs in the Administration.

The new Anti-Federalist combined political party adopted an

Anti-Administration platform, supporting states' rights, the strict interpretation of the Constitution, free markets with no federal regulations of business, and the Tenth Amendment ("the powers not delegated to the United States by the Constitution, nor prohibited by it to the States, are reserved to the States respectively, or to the people"). They also contended that Congress did not have the right to adopt new laws to fulfill the duties of Congress or its mandate.

Within a decade, the Anti-Federalist Democrat-Republican Party would gain political control over the Republic. Once they seized power, they remained the main political force of the nation and operated the federal republic, for almost 25 years.

Friction between feudalism (agrarian south), neo-feudalism (industrialization in the north), and the equality/anti-slavery liberals caused the Republicans to leave the initial coalition in the 1820s, as federal actions for privatizing of profits and socializing the cost began the land-grab era (Manifest Destiny was the nice term from history, while native American genocide and national land grab from Mexico were the underpinnings) and the handing out land to build railroads, canals, and cities was a result.

The Anti-Federalist Cult of Ignorance plutocrats, patrons, and proponents in the northern states eventually joined political forces with the liberals, Whigs, and Federalists to win elections. The new political force eventually revived the Republican Party label, as part of the end of slavery, and the Homestead Act "Populist" land giveaway program.

Lincoln's election in 1860 precipitated the Civil War, the first Anti-Coolie laws (1862), the Homestead Act giveaway, and the three constitutional amendments, ending slavery and restricting state sponsored feudalism on the citizens of the United States.

The amendments that freed men and women also extended American citizenship rights and precluded the states from interfering with citizen's rights (No state could pass a law that took away the rights to "life, liberty, or property). It would take another 90 years after ratification and several more amendments, to insure civil/voting rights were included.

The new post-Civil-War Republican Party remained in political power through most of the Reconstruction period (1870-1900). In many ways, Reconstruction did not go as well as the liberals, reformers, Whigs, and Federalists would have liked.

Corporatism and neo-feudalism produced the robber baron and sleazy carpetbagger eras. The economic transition from the slavery-based, "coolie" and chain gang indentured-servant economy to sharecropping, company towns, and segregation did not occur overnight. Mark Twain and Charles Dudley co-wrote *The Gilded Age: A Tale of Today* in 1873, satirizing the era with its serious social problems, masked by a thin gold gilding, keeping the social turmoil under wraps.

By the 1890s, Republican progressives (liberal reformers) passed the Sherman Anti-Trust Act, for regulating Trusts and Cartels (the Act addressed oppressive business practices and consumer exploitation problems but were mostly used to thwart unions and their demands for better working conditions and higher wages).

The Republican Party progressives also began to realize that "the general Welfare" Constitutional mandate required the government to take steps to ameliorate the economic, social, and healthcare problems being caused by industrialization, urbanization, environmental abuse, immigration, farm bankruptcies, and the political corruption in the cities and states.

President Roosevelt and a reluctant Congress ultimately intervened on the side of labor, for the first time ever, in the United Mine Workers Strike in 1902. The federal government supported the notion of shorter workdays and higher wages for the people. Roosevelt's intervention in the strike did produce a shorter workday and higher pay.

Roosevelt also used the Sherman Act for the first time, to curb the monopoly power of the railroads, and it is said he and Congress destroyed the Big 6 Meat Trust via the Supreme Court and congressional action to create the Pure Food and Drug Act and the Meat Inspection Act. They also stimulated the conservative environmental movement with laws creating 5 national Parks, 51 bird sanctuaries and 150 national forests.

Republican Theodore Roosevelt also got Congress to place the nation's first ever excise tax on corporations and trusts. This tax on production instead of being on consumers and consumption was the first step in pursuit of progressive economic ideas on how to implement Roosevelt's Square Deal and its 3 Cs program: Conservation of natural resources, the government Control of corporations, and Consumer protection.

His progressive (new secrete code word to avoid liberal) actions and his ability to get Congress to regulate big business and trusts, while protecting the environment and consumers earned him a slot on Mount Rushmore; it also began a schism within the Republican Party.

The split between the Progressives/Reformers promoting the "general Welfare" (left), and the neo-feudalist conservatives/Cult adherents still promoting the "accumulation of wealth" model (right) eventually spilt the party into factions for the accumulation of wealth versus for the people.

The schism created a new president (Wilson) and new Congress (Democrats supported by the progressive Republican minority). The new Congress implemented the progressive/reformer ideas that signaled the decline of the neo-feudalism era in America.

The new income tax laws, the death tax laws on accumulated wealth, the Federal Reserve regulating banks and Wall Street, the Clayton Anti-Trust Act, and the statewide election of Senators transformed the nation's consumer-only tax base (excise taxes and tariffs are paid by consumers) to the new production-based capitalism model (income tax and payroll tax are on production, not consumption). The transition to the new ways to socialize cost and make transfer payments to the poor, seniors, and unemployed, transformed the nation's economy and produced the 1917 to 1948 economic results.

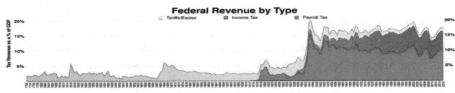

Figure 74 *Federal Revenue by Type*

The progressive spurt at the start of the 20th century also pro-duced the conservative Republican "Return to Normalcy" political era and the roaring 20s, conservative government model (Teapot Dome scandal, income tax cuts for the rich, farmer exploitation, the Wall Street bubble and collapse).

The 1920s also laid out the foundation for how not to "promote the general Welfare" with tax cuts for the rich and government spending cuts that would create unemployment, bankrupt farm-ers, and downsize the GDP, to create a Great Depression.

The progressive agenda to "promote the general Welfare" and its conflict with the neo-feudal corporatism drive to maintain the status quo and facilitate the accumulation of wealth by the wealthy, split the Republican Party for more than a generation, as the conservatives and the Cult patrons purged the progressives from their midst.

The Republican Party "purge of the left" produced nearly 80 years of Democratic majorities in Congresses, in comparison to 4 years of Republican Congresses, before voters adopted the neo-feudal conservative model in the Nixon/Reagan era.

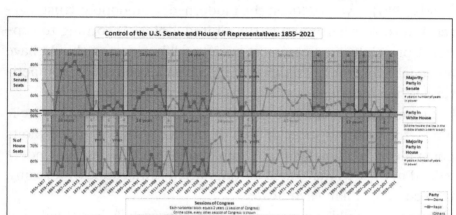

Figure 75 *The Control of the Senate, House, and Presidency 1789-present*

The party's progressive-member death knell in the 1970s also rang in the birth of the Neocon political ideology and the first wave of conservative-driven Congresses that produced the disastrous 1972 to 2013 economic failure for 90% of the people in the nation.

Today, the Neocon, Cult of Ignorance, and caucus movements publicly claim to be staunch supporters of capitalism. The Cult promoters who finance campaigns generally select ultra-conservatives, while the Neocon promoters favor borrowed money (deficit builders) and warmongering (regime change) conservatives.

Reagan outlined the conservative focus and the neo conservative political ideology as a "three-legged stool" that included "fiscal and economic" issues, "social and cultural" issues, and "national security" concerns. While full of issues and concerns and supply-side capitalism, there was virtually no thought given to the constitutional mandate to "promote the general Welfare," protect the environment, or to provide consumer protection (demand-side capitalism).

The process and deregulation of Junk Bonds (1984) and Hedge Funds (1987) have produced the modern-day monopoly, trust, cartel, and robber baron era in the United States. According to capitalist principles in a capitalist society, all businesses should have an equal opportunity to thrive and do business based on competition. When monopolies and trusts exist, competition cannot.

Seems simple. Unfair competition reduces transactions, facilitates the accumulation of wealth by the wealthy, and exploits consumers. Loading firms with junk bonds and seizing the undervalued net worth was called looting, when it was done by an army, instead of a banking syndicate.

Modern Republican candidates have successfully leveraged their traditional minority anti-capitalism party status into the majority party congressional position, at both the state and federal level, in comparison to the Democrats in this Neocon monopoly environment.

The Republican Party's conservatism today involves support for free market capitalism, free enterprise, business friendliness, a strong national defense, deregulation, restrictions on labor unions, social-conservative policies (anti-abortion, gun rights, family values, white nationalism, etc.), all with an evangelical Christian foundation and little tolerance for change and little thought given to promoting the "general Welfare."

The general Neocon misperceptions of demand-side capitalism and the privatizing of profits from transfer payments inadvertently enables the Republican Party to socialize the cost of government in ways that are detrimental to the economy and the "general Welfare" of the people. It also facilitates their efforts to provide tax loopholes, tax cuts, offshore banking advantages for the rich and massive deficit spending, that facilitates the accumulation of wealth by the wealthy model.

The Anti-Federalist Democratic Party that lost the Civil War and the Reconstruction, continued to promote feudalism and conservatism at the start of the last century. Like the Republican Party the Democratic Party would go through a social political schism and political metamorphosis, as a direct result of the progressive Republican agenda that split the Republican Party.

The loss of the Civil War and Reconstruction had initially hardened the anti-federalism, conservatism, and agrarian-based feudalism resolve of the Democrats.

Segregation, states' rights, Jim Crow, the Klu Klux Klan and traditional business-friendly/union-unfriendly/consumer-unfriendly legislators and legislation replaced the original slavery economy and plantation-life model, with poor farmers, poor peasants, poor cowboys and poor vagabonds, in the South and West.

The "dirt poor" segregationists, sod busters, ranch hands, sharecroppers, company town immigrants, and non-evangelical Republicans, eventually partnered with the city bosses and "Bourbon" Democrats in the Northeast, to re-create a base of Democratic Party voters, able to displace post-Civil War urban Republicans, at both the state and federal level.

In general, the Bourbon Democrats and urban southern Democrats both favored *laissez-faire* capitalism (businesses function best when there is no interference by the government, monopolies, cartels, and financial trusts), trying to find a way past the high protective tariffs and monopoly/trust operations, controlled by the Republican plutocrats.

The southern and western non-urban/rural Democrats and Republicans favoring states' rights also teamed up with the northern state Democrat progressives and party bosses, trying to escape the Republican reconstruction and carpetbagger era.

The continued urbanization, expanding Caucasian immigration, and the patronage and party boss model of New York spread westward with industrialization (oil and coal found in Pennsylvania, gold discovered in California, locomotives and train cars in the Midwest, farm automation, electricity, light bulbs, and telephones all appeared before 1900).

The urban party boss model of the North (successfully created by Democrats and gangsters), enabled the Democratic Party to establish a grassroots political movement of voting blocs in the urbanizing/industrializing immigrant/migrating Negro environment.

Many of the Republican progressives, liberals, and abolitionists being shunned by the Republican Party also began shifting allegiances to the party boss model being championed by the northern Democrats.

The city/state corruption flourished in the model, as the mobsters invaded the new political boss and elected-party patronage system. Reformers and progressive candidates often competed against the party bosses in the evolving Democratic Party of the north.

Although the Democrat Party also courted the labor movement in the neo-feudalism-based north, the embrace was as a voting bloc, much like the way Republican plutocrats and patrons had treated unions in the Coal Strike in 1902.

The obvious friction between the party patrons who financed candidates and the unions, the mob bosses, the feudal South, the northern Democrat plutocrats, and party bosses virtually precluded the development of a labor-based Democratic Party.

The northern and southern Democrat Party voting blocs could win in the cities, states, and the House, but hardly ever dominated the Senate (mostly appointed plutocrats from the states before Senate voting was mandated in 1917), and they infrequently won the presidency, until the Republican split manifested itself in 1913.

Wilson, the Democrat reformer, won the White House and got a

Democratic Congress as a result of the Roosevelt/Taft split of the Republican Party votes.

Wilson was a southern neo-feudalist segregationist, academician, reformer, and well-educated progressive. In office, Wilson proved to be almost the exact opposite of the traditional populist presidents (populism is the political approach that deliberately appeals to "the little people," often juxtaposing them against the "elite" know-it-all rascals and intellectuals telling you what is good for you).

The rapid implementation of Wilson's progressive economic tax reforms and policies by the new Congress (modern day liberalism and federalism in action), included the income tax on the rich, death taxes on the rich, the Federal Reserve, state voting for Senators and the Clayton Anti-Trust Act.

As shown earlier, these liberal actions ultimately spurred the economic rebirth and social development of the nation. This rebirth would lift the nation from a middling player status on the world stage to a powerhouse over the next 50 years.

In every way possible, Wilson also chided the general failure of Congress for not doing enough to promote the "general Welfare."

He saw himself as the man of the people and for the people. As an example, he said "No one but the President seems to be expected . . . to look out for the general interests of the country." According to history, the political conflict in Washington was palpable.

Wilson did get Congress to enter World War I in an effort "to make the world safe for Democracy," and he signed the law giving women the right to vote in America, in 1920.

While the Republican "Return to Normalcy" conservative era in the 1920s stifled the liberal Democratic progressivism for a decade, the Great Depression and the election of Franklin Delano Roosevelt and a Democratic Congress in 1932 unleashed it again.

The new Democratic majority in Congress in 1932 passed

thirteen new laws in the first 100 days of what was the New Deal for the people. The Republican minority, big business, and southern Democrats fought against the progressive activities, saying they cost too much and violated the 10th amendment.

Some of the early laws regulating working conditions (hours, days, pay) and some of the transfer payment processes to the unemployed were ruled un-constitutional. Most simply reappeared in the national Labor Relations Act in 1938 and the Social Security law covering poor and destitute seniors, in 1939.

The following 60 years of the liberal progressive New Deal political ideology, laws and the promotion of the "general Welfare" produced the financial and economic results shown earlier, while also facilitating the accumulation of wealth by the wealthy, at the same time.

The liberal progress embedded in the New Deal embraced the union movement, workers' rights, minimum living wage rates, equality, justice, infrastructure builds, and promoting the "general Welfare." These actions created conflicts with the conservative coalition and the southern portion of the party that still embraced feudalism, segregation, and class inequality, since the Reconstruction era.

President Roosevelt's executive order creating the Fair Employment Practice Committee ended hiring discrimination based on race, color, creed, or national origin by the federal government and any corporation contracting with the federal government.

That order set into motion the future hiring of thousands of African Americans and caused what would prove to be the start of an irreconcilable schism between the northern Democrats and the southern Democrats that embraced segregation and social inequality. The Democratic Party schism, like the Republican Party schism did not create a separate or new political party, but it did produce a weakened one.

The social schism between the northern and southern

Democrats continue to grow with Truman's desegregation of the military and ultimately the Supreme Court's decision in the *Brown vs. the Board of Education of Topeka* case.

The impact of the court decision was discussed earlier. It ruled that "separate but equal" legislation was a state sham and that discrimination by the state was unconstitutional and a violation of a citizen's rights to an education.

Within a decade of the court case on education, there would be federal troops marching students past a protesting Democratic governor and a new Declaration of Constitutional Principles (known as the **Southern Manifesto**).

The Manifesto released in February and March 1956 to the United States Congress, formally stated the South's opposition to racial integration of public places.

The Democratic Party internal conflict exposed the progressive conflict with the Southern Democrats to the Cult of Ignorance conservatives, and the traditional conservative plutocrats/patrons in the Republican Party. The Southern Strategy, by Nixon, exploited the ideological gap and successfully leveraged it to generally shift the focus of Congress away from equality and justice for people in the form of civil rights, voting rights, education and healthcare to the accumulation of wealth by the wealthy, at the expense of the people. The success of the Strategy is shown in the 1972-2013 results.

While both parties were internally squabbling over their internal schisms, registered Independents (those without any declared party affiliation) became the largest voting bloc in the country. Moreover, the new Independent bloc leaned toward a political party (Democrat versus Republican) and not necessarily the political ideologies (left "for the people" versus right "for the accumulation of wealth by the wealthy").

The Democratic Party platform over the last 30 years has sought to protect the social programs and transfer payments to the seniors, unemployed, farmers, veterans, the disabled, and the poor while supporting the labor unions and raising consumer protection and workplace safety regulation along with the development of equal opportunities, racial equality, and regulation against pollution of the environment. More recently, they have turned a spotlight focus on human rights, minority groups, and women's rights.

As mentioned earlier, the parties were exquisitely diverse, according to the Brookings Institute chart below and earlier party belief charts (Chapter 6). In 1969, where the red and blue merge in the scatter gram is where most people were at ideologically. As shown, there were Democrats who were more right-wing than Republican conservatives.

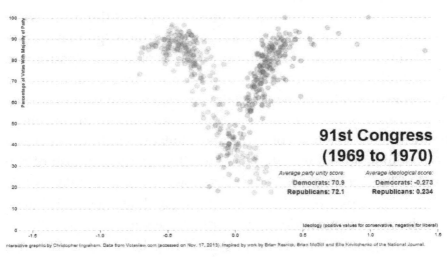

Figure 76 *Ideological Scatter Gram of 91st Congress Members*

To put that time and space (the 60s) in perspective should help clarify today's perspective of the parties. In the 1960s, a higher percentage of Republican legislators voted for the Civil Rights and

Voting Rights Acts versus the Democratic Party representatives who had introduced the bills in Congress.

In retrospect, this progressive-based multi-party model deteriorated from its diversity into the warring feudal fiefdoms of today. The same Brookings Institute scatter map chart in 2012, displays the partisan-politics implications for current voters.

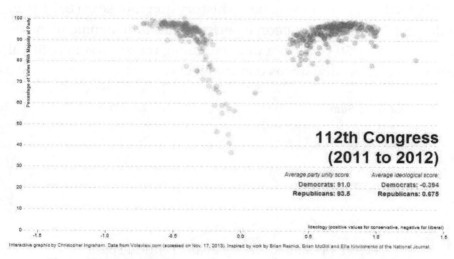

Figure 77 *Ideological Scatter Gram of 112th Congress Members*

During the shift between the two representations, bi-partisanship politics virtually ended, and partisan politics began. This transition and party dichotomy are important for voters to consider in the future.

Members of the VEP, in the past were presented with a non-zero-sum game and little differences in outcome (candidate ideologies with significant overlap). Elections today present a zero-sum game and outcomes with dire consequences for the loser. In the past your vote mathematically did not matter as much, because of the overlap in the outcome between the parties. Both parties win.

255

In a zero-sum game of today, there is no overlap or mutually beneficial outcome for the people.

In the past, the actual candidates who got through the plutocratic party screening and patron funding in the primary and the general elections were a relatively safe bet to represent the people and the nation's best interest, to the best of their ability, regardless of the political party of the Representative.

That safe, non-zero-sum bet in history does not seem to be true today and based on the income performance and income inequality results over 50 years, not understanding the zero-sum political environment has disastrous consequences.

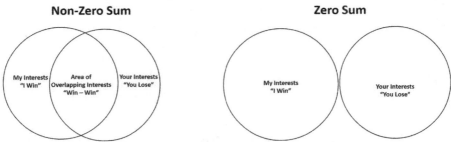

Figure 78 *Gaming Strategies and Political Power*

In the current environment, the typical candidate who gets through the plutocrat party screen and the patron funding today is typically representing the party, the Cult, or the caucus ideology and not the people or the nation.

The Cult of Ignorance and the conservative/caucus candidate patrons were able to leverage the social transformation from the North/South, black/white, and women's rights sociology schism among the Democrats and the progressives to eventually overcome the original conservative left-right ideology schism among the Republicans.

The rise of conservative ideology and the embracing of Nixon, Goldwater and eventually Reagan, began the transitions away from the for the people era and back to the new "for the accumulation of wealth by the wealth era, we are experiencing today. The notion that "In this instance, the government is not the solution to the Problem, the government is the Problem" has produced a generally ill-informed electorate, willing to reject the for the people mandate of the past.

Today, I can only speculate on what voters thought Reagan meant, at that time of his inauguration. In the same vein, I do not know how Reagan got the Democrat-dominated Congress to pass the deficit-creating tax cut for the rich and pass 7 tax increases on the 90% of the people in 8 years.

The first 8 years of tax roulette seemed to work fine, before the first recession hit and Wall street noticed the federal debt had doubled (see chart 80). When put in the perspective of the disastrous 50 years (1972-2013) that were set in motion back then, it should be clear that your vote today does matter, and it will count even more in the future than it did in the past. The Millennial bloc has the numbers to swing the results to the left or even further right toward fascism.

Based on your vote's increasing value to the people, I would recommend that voters give more intellect-based thought to the impact of candidates, especially with respect to their claims and conjectures about people and the "general Welfare." In the same vein, I recommend voters also spend more time vetting candidates, especially those attacking the federal institutions or claiming the institutions like the free press are the problem.

I also recommend voters give more intellect-based thought to the fact-free opinion claims, such as "it costs too much," "the free press is the enemy of the people," "tax cuts for the rich promote the general Welfare," or "a tax cut will somehow pay for itself."

In general, these expressions are bad ideas converted into misleading propaganda and false flags that generate behavior patterns reflecting ignorance and/or the Cult beliefs or political party dogma, versus knowledge of governance, government, or the economic impact of taxes on privatizing profits and the socializing of costs.

The Nixon/Reagan and congressional conservative transformation of the nation produced an inflection point, much like the Wilson transformation. The congressional and voter difference between the liberal versus conservative paths economically can be seen and reviewed in the positive and negative results from 1917–2013, shown on Figure 73 in this Guide.

Clearly, the failure to "promote the general Welfare," while promoting the accumulation of wealth by the wealthy has an impact on the people. Voters in the zero-sum game of today need to consider where a candidate sits on the intellectual continuum based on his or her words and deeds, if you want your children to avoid another 50-year disaster or the doom, as Jesse Ventura called it.

The rise of conservatism and the decline of liberalism in the United States has been examined by numerous scholars over the last fifty years. This chapter cannot do justice to their efforts, insights, and informative information.

On the other hand, this is a Voter Guide to help you assess future candidate behaviors and performance before they are elected into office. The Guide suggests you avoid the Cult of Ignorance proponents and those embracing economically flawed conservative principles for the accumulation of wealth by the wealthy.

The Guide also recommends that you evaluate candidates in your own best self-interest and the interests of the country, and then cast a vote in the federal elections to ensure the elected representatives are not addle-brained in your expressed opinion.

I hope the previous chapters and this one did not convey the idea that conservatives are selfish or stupid people. This chapter strongly suggests they happen to hold beliefs that make them want to maintain the status quo for themselves or their class, and there is nothing wrong with that desire and belief.

On an intellectual basis, they may not comprehend the concurrent drive by similar status quo thinkers is to leverage this class orientation to facilitate the accumulation of wealth for the wealth, at the expense of the people. The greed factor produces bad ideas and bad legislative actions that educated voters can avoid.

Who knows, you could help Congress achieve higher job approval ratings and earn back people's confidence.

CHAPTER 12

Open Question to Some Voters: R U Profoundly Clueless, or is it Dementia?

"To raise questions regarding normality and abnormality is in no way to question the fact that some behaviors are deviant or odd."
—DAVID L ROSENHAN, ON BEING SANE IN INSANE PLACES, JANUARY 1973

This chapter uses the inquiry-based learning method and the scientific processes, based on the Bible, to bring into focus how scientific beliefs, political ideology, determinism logic, deductive logic, religious beliefs, and economic understanding interact and impact voter choices in the election of representatives and the Will of Congress.

The scientific process suggests that the question is never the answer. The question is the impetus for examining the observed phenomenon, checking the facts and then the development of a hypothesis, or a proposed explanation for the phenomenon that can be tested and evaluated to verify its truth.

The question opening the chapter, is seeking to find the root cause (s) that produced the poor congressional Gallup Poll ratings, over the last 50 years, assuming they were a result of the elected Representative's actions.

While it might be some God's plan to persecute 90% of the US population, I do not believe it's my God's plan. Although he may be short and have a Jewish son, my God is just not that vindictive.

The question, though, is the logical first step to seeking the truth or enlightenment (the state of attaining knowledge or insight into the truth). The use of questions and seeking answers is based on the Christian Bible, in which both Matthew and Luke spelled out how the knowledge creation processes works, in relationship to the understanding and the communications processes:

Matthew 7:7-8 New American Standard Bible (NASB)

7 "[a]Ask, and it will be given to you; [b]seek, and you will find; [c]knock, and it will be opened to you. 8 For everyone who asks receives, and he who seeks finds, and to him who knocks it will be opened.

Footnotes:

a. Matthew 7:7 Or *Keep asking*
b. Matthew 7:7 Or *keep seeking*
c. Matthew 7:7 Or *keep knocking*

Matthew encoded the secret formula to finding truth and knowledge and ensconced the "asking principles" for seeking facts, finding truth, drawing conclusions, and sharing the results with "him who knocks."

Matthew focused his New Testament insights on the teachings of Jesus via the process the theologians call the Power of Prayer and scientists call the Scientific Method.

The two uses can get confused, by the "it is God's will"

pre-determinism logic and the "God's law" environment that implies that all events that happened were pre-ordained to happen, and anything that will happen in the future is destined to occur, in god's plan.

While many evangelicals and creationists embrace the religious notion that everything is God's will and God's plan coming to pass, many other people and virtually all scientists and intellectuals disagree with the theological determinism logic (God's will) and pre-determinism laws (God's Plan). Explaining reality, the causes of events and predicting future events does not seem to follow the "will" and "plan" model, very closely.

The four evangelical writers of the New Testament (attributed to Matthew, Mark, Luke, and John in the second century), produced the general teachings of Christ, the notions of sacred scriptures and divine inspiration via their gospels. Over time, these teachings produced dogma (gospel means a thing that is absolutely true, while dogma is the set of principles and laws laid down by a human authority, as incontrovertibly true and immutable (unchanging over time and unable to be changed)).

The intellectualism versus anti-intellectualism conflict between religious dogma and science were initially suppressed by nobility, politics and the churches. By 1000 AD, the Great Catholic Schism was forming over dogma. At the same time, the rise of Islam was producing a different kind of theocracy and dogma conflict. By 1400 AD, the Protestant Reformation and theocracy conflict was underway. By 1600, Baptists were priming theological and dogmatic battles that would create the English Separatists, who would go on to produce a new evangelical group every 100 miles or so, by the 1920s.

In the 17th century, theological determinism, pre-determinism, and even God's omniscience (God knows all past and future) ideas and dogma were challenged. The new challenge to the status quo period was called the "Enlightenment Era."

The Enlightenment Era became that period in man's history that produced a new kind of non-theocratic determinism-based behavior in what today we call the sciences.

The new scientists inadvertently found some things did not work the way theology or dogma suggested. Some such thinkers were called heretics. Others created evangelical religious cults, while some became the founding fathers of the modern age.

The Enlightenment Era produced a new kind of non-pre-determinism economist (people engaged in the development of knowledge about the way a government and people interact to manage and use resources).

People like Descartes, Locke, and Newton and their prominent exponents, including Kant, Goethe, Voltaire, Rousseau, and Adam Smith, extended Matthew's gospel logic and truth-finding process, into the scientific process, for seeking the truth through questioning, understanding facts, experiments to validate facts, rational thinking, and logic (intellectualism). I mention the string of names that contributed to the scientific processes here, just in case you need them to solve a future quiz, on your cell phone.

The new scientific and economic processes they espoused, augmented the power of prayer and they also produced new evangelical theology cults (Methodist, Mormons, Scientology...), and a new scientific understanding of how things work and interact.

These new scientific insights began with questions and new answers and testable hypotheses, replacing the relatively fact-free, theocracy-based, deterministic opinions, deterministic logic, and the anti-intellectualism model, of pre-determination dogma.

The intellectuals of the Enlightenment put into practice the idea of determining what was normal, versus abnormal and recognizing what was deviant or odd and then seeking answers to what caused the abnormal, deviance and odd behavior.

The scientific process, or Scientific Method (which is the Bible verse re-written with modern wording), for seeking the truth, finding the facts, generating new knowledge, and communicating the results to people are straight-forward and self-explanatory and can be found in a variety of forms in virtually every language.

Steps in the scientific process

- Step 1: Ask a question.
- Step 2: Do background research.
- Step 3: Construct a hypothesis.
- Step 4: Test your hypothesis by doing an experiment.
- Step 5: Analyze the data and draw a conclusion.
- Step 6: Share your results

As an example, the scientific process helped <u>economist Isaac Newton (the father of modern science)</u> develop and explain the natural laws of motion and gravity. While the Newtonian math could determine that there must be something there, based on wobbles in the orbit of Uranus and Neptune, the formulas could not predict the actual orbit of Pluto. The lack of a "planet" problem was simply treated as just odd and deviant behavior, of the universe. Other natural anomalies were initially dismissed the same way.

A new scientist (Albert Einstein), patched the equation and added the space-time Theory of Relativity, in 1905. The Theory went through the same scientific process and validation as Newton's, and the difference in the answers became what is known as progress.

Although progress started, in 1905, they still did not "find" Pluto, until 1930. And, when they found Pluto, they also found it did not explain the wobble any better. Today, we still do not know the wobble answer. We call it dark matter instead of Missing Matter. It sounds better than I don't know, while we continue to look for the answer. That is called progress, as well.

The scientific process and progress not only worked for the energy and gravity phenomenon, it also helped a physician/philosopher, John Locke (the father of liberalism), develop the concept of a social contract between people and government, to enable a government operated by representatives of the people, for the benefit of the people.

Likewise, the new scientific process also helped a political economist and moral philosopher, Adam Smith (the father of modern economics/capitalism), unlock the ideas of private ownership of the means of production, the notions of supply and demand and the interworking of consumers and sellers, to produce prosperity for everyone.

His theory of transaction-based exchanges and his hypothesis that the just payment for labor would produce exchange transactions between consumers and sellers was a novel idea. The notion that transactions would produce profits for owners and generate The Wealth of Nations, for the people was even more farfetched. It was economically the exact opposite of the traditional measurements of the accumulated wealth of the wealthy, at the top of the feudal hierarchy. In fact, their wealth in his plan did not matter much, and contributed virtually nothing of value to the Wealth of Nations.

His heretical theory and the wages/transactions based buying and selling hypothesis set-in motion a testing and validation period, over the next several hundred years. The new process of a consumer-driven economy would ultimately produce the largest social, political, and economic shift in the history of mankind.

The interrogatory question opening of this chapter, "R U profoundly clueless or is it dementia" uses the same scientific questioning process, to help the VEP understand how faulty political dogma and anti-intellectualism have contributed to the lack of progress reflected in the mediocre Gallup Poll results and the lack of confidence, in the ability of Congress, over the last 50 years.

Obviously, the lack of confidence in Congress flows directly from the job performance perceptions displayed in the Gallup opinion polls. As shown in previous chapters, the poor perceptions are clearly earned, based on the lack of economic progress by the people, over a long period time.

Whether the poor Congressional performance was a result of the virtual Duopoly offering poor candidates, the VEP making poor selections, or a combination of poor candidates and poor selections, the goal is seeking the causes for the lack of progress.

The initial question in this chapter exposes the idea of a profoundly clueless. Nothing suggests that voters are not making informed decisions when selecting candidates. Analysis does suggest many Baby Boomers are just misinformed and misguided as a result of the psychological bombardment of liberal bad conservative good propaganda. They in turn promulgated and reinforced the same misperception to Generation X. This process produced the multi decade economic disaster for the people. It does not seem logical to most people that the Cult would want to mislead and misinform the nation to support its questionable dogma.

The exposing clues were there and openly discussed. For example, in Reagan's inaugural speech he stated, "In our current crisis, government is not the solution to our problem; government is the problem." Clues were also embedded in his action plans.

If, the federal government for the people, by the people and of the people representatives was the problem, the solution was also clear to Reagan. A tax cut for the rich, to shift the funding of the government's activities to the debt market and stimulate the economy, from an upward distribution of income direct to a class of the society, dedicated to the accumulation and hording of wealth was a bad idea that came to life.

Obviously, the Boomers were not clueless. They debated the issues and seem to have inadvertently bought into the false flag propaganda that our representatives were converting the nation into a Socialist State and only conservatism could solve the problem and save the country.

Although it was factually untrue, it was used as justification for changing the role of government from the "for the people" model, to the "accumulation of wealth by the wealthy" model.

The false flag plant does not explain the acceptance of the inane government plan for an upward distribution of Income to solve citizen's problems. The Reagan tax experiment though proved that Reagan was correct, in this case, the government became the problem.

The not clueless Baby Boomers and their acceptance of the inane tax solution (as evidenced by reelections) was clearly a result of the carryover economic growth of the period, that started before the tax cut and the inability of the VEP or Congress, to grasp the long term downside of the new Income Inequality processes they unleashed and the resultant government shift to debt financing for the ongoing government operations.

The sole purpose of debunking the question of clueless versus dementia is to provide voters with the scientific process experience to help the VEP develop their own insights and hypothesis and use them to evaluate a candidate's perceptions of reality and their political ideology. The need for this skill is increasing, along with the expansion of the dark money forces and the power of persuading and influencing people's decisions, though advertising and promotions of bad ideas and poor candidates.

Obviously, the candidate information needed to make a personal candidate evaluation is usually obtainable and generally available. Cult of Ignorance supporters with the predisposition to facilitate the accumulation of wealth by the wealthy, normally self-identify for electability reasons, like the way Reagan did in his campaign and speeches.

Understanding a candidate's conservative ideology and their accumulation of wealth by the wealthy predisposition, can hopefully stimulate informed voters to cast more ballots for anybody else and hopefully thwart the other voters that favor the Cult of Ignorance advocates. Again, the goal is to select the most qualified representatives being put forward by the political Duopoly and ultimately cause them to run better candidates.

The new not-clueless hypothesis replacing the opening question about clueless did not dismiss dementia (a word that describes a group of symptoms associated with a decline in memory or other thinking and intellectual skills that are severe enough to reduce a person's ability to perform everyday activities including voting in elections).It also did not dismiss the need to better understand normality, abnormality, and the deviant and odd behaviors demonstrated by some voters and representatives, in the United States.

At the beginning of the Representative process, in 1789, there were no effective political parties involved in the House votes, the State appointments of Senators nor the selection of Electoral College Plutocrats for selecting the executive branch.

We also need to appreciate the fact that the plutocrats and the party patrons developed our unique national political party system, after that first election, to facilitate their own Party self-interests, via the developing of a voting constituency power base, to control the House votes. The control of the Senate, by the states and the control of Presidency via the College was already embedded in the constitution.

The new political party process enabled the political patrons (investors who put up the money to run candidates for office) to select the candidates they wanted for their purposes and they managed the elected representative's government actions, by aggregating party line voters, in the Congressional districts to get them elected.

We also need to remember that the Democratic and Republican Parties were the names used to identify the Anti-Federalist special interest groups (slavers and big business) that were formed, in opposition to the new Republic mode of government.

The anti-federalist, Democrat-Republican genes were passed on. The resultant offspring, with the built-in genotypes combined with the new environment, personal developments, national development and mutations, to form new politician phenotypes.

We also need to be cognizant of the fact that over the centuries, Congress granted most adults the right to vote in our federal elections. Although expanding the voter count and gene pool, Congress has not tried to recreate any new role of the federal government.

As a brief refresher, the Founding Fathers set up a republic to govern the nation for the benefit of the people. It based the institutions on the rule of law and precedence versus the traditional accumulation of wealth by the wealthy and dogma-based models.

While the background research of the initial question suggests that cluelessness was not the cause for the down-trending congressional performance, the resulting hypothesis suggests that the down trending Congress performance is more a result of deep-seated, anti-federalist misperceptions of the role of government, or being expressed by the chaos-causing personality disorder, that the Buddhists call Avidya. The Avidya anomaly describes the personal *misperceptions, of some people, that mislead them into what other people identify as deviant and odd patterns of thought* and behavior.

The declining job performance in the Gallup Opinion polls reflects clear observations, measured against the preconceived notions of the role of the federal government and its success in our society. Search engines help produce a consensus understanding of that role of government that is in decline.

Per Google, "The **main function** of the federal government **is creating and enforcing laws to ensure order and stability within society**. And further, according to Google, "the main function is an activity or purpose, natural to or intended for a person or thing" and the representative role itself is "the function assumed, or a part played, by a person or thing in a specific situation."

Bing's answer to the "role of the federal government" is a little more expansive. The United States government is a "federal system in which the federal and state governments share power and the Constitution outlines the responsibilities of the federal government. The **main function** of the federal government **is creating and enforcing laws to ensure order and stability within society**."

While both engines did a good job of explaining "creating and enforcing laws to ensure order and stability within a society," the Constitution's actual preamble granted authorities and responsibilities that were a little broader than just "to ensure order and stability" within our society.

As mentioned in previous Chapters "...in order to form a more perfect Union, establish Justice, insure domestic Tranquility, provide for the common defence, promote the general Welfare, and secure the Blessings of Liberty to ourselves and our Posterity" specifies goals for the government and its laws that go beyond the generic notions of creating and enforcing. Establish justice, insure domestic tranquility, promote the general Welfare and secure the blessings of liberty notions have also been incorporated into the State government charters, as well.

How to determine the normality or abnormality of any actual government legislative is somewhat embedded in its accomplishment of the goals of the government that are clearly annunciated in the Preamble. The success of the Federal government in achievement of its goals, is measured in the trust level of the Branches.

That trust of people and their perceptions of the three branches of government, is undergoing declines and stress, after the shockingly poor legislative performance over the last 50 years. Trust in all three branches are declining across the board, according to Gallup polling and the responses they are getting.

Trust in Three Branches of U.S. Government

Figures are percentages with a great deal/fair amount of trust in the branch

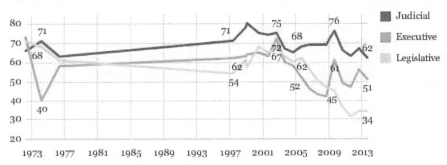

Figure 79 *Trust in the Three Branches of Government*

Trust in the three branches of government, like the opinions on the performance of Congress and the executive branch, has generated new government behaviors among certain representatives and even certain groups of representatives (caucuses).

Clearly, the Government Branch opinions are declining and moving toward the same negative environment as the legislative journey. Moreover, the declining level of trust in the Federal government has produced other negative artifacts. For example, 27 states have called for a "Constitutional Convention" to amend or rewrite the constitution.

It should also be noted, the last time the nation-states generated a Constitutional Convention was 1787. The Convention called to do amendments, in fact, replaced the Articles of Confederation

Constitution that was initially favored by the States, in 1781.

As discussed in earlier chapters, 1,071 plutocratic Federalists positively responded to the new Constitution proposal. They voted to replace the Articles of Confederation Constitution, with the experimental "for the people" federal republic Constitution.

The new experimental model that the Constitutional Convention proposed and the States adopted, clearly violated all traditional norms of national government that had, until then, promoted the accumulation of wealth by the wealthy model and the special interest groups that operated the government processes, for the wealthy and nobility.

Because no evidence exists in the current environment, there is no way to predict what would happen at a new Constitutional Convention. On the other hand, the brain power of informed voters, who understand the Intellectualism versus anti-intellectualism continuum, does provide ways to assess the poor legislative actions from Congress and repair it every two years. The process also provides the means to address new problems quickly, if you, the voters can perceive them and select representatives to address them

The VEP hopefully knows from the voter guide that they need to start avoiding candidates suggesting tax cuts for the rich and the upward distribution of income it produces, on the way to facilitating the accumulation of wealth by the wealthy processes.

Likewise, the VEP should now have a least a basic understanding that decreasing the taxes on big business, Trusts, Monopolies and monstrous estates, only increase the after-tax income for the owners, on the already profitable transactions. It does not increase incomes of 90% of the people or the primary transaction makers in our economy.

Both "for the rich processes" also clearly violate the core principles of capitalism, determinism logic, and deductive logic. And, in this same vein, the deregulation of big business and banking also violates sound economic principles and logic and has virtually never resulted in an environment promoting the "general Welfare."

The initial spurt in intellectualism at the beginning of the last century (1900-1920) kicked off by the Republican Party, produced the then new income and paycheck taxes. Congress eventually produced a 65-year interval of legislation for the people (as shown in the previous chapter from 1917 to 1973). As shown below, there was no current crisis in 1981 and the misguided tax cut experiment has ultimately reversed the long-term trend of promoting the general Welfare for 90% of the transaction makers (consumers).

Chart 5: Distribution of wealth in the US since 1917

Source: BofA Merrill Lynch Global Investment Strategy, Emmanuael Saez & Gabriel Zucman - 2015

Figure 80 *Distribution of household wealth distribution 1917-2017*

The *Roe vs. Wade* (1973) court decision, like the election of Nixon (1968 and 1972) and Reagan (1980 and 1984) serve as time line beacons, marking the high-water mark of "for the people" government and the start of the new anti-intellectualism Cult of Ignorance movement in the United States. This movement and the rise of the conservative ideology favoring the "for the accumulation of wealth by the wealthy" model has dominated congressional legislation, over the last 50 years.

The re-invigorated pre-determinism dogma and the Anti-Intellectualism processes of the Cult of Ignorance, presented as economic facts, have produced a unique constituency group of voters that believe in trickle-down economics, the deregulation of Wall Street, the deregulation of banking and the support of special interest groups.

The anti-Intellectual Cult of Ignorance constituency has also merged with other constituencies (Conservatives, Nationalists, Tea Party, evangelicals, Fascists...). This combination has produced the election of legislators supporting the rich, the Big Business Plutocrats and special interest Plutocrat groups under the Republican Party banner.

The following chart summarize the Intellectual and Political Ideology end points that help explain the scatter diagram party results in the last chapter, along the attitudinal conflict, facing the VEP in the national election.

Intellectualism	Intellectual Continuum	Anti-Intellectualism
Self-improvement by the people, government for the benefit of the people by dealing with the abstractions for societal class advancement and the economic improvement in the quality of life of all the people.		Self-improvement by the people, government to maintain the status quo, neofeudalism social order and facilitate the accumulation of wealth by the wealthy.

Liberalism		Conservatism
The "for the people" political ideology and liberal bias based on the ideas of individual liberty, individual equality under the law, justice and the general belief that Representative based government is needed to enhance personal freedom, promote the general welfare and protect the individual from harm caused by big business, the environment, the economy, the government itself and other people in the global society.	The Political Ideology Continuum 	The "for the accumulation of wealth by the wealthy" political ideology, based on hierarchical plutocratic authority, property rights, the maintenance of the status quo and the general belief that the role of government is to facilitate the accumulation of wealth by the wealthy and provide the resources to protect the economic and social status of the plutocrats via the conservative model of government operations.

Figure 81 Intellectualism Ideology Continuum

The VEP and the voters all have a combination of their own unique mix of the intellectual and political ideology. Many of them contain their own form of political dementia and avidya when they vote and select representatives.

As hypothesized in this chapter, the combination of misinformed voters and their abnormal and deviant behaviors, (Dementia and Avidya impacted votes) is probable the root cause of the poor Congressional job ratings, the lack of trust and declining Branch of government evaluation that all seem to be highly correlated to the legislative track record and economic results over the last 50 years.

Figure 82 graphically displays the normal curve of the voter population going into an election and the after-election normal curve of the Representatives expressed in terms of their Intellectual and Political Ideology.

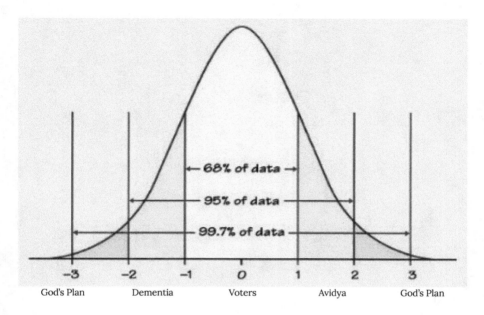

Figure 82 *Voters Dementia, Avidya and God's Plan*

This expected voter population and elected representative chart uses the terms Dementia and Avidya and potentially God's Plan to describe the other forces that are influencing and creating the mediocre performance of Congress and the declining performance of all three branches of government.

The next chapter explores the question, why did the VEP produce the new concentration of wealth and accumulation of wealth by the wealthy government role that is obviously not in the best interest of the people.

CHAPTER 13

Why did the VEP Produce the Concentration of Wealth and Reduce Their Quality of Life?

"Concentration of wealth yields concentration of political power. And concentration of political power gives rise to legislation that increases and accelerates the (wealth) cycle."
—NOAM CHOMSKY

Facts covered in earlier chapters summarized the congressional performance decline, created by the VEP and the poorly performing representatives they selected. The representatives who ran up the deficit via tax cuts, tax loopholes, and corporate subsidies are spread across both major political parties in Congress, although the preponderance of the perpetrators came out of the conservative led Republic party.

The poor legislation was also coupled with poor executive branch performance, via the Executive Order driven deregulation of Wall Street-Banking (allowing junk bonds, hedge funds, sub-prime loan securitization, poor rating agencies, the relaxing of federal regulation on Business), coupled with the poor performance of the oversight agencies protecting consumers, reflect the direct executive branch efforts to facilitate the Income Inequality and the accumulation of wealth by the wealthy, at the expense of the people.

Together the poor legislation and the poorly performing executive branch office holders have clearly shifted a larger portion of the Federal tax burden to the general population, while, stagnated wages for 90% of the population.

The last 50 years of "conservative" Republican driven legislation, regulations, and stagnant wages have virtually wiped out the first 50 years of economic progress in the nation and has actually reduced the share of household wealth owned by 90% of the people of the United States, according to Bank of America and Merrill Lynch.

Chart 5: Distribution of wealth in the US since 1917

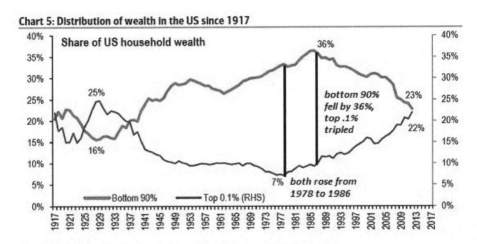

Source: BofA Merrill Lynch Global Investment Strategy, Emmanuael Saez & Gabriel Zucman - 2015

Figure 83 *Distribution of wealth in the US since 1917*

The scientific question opening this chapter "Why did the VEP produce the new concentration of wealth in the hands of the wealthy" is not intended to be at all like asking a suicidal dying person, why they took the poison.

The distribution of Wealth Chart, like all of those charts, graphs and lines displayed before it is intended to help you the members of the VEP better understand reality, the role of the Federal government issue in our society and your VEP responsibility to select representatives that will help the government fulfill its purpose.

The century long chart of results reflects an interval of time, where the Federal Government was clearly fulfilling its Constitutional role to promote the general Welfare. The chart even shows an extraordinary success rate, between 1978 and 1986, before the extraordinary failure from 1987 to today.

Mr. Chomsky's observation that the concentration of wealth yields concentration of political power may be the answer. His use of the term yields is extraordinarily insightful and valuable to your understanding of yielding political power. In financial circles yields are a measure of cash flow that an investor gets on the amount invested. At a 4% yield it takes 18 years to double your investment. AT 8% it takes 9. Yield is also used to describe what comes out in volume such as bushels per acre.

The 1981 tax cut for the rich yielded a new Government dynamic that stimulated the VEP to select anti-Federalist conservatives and Republican candidates at new rates that ultimately altered the political power of the nation, as demonstrated in the makeup of the Congress over the period from 1986 to today.

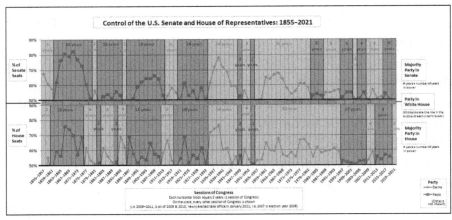

Figure 75 *The Control of the Senate, House, and Presidency 1789-present*

Baby boomers became the largest voting bloc age group, in the late 1970s. As a group, they had virtually no hands-on experience with the anti-Federalist Cult of Ignorance genes, the aristocracy based Plutocracy psychology, nor the political ideology for the preservation of the status quo and the accumulation of wealth by the wealthy role of government.

Moreover, they had not learned much about or from the Republican schism earlier in the Century and the ongoing purge of the Republican Party progressives. Boomers also had virtually no idea of the inherent strength of the Cult of Ignorance or the political power of the dark money special interest groups and lobbyist groups, inundating Washington D.C.

Benjamin Franklin understood the young adult problem from his era in turbulent history. And, one of his quotes described the late 1970s Baby Boomer political issues quite well. "An empty mind has no power to critique ideas, but since it is not always a stupid mind, it is able to absorb them like sponges absorb water if those ideas come from someone who they admire and listen to. This would not be hurtful if people spoke the truth, but many people in power, tend to put their interest above everyone else's."

With nearly 20 years of Pavlovian bell training to their credit, one thing many Boomers believed was the misstated fact that Democrats were liberals, liberals were socialists and socialist were communists. When the bell rang for the 1980 Presidential vote, the new conservative ideology seemed to fit well - "in this case, the government is not the solution to the problem, the government is the problem" message closed the deal. Reagan was clearly someone they respected, and he was swept into office with a 44 state land-slide victory in the Electoral College.

Although George Orwell's Animal Farm had existed their whole life (it was published in 1945), few Baby Boomers could make the intellectual bridge to the fact that people's ignorance could contrib-ute directly to their political and social oppression. Much as the 7 commandments had changed on the farm, the goals of the govern-ment began to change. The Contract with America spelled them out in 1994. The Great Society program and ideals to foster education, end poverty and put a stop to social injustice in the 1960s, became the freebees and Welfare Queen environment, while social Security and Medicare Pavlovian training expanded to reflect they were the socialist programs bankrupting government by the 1980s. The living wage principles of the past also got updated to the minimum wage ideas and tax loopholes, offshoring jobs and shifting production to other countries, to increase profits in the 1990s, established the path to today's gig economy of independent contractors.

The income inequality explosion in the 1980s and 1990s (tax cut for the rich, 8 tax increases on the non-rich, deregulation of bank-ing and Wallstreet) accelerated the wealth accumulation by the wealthy and the decline in the share of income by 90% of the pop-ulation. The wealth accumulation by the wealthy also strengthened the conservative political power, within the "purged" Republican

Party. The attempt of Ross Perot to purge President Bush in 1992, inadvertently produced a Democratic President and Congress, in 1992 (Clinton).

The 1993 Democratic Party tax increase caused a minor blip in the downward wealth spiral for 90% of the people (see Figure 83). The reprieve lasted for eight years and produced the first surplus in almost 50 years. The 2001 Republican led tax cut reversed the reprieve process and accelerated the decline in wealth for 90% of the population.

The historical facts reflected by Figure 83 speak volumes in terms of political and economic information about the Distribution of Wealth in the US, since 1917. The available information and understanding how it occurred should you, as a member of the VEP. I should also generate some thoughts in your mind on how you might help the VEP redirect the process for yourself, your family, your nation and posterity.

The facts in the charts speak for themselves in terms of political and economic information. Available information, though, is not the same as understanding.

Understanding the transformation problem from the "for the people" model to the "for the accumulation of wealth by the wealthy" model should result in improved candidate selection behavior in the VEP. This better assessment and selection process will hopefully generate the future congressional skills to repair the damage, in time to save the Millennials, their children, and our posterity from the inevitable collapse of the Wall Street bubble, created by the recent tax rate cut and stock buyback salting of the stock market, using the newfound after-tax earnings at the expense of increased deficits.

Understanding the issues begins and ends with thinking. In fact, thinking and processing of the arriving sensory information from the environment, understanding it, and integrating it with previous knowledge are all core attributes of the human mind.

Thinking probably first occurs in the womb, although sensory information processing probably starts with cutting the umbilical cord to get your attention and the butt slap that generates the breathing and crying behaviors.

The other problem with thinking is grasping the facts and developing the truth. Marcus Aurelius warned everyone how hard it is with his admonition that "everything we hear is an opinion and not a fact. And, everything we see is a perspective, not the truth."

In any case, thinking, understanding, recalling, creating new knowledge, and thinking before acting are the key attributes of most personal behavior in society. They also generate a need to know the facts and the truth that can best be satisfied by using the scientific processes.

Lastly, thinking about ways to reverse the current cycle is the subtle unasked question, driving this chapter, while helping the reader better understand why would the VEP wants to lower the quality of life of most Americans and our future posterity.

A hypothesis that it is a mass, non-suicidal, self-injury need of the people does not seem to be a reasonable conjecture explaining the behavior of the VEP. Neither does a pathological social submission hypothesis.

Obviously, it could be the vaccination causing a mass sociopathic personality disorder, that is manifesting itself in a form of extreme antisocial attitudes and odd behaviors that want the rich to be happy and pay no taxes to boot.

Given 45% to 50% or more of the VEP does not vote in federal elections, the prime suspect causing the lower quality of life for the people is probably a result of voters not knowing any better. In general, the only rational explanation and hypothesis for such results is a high preponderance of low-quality thinkers suckered into the conservative socialism propaganda and inadvertently selecting the representatives to protect the people from wealth.

The distribution of low-quality and high-quality thinking among the VEP probably follows a "normal curve" and distribution. The distribution of voters gets skewed toward the low quality of thinking by too many high-quality thinkers thinking they do not need to make candidate assessments and voting decisions. Let the low-quality thinker do it.

The quality of thinking distribution explains the large number of VEP members who consciously make the decision to not vote in federal elections. It also explains how the low quality of thinking in voters helps a minority political party to have significant influence on many actual voters that vote against their own best interests.

The scarcity of high-quality thinking among the actual voters could also be the root cause that produces the mass, non-suicidal, self-injury of the American people and our posterity from the actions by the elected representatives, over the years.

The book *Thinking Fast and Slow* by Daniel Kahneman implies that people use two primary modes of thinking to process information, create understanding, and make decisions in everyday life. He calls them Mode 1 and Mode 2.

Mode 1 is intuitive, instant, virtually unconscious, automatic, and emotional.

Mode 2 is slow, rational, conscious, reflective, reasoning, and deliberate.

Your active thoughts and your actions, and those of the elected representatives, vary depending on what mode is running and the situation that is causing the action and behavior. Obviously, the operating thinking mode also impacts fact assessment.

In most daily situations, Mode 1 is typically running in real time with reality. People take in the real-time sensory information and typically look at first-order consequences. Some activate Mode 2 more often than others. Statistically, some never activate Mode 2.

The Mode 1 process is referred to as "shallow" thinking. It rarely goes beyond the obvious. Information is taken at face value. In most cases, slow, deliberate, focused, and logical thinking (referred to as "deep" thinking) is reserved and only applied to complex problems. Given many voters do not invoke deep thinking processes, their understanding of the information is "shallower" than those who do invoke Mode 2 to assess information.

In terms of the VEP and the representatives, shallow thinkers strongly believe their shallower understandings are correct and that Mode 2 behavior is overthinking the problem of facts. Given the false sense of correctness, shallow thinkers also believe that they have acquired enough depth of knowledge, facts, and understanding to stand behind and support their opinions, actions, and behaviors. Sharpie marking on weather maps depicting hurricane movement is a sample of shallow thinking, in action.

Mode 1 thinking is also more simplistic, somewhat superficial, and just about everybody can do it and does do it. Mode 1 shallow thinkers clearly believe their knowledge and understanding is based on the truth and indisputable facts, although shallow thinkers are generally incapable of looking at all sides of an issue or exploring issues deeply, before making judgments or decisions leading to actions and behaviors.

Shallow thinkers generally take in facts, statistics, and information that fortify their own pre-conceived biases. They do not question the rationale behind any new information, nor do they make much effort to analyze what they have seen, read, heard, or been taught.

Contradictory facts, information, and opinions create ambiguity that shallow thinkers generally dismiss, using a self-worth protection response, while claiming social and religious justifications via euphemisms, misconstrued facts, and partisan preferences.

Most people in the VEP are generally operating in the shallow-thinker mode. The Mode 1 is a direct byproduct of our unique electronics-enabled mass-market social environment and the basic educational processes that focus on regurgitation of pre-approved facts, from school board approved books. As a society, we do not directly promote deeper thinking skills until college, grad school, and mid-level management assignments in a business, science or technical fields.

The deeper thinking skills reflected by Mode 2 are ultimately learned from the educational system, training, and experience and are somewhat "self-taught" through interactions with people and the personal use of the scientific process.

Deep thinking processes are often applied to complex problems, even by generally shallow thinkers. While not necessarily skilled in the process, most people try.

Deep thinkers, on the other hand, use the Model 2 processes more often, in more ways than shallow thinkers, and they even use them in moments of reflection on the information they receive. The more one uses the Model 2 processes, the more they hone their thinking skills. Eventually, deep thinkers develop different mental models of reality and even behavior patterns in comparison to shallow thinkers.

These diverse thought models, analyzed from different perspectives, help develop skills for seeing things from different angles. These deeper thinking skills often generate a clearer understanding, even among deep thinkers, although focus, strategy, and logic muscles can also produce convoluted contrarianism and conspiracy theory advocates.

The economic, political, and social culture in the US is predicated on a great deal of advertising, hype, promotion, and marketing, to persuade and influence attitudes and behaviors of shallow thinkers.

The general fakeness, phoniness, subtle misinformation, bold-faced lies, and illusions make shallow thinkers less trusting (they understand the information they are receiving is suspect) and more closed to new ideas and less adept at dealing with conflicting information.

Politically, the somewhat jaundiced view of new information and the bias toward their own intellectual self-worth protection (belief in what they think is true is true, otherwise, they are wrong and less worthy) is infectious. This jaundiced view produces a more conservative behavior pattern among the shallow thinkers in comparison to deep thinkers.

The conservative tendency also makes shallow thinkers generally more prone to herd or gang mentality (embrace facts and follow similar-minded peers and groups), evangelical cultism (the sovereignty of God, the infallibility of the scriptures, illumination by the Holy Spirit, the sinfulness of humanity, salvation by grace and faith in Christ) and the acceptance of an emotional, populist political appeal, especially one pitting "us," our group, against "them," the enemy and know-it-all, deep-thinking "elitists" who think they know better.

While the political party platforms reflect their most recent patron-approved marketing programs to differentiate the party product, the candidate campaigns are conjuring up their own fakeness, phoniness, subtle misinformation, bold-faced lies, and illusions, on a personal scale in the two-, four-, and six-year cycles of the House, Presidency, and Senate.

The plutocratic patrons evolve and fund plans to influence and exploit the shallow thinkers and mislead the deep thinkers. You can review **Chapter 10 Introduction to political Anti-Intellectualism, Ignorance and the rule of law** for an in-depth discussion of conservative/secessionist agendas and the political movement to restore the class structure supporting the "accumulation of wealth by the wealthy" government role.

Whether you are a shallow thinker or a deep thinker, the

commonality is thinking about something. This chapter, for example is exploring "Why did the VEP produce the concentration of wealth and reduce their own quality of life?"

There is no dispute of the financial facts from the Bank of America and Merrill Lynch, shown earlier and in Chapter 13. There is also no rational dispute that the will of Congress and its legislation were the prime contributor to these results for the people.

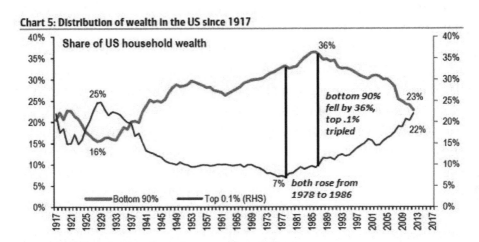

Chart 5: Distribution of wealth in the US since 1917

Source: BofA Merrill Lynch Global Investment Strategy, Emmanuael Saez & Gabriel Zucman - 2015

Figure 83 *Distribution of wealth in the US since 1917*

The VEP has been informed enough to understand and think about the problem. The Gallup Poll opinions of congressional performance certainly reflect the voter understanding

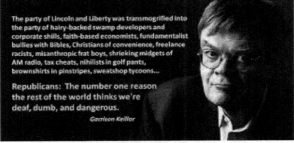

Figure 84 *Garrison Keillor on Republicans*

and disdain. Many people, like Garrison Keller and others, have already concluded the Baby Boomer generation and the political party system failed the people, their own children and our posterity.

Some commentators and deep thinkers have publicly proclaimed the failure and what caused it (the last phase of the scientific process and potentially the root cause of shallow thinkers proclaiming that the free press is the enemy of the people).

State legislators in 27 nation-states that are members of the United States want to rewrite the Constitution, which suggests they see the government failure being a result of the Constitution itself and not the transmogrified political party that gerrymandered the voting processes and produced the poor job performance.

"Make America Great Again" (MAGA) is a political slogan and a great example of how to capture shallow thinkers who will not ask themselves what has made us not great.

"Build the wall and Mexico will pay for it," "She [Hillary Clinton] let Benghazi happen with a stand-down order," and "In your guts, you know he is nuts," were some of the other shallow-thinker marketing and sales programs in the 2016 federal election.

"Low energy," "small hands," "not a hero," and "wacko bird" may all be political plants from Russians interfering in the 2016 elections. Championing victories that never happened, claiming things that are not true, and complaining about threats that do not exist, all became part of the plutocrat and patron produced political party misinformation lexicon directed at the shallow thinkers in the 2016 and 2018 elections. And, they will be recycled in various forms for the upcoming 2020 election.

Many shallow thinkers embrace the misinformation, the misconstrued data, and even the blatant lies via their personal bias toward their own herd that offers them personal intellectual self-worth protection. The plutocrats and patrons in the political party system and even many of the party representatives promote the same programs to reinforce the Mode-1 behavior and shallow-thinking supporters for their own political self-interests.

Some of the misconstrued information is so farcical that they produce inappropriate laughs. As an example, at a speech to the United Nations in September of 2018, the president championed a victory that never happened:

"My administration has accomplished more than almost any administration in the history of our country," Trump told the local live and TV audiences. "So true," he said, as laughter broke out among the dignitaries in attendance.

"Didn't expect that reaction, but that's okay" the president concluded in shallow-thinking recognition of the audience's response to the absurd false claim of victory.

Some of the misinformation is so patently false that the degree of misconstrued inaccuracy must be intentionally misleading lies being told to facilitate shallow thinking, populism, and the fortification of erroneous ideas as somehow being factual.

As an example of such behaviors:

"When people or countries come in to raid the great wealth of our nation, I want them to pay for the privilege of doing so...We are right now taking in $billions in Tariffs. MAKE AMERICA RICH AGAIN," December 2018, Trump's personal tweet to 33 million followers.

Buying and selling is an "exchange transaction," not a raid on wealth, according to Smith and the theories of capitalism. Tariffs are government fees on the exchange. The fee is paid by the US buyer, not the foreign seller. The tariff is, in fact, a tax on the consumer in a consumer driven economy, and most consumers are in the lower 90% of income and earnings.

Lastly, economic theory suggests that increasing prices reduces potential demand, which reduces exchange transactions, which reduces profits and wealth. Factually, the tariff raid on the US consumer was produced by our government's focus on the accumulation of wealth by the wealthy. Blaming the suppliers was a diversion false flag and the intentional misinformation about tariffs was prepared and propagated especially for the shallow thinkers.

It should also be noted that misleading, misinforming, and even lying to shallow thinkers or deep thinkers is not illegal in the United States. In fact, the only thing virtually wrong with such immoral actions and intellectual transgressions is that they increase the risk of government collapse, by jeopardizing the Constitution of the United States. The other potential problem is that they tend to drive the government and the economy toward the accumulation of wealth by the wealthy at the expense of most of the people. Mr. Adams points out the impact of such behaviors.

Figure 85 *John Adams on the Constitution*

Clearly, in 2016, no deep thinker believed that our nation would build the wall and Mexico would pay for it. I would also suggest few, if any, deep thinkers favored the ideas of significant personal tax cuts, or the cutting of the business tax rates, with the largest benefits, in dollar and percentage terms, going to the highest-income households and 500 largest private firms, for the accumulation of wealth by the wealthy.

The shallow thinkers who bought into these aspects of the federal campaign to elect a Republican House of Representatives and a Republican Senate, in 2016, to serve in the 115th congressional session, worked. The tax cut that was supposed to pay for itself did not do so in 2018 and never will, based on the cash-debt environment of at the time of the cut. Surprised?

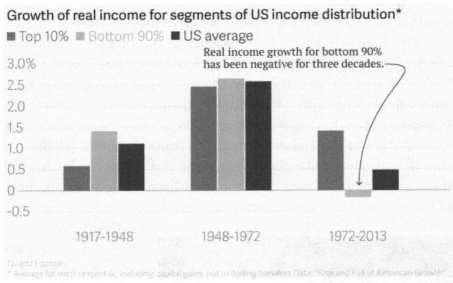

Figure 86 *Growth of Real Income and Income Distribution*

Approximately 54% of the VEP voted in 2016. A little over 63 million voters created 247 Republican districts, while 61 million created 194 Democrat districts. One of the lowest-rated Congresses of all time (114th) lost only 6 Republican districts to Democrats. One Democrat district in the one of the worst ever 114th Congress converted to Republican in the 115th Congress.

34 Senate seats were up for a vote (10 Democrat and 24 Republican) in 2016. Two Republican seats changed to Democrat. Republicans received 40 million popular votes, versus 51 million popular votes for the Democrats.

The newly seated 115th Congress passed 442 laws, including the 2017 tax cut for the rich. The 2017 tax cut was passed under the intellectual proposition that it would pay for itself based on the notions of elasticity and supply-side economic theories. Deep thinkers laughingly refer to these ideas as the "Laffer curve" and "Voodoo Economics."

Similar tax cuts for the rich structured to facilitate the accumulation of wealth for the wealthy and maximize shareholder returns have typically produced a decline in real income for most people and a decline in the quality of life of the American public.

Three decades of legislative productivity in U.S. Congress

Number of public laws enacted by each Congress, by type

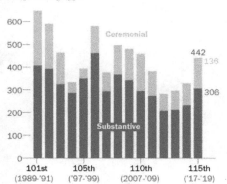

Figure 87 *Recent legislative productivity*

As demonstrated by the following chart, whether you are a consistent shallow thinker, an occasional deep thinker, or a general deep thinker, you need to consider the fact that the Congresses elected by the VEP have negatively impacted the average Real Income of the middle class, the Real Income of 90% of the population, and even the income performance of the top 10% through misguided conservative-driven legislation that is hurting the national economy, reducing the GDP, and poisoning the moral fiber of the nation in ways that jeopardize the Constitution (27 states want to rewrite the Constitution in order to facilitate more of the ideas that produced the disastrous 1972-2013 results).

The general hypothesis derived from the question opening this chapter is that the ever-changing VEP has done what it has done in the past, because it did not know any better. The alternative hypothesis that will be tested is that the VEP may have contracted a new political, racial, and sexual Mode 1 thinking abnormality that is limiting their ability to think logically or rationally, when casting votes in the gerrymandered states.

EPILOGUE, SUMMARY, AND CONCLUSION

"All good things must (come to an) end."
—FARLEX DICTIONARY OF IDIOMS.
© 2015 Farlex, Inc, all rights reserved.

The past produced the present. The current eco-system, the current political environment, and the current cultural milieu owe their existence to the past and the past continues to make significant contributions to the eco system of the future.

Both good and bad things have happened in the past. Based on the economic graphs and charts presented in the Guide, for example, the quality of life of an average America that was dramatically improved from 1917 to 1972, has dramatically declined, since then. That is a fact, even though the accumulation of wealth by the wealthy improved dramatically.

While the indices reflecting wealth accumulation process are near record level highs, the average American and the

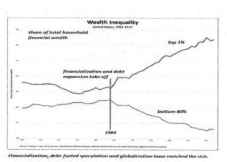

Figure 87a The Wealth Paradox

average American family inflation adjusted earnings and wealth has been declining for nearly 25 years. The decline is a result of the Congressional actions, the failure of both the Federal and State government to protect the people from predatory business practices and the Federal Government's inability or unwillingness to promote the general Welfare, in comparison to facilitating the accumulation of wealth by the wealthy.

Moreover, the government failure to "promote the general Welfare" has not only hurt the Average American consumer, it has also reduced the nation's Production Possibility Curve, while running up a massive loan balance, that is now larger than the annual GDP itself.

Members of the VEP and the actual voters in elections that do not heed Jessie Ventura's warning and learn from the past, are doomed to extend the failures into the future. The extension of the doom is not a forecast. It is in fact and a law of science.

According to Newton's law of motion, an object in motion will remain in uniform motion in a straight line unless compelled to change its state, by the action of an external force. The only external force strong enough to change the direction of the economic and cultural decline in America is the representative-based federal republic, that created it.

Moreover, in this same context, you, as a member of the Voter Eligible Population (VEP), are the only force with the potential to change the direction of our representative based federal republic and return it to the path that promotes the general Welfare.

The Guide has provided historical information and insights to assist the VEP to learn from the past and avoid the doom of a worse-off average American, over the next 20 years. Although changing the direction of a government is not easy, the Baby Boomer generation did it almost by accident, with their poor selection of representatives and their embracing of the conservative political ideology and worldviews, on the role of government in the United States.

The inadvertent decline, clearly began with the cultural rejection of the liberal Kennedy/Johnson era and the Great Society cultural efforts to eliminate poverty, improve educational opportunities and end racial and gender inequality. In 1973, at the start of Nixon's second term, only 11.2% of the US population lived below the poverty line, according to the US Census Bureau. 28 States had adopted the Equal Rights for women amendment by 1973, three years after Congress passed the amendment. By 1984, the year that Regan won his second term in office, the poverty rate was up to 15.2% and the Equal Rights amendment had failed to be adopted.

Generation X members of the VEP fanned the conservative flames with the Baby Boomers, via the election of conservative Republican Congress, in 1994, and the election of conservatism in the Presidency and Congress, in 2000. The poverty rate at the start of the new century was back to only 11.3%, at the end of the Clinton's Presidency, in 2000 and it went back to 15%, by the time Obama was bailing out the nation, in 2009.

The good news about this rapid adoption rate of conservative ideology and the embracing of their worldviews on the role of government for the accumulation of wealth by the wealthy is that it can be replaced just as fast. In fact, the House cleaning in the 2018 elections may well be an indication of the "for the people" governance recovery.

Going into the next election cycle (2020), the Millennials will represent the largest voting bloc in the VEP and be a key contributor to whoever wins. Moreover, they have almost a whole year left to learn from history and better understand the Political and Intellectual continuum differences, among the candidates.

While honing their candidate assessment skills during the campaign cycle is important, the newest members of the VEP need to turn out and vote, if they want to help the older generations fix the economic and social disaster, produced by the VEP over the last 40 years. That turn out of young adults alone could provide the momentum and vote count, to recover from the Baby Boomer and Generation X disaster.

The starting block to voting success is understanding the voting contribution issue and recognizing that voters in the VEP need to show up and vote, if they want to elect better-performing representatives, to serve in our government institutions. Circumventing the gerrymandering and voter suppression is needed to avoid the doom.

The other side of that effort to circumvent the gerrymandering and suppression coin is not voting, which in the scheme of things is in reality, a vote for whoever wins, and if that does not matter to you, that is OK, too. Shallow thinking is not a crime.

The first step in replacing the political ideology process is making better future candidate assessments, by increasing your knowledge and understanding of the past to improve your voting skills. Hopefully, the 13 chapters help in taking that first step.

In addition to fixing the economic/social disaster, these improved voting skills can also help recycle the older generation's mis-concepts of progress and their inexplicable movement toward the future of Americanized fascism. Aryan ethnic beliefs, white supremacy and misguided "us versus them" nationalism versus "We the People" patriotism will ultimately be one of the hardest social issues to reconcile.

One vote for the correct candidate produces love of country principles, while one vote for the wrong candidate will reinforce the role of fascism in our Country.

Hopefully, the chapters have provided the information you need to help you recognize which candidate is which.

As a reminder, fascism is a form of right-wing conservative

governance and government, featuring authoritarian, eth-nic-oriented, ultra-nationalism that liberals call ethnic-oriented, ultra-nationalism and "racism" today.

In an economic environment, fascism is characterized by the suppression of the opposition and dissenting opinions, coupled with the suppression of the press and ethnic groups by race, color, creed, religion, and gender are all clearly the attributes of a political ideology, supporting the accumulation of wealth by the wealthy, at the expense of the people.

The historical and pre-historical events covered in the Guide are memorialized facts, descriptions, and recorded observations of events that occurred. Associating them with the political and intellectual continuum is intended to clear up any misperceptions that have been introduced by historians trying to cleanse some of the behaviors of people, cultural groups and downplay some of the outcomes from their actions.

Logically, relating this information to today's candidate assessment and voting is tantamount to the Guides attempt at proving information for honing your voting skills. The Guide's various chapters were arranged to expose you to a variety of memorialized facts that contributed to our past and determined the current environment.

As the facts, descriptions, events, observations, and opinions from the guide came into your consciousness, they were being assessed and evaluated within the context of your own previous personal beliefs, your own personal liberal/conservative ideology mix, your own personal economic views, your own political party views, and your own learned behaviors, that came from your previous training, learning, and understanding.

The new knowledge you picked up from the Guide is now a part of honing your knowledge and voting skills.

The didactic compilation of history and pre-history that most people had before reading the guide came through school lectures and textbooks that taught you something about many of the same key events.

As an example, Fascism, Hitler, and the defeat of Germany in World War II, should be key takeaways from any didactic teaching, while Auschwitz, Dachau, Roma persecution, slave labor, ethnic cleansing, the final solution, and the Holocaust's contribution to the 78 million World War 2 deaths are hardly ever addressed as a subject.

While you may have gotten a passing grade in school via the dates and the key points, you might not have perceived the full impact of the ethnic-oriented, color of your skin, nationality or gender issues of the ultra-nationalist attributes, in history.

The attributes were not being hidden from you. The didactic teaching model does not normally mention that the fascist form of plutocracy and the hierarchical conservative government model for the accumulation of wealth by the wealthy is by its nature, exploiting the people, on variety of social and cultural issues.

Many teachers do not even point out that fascism was voted into office, in a federal republic government model, just like ours, in Germany, in 1934. Even fewer teachers would point out that the German voters produced the same doom that plutocracies and conservatism have produced, throughout the history of Republics, since 1789. Moreover, only a few teachers would point out that fascism was voted into other countries or that Communism in Russia has transformed itself into fascism, with the privatization of the means of production.

The discourse in this Guide is intended to be a little different than the didactic learning model. It is intended to provide you a clearer understanding of what was happening to the people and how the didactic packaging of events of history and pre-history impacted your teachers, your parents, your neighbors, other cultures, and ultimately your learned behavior and the behavior of other people, in the current eco-system and cultural milieu, where you now live.

The didactic model inadvertently "cleans up" history in ways that can sometimes mislead and inadvertently misinform people, who then make poor decisions based on the misinformation they took away from the learning sessions. The Thomas Jefferson, Robert E. Lee, and even Andrew Jackson ethnic and racial controversies of today are samples of dichotomies of thought, that the didactic process of teaching creates.

Was Thomas Jefferson a liberal plutocrat who owned slaves and seemingly sexually exploited one in particular? Was he also well versed in liberal thoughts of John Locke, as evidenced by the Declaration of Independence and his signature?

He was clearly a patriot, liberal, founding father and an anti-Federalist conservative plutocrat, and he personally opposed the second Constitution, and government for the people concepts, as evidenced by his arrangement with Madison to lead the Anti-Federalist Democrat-Republican Party.

Jefferson's election in 1800 was viewed at the time, as a transfer of power from the liberal plutocrats to the conservative plutocrats, by most of the nation's plutocrats, that controlled most of the federal votes in 1800.

Was Jefferson a liberal plutocrat, a conservative plutocrat, or just a mixture of both ideologies with a primary focus on the accumulation of wealth by the wealthy?

He was probably motivated by the accumulation of wealth by the wealthy issues, while supporting the for the people principles. Was he a slave holder? Definitely. Did he have a mistress? Yes. Was she a slave? The facts say yes. Was he a racist? I doubt it. Was he supporting the for the people ideals or just going along with them, until they collapsed on the weight of their conjectures? I do not know, and history cannot reveal it.

Didactic learning processes of today, seem to have inadvertently interwoven skin colors, ethnicity and gender issues with the economic and social ones.

Given Jefferson's scientific era, he may not have even considered his mistress to be a human being, although he certainly had no problem with the color of her skin.

Although modern didactic training could mislead some into thinking he was a racist, it is hoped that this Guide has taught you that he was not any form of racist in his time and that the question itself is derived from a faulty hypothesis with no logic supporting it.

In the same confusing manner, can a person like General Lee, who broke his oath of office, operated as a traitor attacking his own countrymen, and lost the war to boot, somehow be a great soldier and statesman memorialized in bronze statutes to a traitor?

The didactic teaching efforts to clean up this conflicted history have certainly made the question a possible historic set of events to evaluate.

Like Jefferson and Lee, Andrew Jackson, had his own brush with didactic history-cleansing as a process to avoid overexposure of the genocidal ethnic purge of Native Americans, by the first natural-born American President.

Does the didactic cleansing process of history matter with respect to the Guide? The answer is yes and no. The cleansing may or may not impact the VEP, although awareness of it may be enough knowledge in evaluating candidates and selecting representatives.

Clearly, the didactic cleanup of the never-ending struggle and conflict between "for the people" liberalism in government actions versus the "for the accumulation of wealth by the wealthy" conservatism in government actions has and still does cause people to be misinformed and supporters of political ideologies that support their purposes.

Given better clarity of thought from the Guide will hopefully help voters and the VEP make better-informed decisions, when it comes to vetting candidates, assessing the candidate's future behavior patterns, and evaluating their probable voting proclivities.

How a candidate thinks about the two schools of ideological thought with respect to liberalism for the people and conservatism for the money is also a good indicator, of how they might work across the aisle to bring together the Will of Congress via legislation.

Armed with this new insights and knowledge of people, the past and the related salient facts of behavior and history should help you produce a better grasp of how voters can help shape the future and avoid the economic-average American doom, produced by the parents and grandparents of the Millennials.

It is also hoped the material in the guide will stimulate Millennials to go to the polls in greater number and help the older generations of voters repair the institutions they damaged, or at least fix the Gallup Poll Opinion ratings, by reversing the declining trend lines and restoring a higher level of confidence in the Congress of the United States.

The various chapters in the Guide examined a variety of events, people, and the outcomes from their actions through the lens of history, using the eyes and intellect of a non-partisan, objective observer, to describe what he saw and read about. The ideas were designed to be non-biased and not political-party-oriented.

The fact that the observations of the recent past turned out to be somewhat party-oriented is the result of the history and actions by plutocrats and patrons, and not a biased opinion about the political parties or the plutocrats and patrons running them.

The author's recognition that conservatism was a learned behavior of plutocrats in plutocracies (tribes, cities, states, nations, and even continents that were ruled, governed, and controlled by a small number of people of great wealth and income seeking to increase their wealth) was a rude awakening. My history and Civics classes avoided the issues and made every government entity sound like it was for the people.

Understanding how the conservative behavior became the primary government attitude that created and drove virtually every nation-state in history toward the accumulation of wealth by the wealthy was a relatively unique surprise.

The very goal of political conservatism and its resultant behavior is and always has been the preservation of things as they are for the creation of wealth by the wealthy, and the higher you were in the economic hierarchy for the accumulation of wealth by the wealthy plutocracy, the more conservative you became.

Conservatism was and is the attitude of the plutocracy model and the governing hierarchy and not the form of government or even a philosophy of government.

Conservatism and the plutocratic drive to keep things the way they are became the constant economic force, that drove the development of virtually all societies and eco-systems, prior to the American Revolution.

The historical notion of agrarian societies paying taxes to the king for using his land and local plutocrats paying tribute to the king as an alternative to the king's military looting and pillaging, all seems to have been inadvertently unraveled, by religious beliefs and the Godly ideas about "saving the people" and earning a shot at a good afterlife.

The New Testament Christian "save the people" idea, coupled with the notions to feed the poor, clothe the naked, tend the sick, and educate the young grew into a religious-born reality of life in a large part of the world.

In other parts of the world, the awareness that actions have consequences and change is possible (Buddhism) was augmenting the traditional religions that focused on the issues of how to survive conservatism (Hinduism and Paganism).

Section 2 in the guide described how science, schisms, the Protestant revolutions, the rethinking of the nature of man, the recognition that conservative plutocracy governments were the main stumbling block to individual freedom and success (classic John Locke liberalism), and ultimately, the empowering of government by the governed replacing the Godly grant to the plutocrats, were all signs of change and progress, brought on by the "save the people" principles of the Middle East and Western Religions.

The notion of voting, a representative-driven government and a federal republic government sharing power with the individual nation-states, generated the force that converted straight-line conservatism from an attitude and behavior pattern of plutocrats into elected plutocracies, and a unique new governance and government strategy for the people, versus for the accumulation of wealth by the wealthy.

The initial voting-based decision by all 56 men to sign off on a document stating "We believe these truths to be self-evident that all men were created equal..." was a religious heresy, introducing liberalism's initial attack on the traditional conservative divinity-based plutocracy and its governing hierarchy.

The liberalism "stake in the ground," publication on July 4, 1776, initially set in motion efforts and forces trying to create a new man made "rule of law" form of government replacing the divinity, dogma and the church model, with a new plutocracy control model (small group of the wealthiest plutocrats).

The first new constitutional model would not go on to replace the divinity, nobility, aristocracy and church-based model for the accumulation of wealth by the wealthy. It was put in place when

48 people signed off on the Articles of Confederation govern-ment model in 1777. For a variety of reasons, only 16 liberal sign-ers of the Declaration of Independence also signed the Articles of Confederation government formation proposal.

Thirteen conservative colonies, operating as free nation-states, approved and adopted the new national model by 1781. The new decentralized government model of 13 states virtually jettisoned the centralized model of government that was successfully prose-cuting the war against Great Britain and the colonies.

The new Articles-based Constitution was not working out so well, in the 1780s. After 6 years, the liberals got the opportunity to amend the Articles, in 1787. They ended up replacing virtually every word of it, with the then-new second Constitution.

This new "Law of the Land" also generated the new representative model of sharing power and authority with the traditional nation-states, for the good of the people. The new "We the people and For the People" principles of government formally replaced the unstated conservative goal "for the accumulation of wealth by the wealthy."

The basic ideological conflict between "for the people" and "for the accumulation of wealth by the wealthy" did not go away with the electing and selecting of representatives processes, of the new Constitution.

While the ideology conflict remained, the newly created gov-ernment institution processes produced a variety of positive results over time and numerous varieties of this new institutional model spread across the world, as every plutocracy was forced to come to grips with the newly posed "for the people" issues.

The chapters in Part 2 sorted through the political party conundrum created by the second constitution, as the plutocrats and the patrons of the various states developed their national voter constituencies through didactic processes that converted anti-federalism into the Democrat-Republican Party, in an effort to gain control over the new representative-based federal government model, created by the second Constitution.

In the nearly two and a half centuries of its existence, the rule of law model has passed thousands of laws and has expanded its voting processes from its original plutocrat only VEP, to the current large percentage (80%) of all-adults VEP.

The economic cycles and the ideological imperatives have commingled and coalesced into the current mix of political party patterns, with the liberal-versus-conservative ideology conflict, shifting to various sociological issues, that make it difficult to recognize the ongoing conflict of for the people versus for the accumulation of wealth.

While the ideological conflict between for the people and for the accumulation of wealth by the wealthy remain as the core, the following didactic political summary reflects the general ideological and legislative behavior differences of people at work today.

Liberals, since 1776, believe in and embrace the notions that all men are created equal and born with inalienable rights, including the right to empower government for the best interest of the governed. They also believe the law that was passed and the amendment that failed to extend all constitutional rights to women and the LGBT community should be revived and adopted. They also still demonstrate a strong belief in the need for government actions to achieve a more perfect union, establish justice, protect the people, and promote the general welfare through equal opportunity and equality for all the people, regardless of ethnicity, color, religion, gender, or economic status.

In addition to these concepts, liberals clearly still promote the idea that to protect the people and embrace the general welfare, to place political demands for government action to alleviate social ills, to protect civil liberties and to provide individual and human rights, while shielding the people from economic threats, national disasters, other countries, and even the bad behaviors of some people within our nation-states.

Liberal principles also emphasize the need for the government to solve both personal security and social problems, and they bundle the general principle of separation of church and state, while adopting the basic Christian principles to feed the hungry, tend the sick, clothe the naked and educate the children, as demonstrated in the citizens' rights laws, the Great Society legislation and even as recently as the Obamacare protection of the uninsurable and poor.

Portions of these liberal beliefs, ideals, and cultural principles have been accepted and imported into the behaviors of many Americans, to a degree, although they can be still be contrasted with conservative principles used to attract conservative constituencies.

Conservatives stress personal responsibility, limited government, free markets with no government protection of people or consumers, individual liberty, traditional evangelical American values as they perceive them, the preservation of the way things are, and a strong, active, national military.

Conservatives also suggest the role of government should be to provide people the freedom necessary to pursue their own goals while relying on the profit motive of business, to resolve any social or economic issues for the people and consumers.

The conservative ideology also emphasizes the empowerment of the individual to solve problems as opposed to the government mandate to promote the general welfare. In this vein, Conservatives generally reject the liberal ideas and use of government legislation to solve social and economic problems for the people.

In general, most conservatives also reject the liberal notions that government needs to promote the general welfare, form a